# Poetry
## and
# Fairy Tales

CLEAR Curriculum Units From the University of Virginia
**FOR GRADE 3**

# Poetry and Fairy Tales

## LANGUAGE ARTS UNITS FOR GIFTED STUDENTS IN GRADE 3

Amy Price Azano, Ph.D.,
Tracy C. Missett, Ph.D., &
Carolyn M. Callahan, Ph.D.

PRUFROCK PRESS INC.
WACO, TEXAS

Prufrock Press Inc.
P.O. Box 8813
Waco, TX 76714-8813
Phone: (800) 998-2208
Fax: (800) 240-0333
http://www.prufrock.com

# TABLE OF CONTENTS

**Poetry and Fairy Tales**

Lesson 13: Re-Tellers ............................................................................ 255

Lesson 14: Literary Tellers ................................................................... 259

Lesson 15: Literary Tellers 2 ............................................................... 265

Lesson 16: Festival Prework ................................................................ 271

Lesson 17: Festival Prework, Seminars ............................................ 277

Lesson 18: Festival Prework, Final Prep ......................................... 283

Lesson 19: Folklore Festival and Assessment ............................... 285

**References** ................................................................................................ 291

**Appendices: Unit Resources**

Appendix A: Unit 1 Resources ........................................................... 296

Appendix B: Unit 2 Resources ........................................................... 303

**About the Authors** ................................................................................. 307

**Common Core State Standards Alignment** ................................... 309

# ACKNOWLEDGMENTS

Special credit and acknowledgment must go to the many faculty, researchers, and graduate research assistants who played roles in the development of the CLEAR Curriculum Model; the poetry, research, and folktales units that are included in this series; and the assessments that accompany those units. The CLEAR Curriculum Model was the brainchild of Dr. Catherine Brighton and Dr. Holly Hertberg-Davis. Their original conception of the model led to the drafts of the units mentioned above by then graduate research assistants: Jennifer Beasely, Marla Capper, Jane Jarvis, Maureen Murphy, and Mary Beth Samsa-Hes. Further revisions of the folktale unit were made by Mindy Labernz. Dr. Tonya Moon was a contributor to the development of the performance assessments included in the unit. After field-tests and initial implementation of the units by the teachers involved in the study of the units, Dr. Kimberly Landrum worked with the team to further refine the units with the authors of this series. Without each one of them this publication would not have been possible.

And, of course, we must acknowledge the work of Dr. Sandra N. Kaplan, Dr. Joseph S. Renzulli, and Dr. Carol A. Tomlinson whose foundational work in gifted education guided our thinking in the conceptualization of the model and in the development of units that would challenge and engage gifted learners.

# Part I

# Introduction and Using the CLEAR Curriculum Units

# Introduction

As researchers at the National Research Center on the Gifted and Talented, we recently completed a 6-year study of the effectiveness of two units based on the CLEAR Curriculum Model. The CLEAR (Challenge Leading to Engagement, Achievement, and Results) Curriculum Model incorporates elements from three widely-used, research-based models in gifted education—differentiation, Depth and Complexity, and the Schoolwide Enrichment Model—by Carol Tomlinson, Sandra Kaplan, and Joseph Renzulli, respectively. The CLEAR Curriculum Model addresses the recognition by leaders in the field that the heart of effective programming for gifted education services lies in the development and the implementation of curricula and instructional strategies that will challenge and enhance learning outcomes for high-ability learners.

The CLEAR Curriculum Model is comprised of five foundational elements:
1. continual formative assessment,
2. clear learning goals,
3. data-driven learning experiences,
4. authentic products, and
5. rich curriculum.

These elements are integrated into a curricular framework that reflects both the language arts Common Core State Standards and the National Association for Gifted Children Pre-K to Grade 12 Gifted Programming Standards. This integration ensures layers of challenge, opportunities for more in-depth study, and the production of authentic work resembling that of professionals within a discipline.

Teachers who participated in our study implemented two language arts units, one in poetry and one in research, in their third-grade gifted classrooms. The poetry unit, "The Magic of Everyday Things," received the 2012 Curriculum Award from the National Association of Gifted Children. As researchers for the study, we visited more than 100 classrooms across the country and interviewed more than 100 teachers who implemented the CLEAR units. We observed their teaching, their interactions with the curriculum, and student engagement. We also analyzed student achievement data, which indicated that the CLEAR Curriculum works! That is, students who were exposed to the units outperformed peers in gifted classrooms who did not have access to the curriculum.

We also listened to our participating teachers throughout the study. These teachers reported not only that students thrived during the poetry and research units but also that they—the teachers—learned a great deal about best practices in the field of gifted education. Teachers shared that for the first time they finally understood how to differentiate instruction for their students. Buzz phrases like "authentic products" and "formative assessments" came to life, providing a unique source of professional development for teachers whose endorsement credentials vary from state to state. Because no other available curriculum integrates the most popular models of gifted instruction in a way that the CLEAR Curriculum does, these teacher reports provide extraordinary testimony.

Finally, we worked with gifted coordinators who shared their frustrations about the loss of personnel and professional development opportunities vital to the livelihoods of their gifted education programs in the context of a tough economic climate that devalues gifted education programs and the students served in them. We heard their expressed appreciation for the opportunities for professional development embedded within the poetry and research units themselves.

Throughout our research, we fielded countless e-mails and telephone calls from our participating teachers, their principals, and district coordinators and, resoundingly, they asked: *Where can we get more?*

This three-part series answers that question.

## CLEAR CURRICULUM UNITS FOR GIFTED STUDENTS (GRADES 3–5)

The CLEAR Curriculum Units for Gifted Students (grades 3–5) offer two units per grade level for a total of six distinct units based on the CLEAR

Curriculum Model. All units put theory into practice and provide teachers with research-based curricula. What's more is that these units are based on a tested model that has been shown to work. For more on their effectiveness, see an article in the *American Educational Research Journal*, in which Callahan, Moon, Oh, Azano, and Hailey (2015) presented the achievement data documenting the success of the poetry (grade 3) and research (grade 5) units for students exposed to them.

## WHAT IS INCLUDED?

Each book in the series contains two grade-level appropriate language arts units based on the CLEAR Curriculum Model, including the award-winning and empirically supported poetry and research units. Each unit incorporates best practices from the field of gifted education while promoting critical literacy skills for the gifted student. Although each book can stand alone, the units are also vertically aligned so that a student advancing through all three grades can encounter innovative and challenging language arts lessons that have clear scope and sequence of learning outcomes that extend the Common Core State Standards (CCSS).

Let us tell you more about the CLEAR Curriculum Model.

## THE CLEAR CURRICULUM MODEL

The CLEAR Curriculum Model is a synthesis of fundamental and compatible curricular features from (a) the Differentiated Instruction Model (Tomlinson, 1995, 1999), (b) the Schoolwide Enrichment Model (SEM; Renzulli & Reis, 1985, 2001); and (c) the Depth and Complexity Model (Kaplan, 2005). The CLEAR Curriculum Model was developed as part of a Jacob K. Javits research grant authored by Carolyn M. Callahan, Tonya R. Moon, Holly Hertberg-Davis, and Catherine M. Brighton.

The Differentiated Instruction Model (Tomlinson, 1995, 1999) aims to address the diverse learning needs of students across differing ability levels, interests, and learning profiles. Its success is grounded in modifying three key elements of curriculum—content, process, and product—based on variations in student learning characteristics. As such, differentiation is a flexible instructional model for a broad range of students, including those who are gifted, based on the incorporation of a variety of both curricular and instructional arrangements. Several concepts from differentiation, as conceptualized in Tomlinson's model, lie at the heart of the CLEAR Curriculum Model. For example, the use of continual formative assessments supports teachers in differentiating the academic experiences included in the curriculum and aids teachers in acting on their recognition that gifted students learn and express learning in unique and diverse ways. More specifically, the continual formative assessments provide valuable feedback, or data, to teachers about individual student readiness and inform "next steps" instruction for diverse gifted learners. Thus, the data derived from continual formative assessments allow for tailoring of the curriculum to each student.

Differentiation is also evident in the flexible grouping arrangements provided in the CLEAR units. The use of flexible grouping arrangements facilitates matching the pace of learning, matching degree of challenge and interests of students to instructional tasks, and allowing students to create individualized products that reflect their learning (Tomlinson, 1995, 1999). Whole-group, small-group, and independent activities simultaneously build community and foster autonomy.

The SEM (see Renzulli, 1977; Renzulli & Reis, 1985, 2001) represents one of the most important contributions to the field of gifted education, and SEM has been adopted by many school districts across the county. At its core, SEM stresses the creative process and encourages academic experiences that mirror the work of "real-world" professionals. SEM promotes student engagement through the use of three types of enrichment experiences, which include (a) exposure to extensions of traditional content within the context of its use by real-world professionals (Type I learning experiences), (b) development of process skills that are applied to solving real problems (Type II learning experiences), and (c) investigations of topics and/or creation of products that reflect in-depth investigations into solving real problems in areas of student interest and ability (Type III learning experiences). The feature of SEM that is differentiated at the highest tier is student choice of independent topics for investigation, where students can engage in meaningful learning within the context of real problems in a field and create products demonstrating the skills of an expert in that field. The elements of student choice and authentic investigation are evident throughout the CLEAR units.

The underlying principles of the Depth and Complexity Model (Kaplan, 2005) characterize the CLEAR units and contribute to building layers of challenge and meaning for students. Depth and Complexity employs standards-based curriculum as the basis for promoting academic rigor. The model develops advanced levels of understanding by integrating elements of Depth and Complexity. To provide depth, CLEAR units focus on big ideas, language of the discipline, details, and patterns, and then those concepts are coupled with a focus on complexity, including multiple perspectives, interdisciplinary connections, and ethical issues (Kaplan, 2005). The dimension of complexity affords teachers and students multiple opportunities to think deeply about the content and identify associations and relationships that exist within, between, and among areas of study. Accordingly, the CLEAR units are designed to ensure that

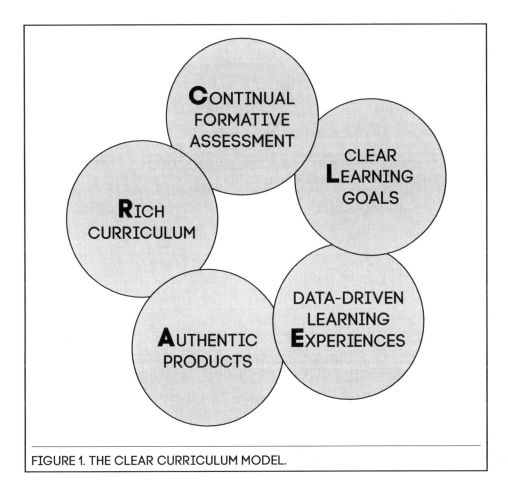

FIGURE 1. THE CLEAR CURRICULUM MODEL.

students recognize that big ideas and principles are rarely simple. Using these elements of the model also allows for the development of critical literacy skills, as students learn how to "read" bias—their own and others.

Based on the compatible theoretical underpinnings of Tomlinson's, Kaplan's, and Renzulli's curriculum models, as well as principles of exemplary curriculum development in general, the units reflect five foundational elements (see Figure 1) evident throughout all of the CLEAR units.

## CONTINUAL FORMATIVE ASSESSMENT

The CLEAR units use formative assessments throughout to provide valuable feedback about students to teachers. Formative assessments serve as a guide to planning instruction with student responses to the assessments informing subsequent instruction. Each unit includes both the formative assessment tool as well as thorough instruction on how assessment data from that tool can be used to differentiate lessons. Use of formative assessment in this manner allows teacher flexibility with the curriculum, thus allowing the instruction to meet students where they are in terms of readiness, interests, and learning profiles.

---

### PREPARATION: FORMATIVE ASSESSMENT 3

In their journals or as an exit card, have students answer one of the first two questions. Have all students answer Question 3.

1. Before you begin looking for the answers to your research question, what should you do first?

2. What is a source?

3. How does what you already know about a topic (your prior knowledge) influence how you will go about researching it?

---

FIGURE 2. SAMPLE "EXIT CARD" FOR FORMATIVE ASSESSMENT.

---

Exit cards, journal entries, and multiple choice responses are examples of formative assessments provided to teachers throughout the units. Figure 2 is an example of an exit card used in the fifth-grade research unit.

## CLEAR LEARNING GOALS

The units in this series have clear learning goals consistent with the Pre-K to Grade 12 Gifted Programming Standards (National Association for Gifted Children [NAGC], 2010) and the Common Core State Standards (CCSS). For example, in the poetry unit, third-grade students read the poem "The Fish," a poem more advanced than third-grade students are likely to read. Students are asked to determine the central message and explain how it is conveyed through the details in the poem, to distinguish literal from nonliteral language, refer to parts of the poem and describe how each successive part builds on earlier parts, and explain how the poem conveys mood. These components of the poetry unit integrate multiple standards for third grade in the English Language Arts Standards, Reading: Literature strand of the CCSS. However, these standards are applied to more advanced content to address the advanced readiness levels of gifted students. Throughout all units close attention has been paid to basing lessons on both the CCSS and the NAGC standards.

## DATA-DRIVEN LEARNING EXPERIENCES

The philosophical principle underlying the CLEAR units is that gifted learners are diverse in their readiness levels and interests and they learn best when their diverse needs are met in the classroom. Consistent with this philosophy, the units include ongoing formative and summative assessments that provide data for teachers to use in effectively differentiating instruction and learning opportunities for students and assessing student learning.

## AUTHENTIC PRODUCTS

In keeping with the Schoolwide Enrichment Model, the CLEAR units provide multiple opportunities for students to create authentic products, to develop real-world skills, and to apply knowledge in relevant contexts. These authentic products take the shape of poetry readings, debates, research presentations, letters to the editor, rhetoric (persuasive arts) journals, and so forth. Students not only acquire knowledge but also use the skills and content they have learned as experts in fields such as poetry, research, and fiction writing.

## RICH CURRICULUM

A focus on "big ideas" in the various CLEAR units allows for the achievement of deep understanding. For example, a big idea in the poetry unit is: "Poetry helps readers see the extraordinary (the magic) in the ordinary." A big idea in the research unit is: "Values, experiences, and motivation contribute to the development of an explorer's (reader's) perspective and purpose." In each unit developed using the CLEAR Curriculum Model, students are challenged to question, to investigate, to answer unanswered questions, and then to question what they find. The CLEAR units stress that there are rarely "easy" answers to hard questions—as such, students will sharpen critical literacy skills as they begin to consider varied perspectives and ethical issues within a unit of study.

# CRITICAL LITERACY

Literacy skills are no longer limited to the tasks of reading, writing, and speaking. Students are inundated with nonfiction texts and media messages and must have the necessary skills to interpret those messages. Paulo Freire argued that literacy is always political and redirected the field of literacy instruction to consider social justice and the transformative power of literacy. The CLEAR units will emphasize critical literacy skills, challenging students to consider the political and social implications of the topics and concepts taught. Students are media consumers and must learn to do what Freire described as reading the "word" and the "world."

# EVIDENCE-BASED PRACTICE

In the current educational environment of accountability, educators, researchers, and policy makers increasingly expect the development and adoption of evidence-based practices, or those that are proven to be effective in raising student achievement. At the same time, a principle contention in the field of gifted education is that gifted students require comprehensive differentiated curricula and instruction to develop their abilities effectively. Thus, the field of gifted education has urged the development and deployment of rigorously conducted curriculum intervention studies to demonstrate that recommended curricula and practices for gifted learners are evidence-based and have demonstrated measurable academic growth for gifted learners.

It was in the context of accountability that the National Research Center on the Gifted and Talented sought to draw from curriculum models with features that had research support and create a new model that could itself demonstrate effectiveness in raising student achievement. As indicated above, the developers of the CLEAR Curriculum Model synthesized components of SEM, differentiation, and depth and complexity that were shown to positively impact student learning outcomes.

Specifically, theoretical support for differentiation comes from learning and development theories that propose (a) optimal learning is achieved when learners are exposed to tasks slightly above their current level of performance (Csikszentmihalyi, 1990; Csikszentmihalyi, Rathunde, & Whalen, 1993; Howard, 1994; Jensen, 1998; Sousa & Tomlinson, 2010) and (b) learning should focus on understanding of key knowledge and principles of the field of study rather than rote memorization of information (e.g., Donovan, Bransford, & Pellegrino, 1999; Wenglinsky, 2002). Studies have documented positive effects of the model in student achievement across subject areas, grades, and performance levels and higher level thinking skills with diverse learners in a variety of school settings. Research on the effectiveness of depth and complexity (cited in Kaplan, 2013) has documented academic growth in social studies and language arts among elementary students at all ability levels including gifted students. The effectiveness of SEM has been shown in raising student creative productivity, student personal and social development, and student self-efficacy (e.g., Burns, 1987; Olenchak, 1991; Reis, 1981; Schack, Starko, & Burns, 1991). Moreover, investigations of SEM as a curricular framework in a reading intervention for elementary students of all ability levels including advanced learners have shown higher scores in reading achievement, reading fluency, and students' attitudes toward reading.

The National Research Center on the Gifted and Talented then investigated the effectiveness of the two language arts units—poetry and research—developed from the CLEAR Curriculum Model. After implementing the work in more than 100 classrooms over a period of 4 years, researchers analyzed observations, interviews, teacher logs, surveys, student products, and student outcomes to conclude that students who were provided instruction with the units earned significantly higher achievement test scores than students in classes where the units were not used. A more detailed report of the impact of the units studied can be found in Callahan et al. (2015). Importantly, these positive results were observed in both full-time inclusive gifted settings and pull-out gifted settings. Because the most prevalent service option for gifted learners is pull-out programs with instructional blocks of 45–60 minutes once or twice a week, the units were designed so the whole unit could be completed during the fall/winter or winter/spring sessions in a typical pull-out classroom, including time for ongoing assessments and the creation of an authentic product for each unit. However, the units are structured so that they can also be used daily in self-contained gifted classrooms or with the frequency deemed appropriate by teachers in that setting. Thus, the CLEAR units can be used in a variety of group and classroom arrangements.

## OVERVIEW OF THE BOOKS

These books are for gifted education teachers, gifted education coordinators, and regular education teachers who serve gifted students in their classrooms. Each grade-level book offers two complete units of study. Each unit contains 10–20 lessons designed for 45–60 minute classes. Within the units, content and skills are developed to reflect a clear scope and sequence of learning opportunities. The following outline details the organization of the grade-level units based on the CLEAR Curriculum Model and identifies the relevant Common Core State Standards in English Language Arts, Reading: Literature (CCSS.ELA-Literacy.RL) and relevant Common Core State Standards in English Language Arts, Writing (CCSS.ELA-Literacy.W) addressed and extended in each unit.

## GRADE 3 UNITS: POETRY AND FAIRY TALES

### LITERACY AND CRITICAL LITERACY SKILLS IN GRADE 3 UNITS
(CCSS.ELA-Literacy.RL.3.1—3.10; CCSS.ELA-Literacy.W 3.3—3.6, 3.10)
  ≫ All texts/sources are influenced by author's purpose and perspective
  ≫ Information comes from multiple sources
  ≫ Understanding bias and cultural contexts
  ≫ Informed consumers of information

### POETRY
In this unit, students will read and analyze various forms of poetry and write their own poetry anthology. They will learn how to identify and use figurative language to create concrete images from abstract ideas.

### FAIRY TALES
In this unit, students will study fairy tales and folklore to understand how and why societal norms and mores are culturally transmitted.

## GRADE 4 UNITS: FICTION AND NONFICTION

### LITERACY AND CRITICAL LITERACY SKILLS IN GRADE 4 UNITS
(CCSS.ELA-Literacy.RL.4.1—4.10; CCSS.ELA-Literacy.W 4.1—4.10)
  ≫ Understanding texts as reflections of culture (politics)
  ≫ Understanding informative/explanatory texts contain personal opinions and points of view
  ≫ Authors manipulate details
  ≫ Readers have filters for information (implicit bias)
  ≫ Fiction and non-fiction are equally biased/loaded

### FICTION AND SHORT STORIES
In this unit, students will read and analyze short stories, develop an understanding of how short story writers develop plot and characters in a concise narrative setting without sacrificing compelling storytelling, and write their own short story.

## NONFICTION AND MEMOIR

In comparison to the fiction (short story) unit, students will study nonfiction (and creative nonfiction) texts to examine how writers use many of the same devices to tell nonfiction stories. Students will read a variety of nonfiction texts and will write their own memoir.

# GRADE 5 UNITS: RESEARCH AND RHETORIC

## LITERACY AND CRITICAL LITERACY SKILLS IN GRADE 5 UNITS

(CCSS.ELA-Literacy.RL.5.1—5.10; CCSS.ELA-Literacy.W 5.1—5.10)

- ≫ Creating texts for purpose
- ≫ Speakers manipulate audiences
- ≫ Yielding and wielding bias
- ≫ Understanding the speaker's perspective
- ≫ Understanding the audience's perspective

## RESEARCH

In this unit, students will learn and employ advanced research skills from crafting open-ended research questions to discerning between reliable sources. They will carry out their own research study and present findings at a research gala.

## RHETORIC

Students will engage in a study of Aristotle's *Rhetoric* to answer the question: *When do you appeal to one's intellect, emotions, or sense of morality when trying to persuade?* Students will learn to identify and analyze a variety of rhetorical devices to better understand the art of rhetoric.

# Using the CLEAR Curriculum Units

In the introduction, we provided an overview of the three foundational models used in the CLEAR Curriculum Model (Differentiated Instruction Model, Schoolwide Enrichment Model, and the Depth and Complexity Model), the five foundational elements of CLEAR (continual formative assessment, clear learning goals, data-driven learning experiences, authentic products, and rich curriculum), evidence from a multiyear research study, and an overview of the units in this curriculum series. In this section, we offer more specific information about the elements you will find in each unit, including information about how the CLEAR Curriculum Model comes to life in the teaching of these language arts units.

## THE SCOPE OF EACH UNIT

Each unit emphasizes "big ideas" within a major focus area in language arts instruction: poetry, storytelling, fiction, nonfiction, rhetoric, and research. Consistent with national standards, these big ideas are then delineated by objectives and vocabulary terms For example, a big idea in the poetry unit is for students to see the extraordinary in the ordinary. For students to grasp that abstract notion, they must practice reading and writing many forms of poetry. They need to understand how poets use figurative language to render the abstract concrete or the inanimate animate. And they do this while becoming poets—collecting ideas, reading as writers, workshopping their poems, and publishing their work. These big ideas allow teachers and students to concentrate efforts on the "how" and "why" of literacy instruction.

Each unit begins with an overview of the big ideas, learning objectives, and a unit outline that gives an overview of each particular lesson, the related big idea(s), and the targeted skills. The units also begin with a section on "preparing to teach" which provides teachers with information related to resources, materials, classroom environment, classroom management, and ongoing assessments as they relate to that particular unit.

Instruction in each unit is based on a preassessment that is the lead-off activity. Each unit contains several formative assessments that are integrated throughout, and concludes with performance and summative assessments. In each unit, students will produce an authentic product (collection of poems, short story, memoir, etc.). The units also include rubrics for assessing these authentic products.

# THE ICONS USED THROUGHOUT THE UNITS

Integrated throughout the lesson plans are a series of icons or symbols intended to draw your attention to the particular content focus, learning objective, or instructional configuration of each learning activity. Some of these icons are derived from Sandra Kaplan's Depth and Complexity Model, while others have been developed specifically for the CLEAR curriculum model used in these units. Icons fall into five major categories: Lesson Organization, Literacy Focus, Differentiation, Discipline Exploration, and Subject Analysis. These icons serve as a "quick glance" roadmap to guide instruction. Here we will explain the icons and how they are used throughout the units.

## LESSON ORGANIZATION

There are four icons used to indicate how students should be grouped for instructional activities.

 **Whole-Class Instruction.** The teacher leads an activity with the entire class together.

 **Small-Group Work.** Students engage in a learning task in pairs or small groups of 3–5.

**Independent Work.** Students work on their own in identifying a topic of study, conducting research, and writing or using other modes of expression to present information or demonstrate understanding.

**Anchor Activity.** As students work at different paces, there will be times when some students finish a task sooner than others. An anchor activity is a task on which students work (usually independently) after they complete other class work. An anchor activity is meaningfully related to the learning objectives of the lesson or unit, allowing students to explore essential ideas, rather than simply a time-filler. All students will have a chance to work on anchor activities over the course of a unit.

## LITERACY FOCUS

There are four icons used to indicate the literacy focus of instruction.

**Word Study.** Students are engaged in learning and practicing how to decode words by breaking them down into their component parts such as sounds, syllables, roots, prefixes, and suffixes. Each student works with words that match his or her own readiness level.

**Reading Comprehension.** Students are reading for the purpose of understanding and practicing comprehension strategies.

**Writing.** Students are engaged in one or more stages of the writing process.

**Critical Literacy.** Students are engaged in thinking about the political and/or social implications of the topics and concepts being taught. They are reading the "word" (text) and the "world" (context).

## DIFFERENTIATION

There are four icons to indicate how teachers can differentiate a particular activity.

**Differentiation by Readiness.** Readiness-based differentiation is the process of adjusting learning experiences to match individual students' levels of past achievement and point of development. Readiness refers to what students already know, understand, and can do related to the learning objectives for a particular task, lesson, or unit. A student's level of readiness might vary depending on his or her background knowledge, prior learning experiences, and profile of competencies related to different topics or kinds of activities. When learning tasks are matched to a student's level of readiness (i.e., within the student's zone of proximal development), the student has the opportunity to work at something that is both challenging and rewarding. When a task is too challenging or not challenging enough for a student, learning is unlikely to occur. Thus, it is essential that general lesson plans be adjusted to better tend to differing levels of readiness among students. Students might work in readiness groups or independently on tasks that are differentiated by readiness.

 **Differentiation by Interest.** Interest-based differentiation refers to the process of adjusting learning experiences to match individual students' interests. When students have the opportunity to work in an area of personal interest to them, they are more likely to become motivated to learn and therefore actively engaged in the learning process. Teachers can attend to students' interests by offering a choice of several materials or topics, by inviting students to suggest their own topics for study, or by allowing students to sometimes work in interest-based groups.

 **Learning Profile.** Learning-profile-based differentiation is the process of adjusting learning experiences to match an individual student's pattern of strengths, weaknesses, and preferences that determines how he or she takes in, makes sense of, and expresses information. Learning profile is shaped by factors such as culture, gender, and learning style preferences. Teachers can provide opportunities for students to work in ways that match their learning profile preferences by incorporating multiple modes of expression and ways of working into the life of the classroom.

 **Twice-Exceptional Learners.** Some students in gifted classrooms also have a disability—such as a specific learning disability, Attention Deficit/Hyperactivity Disorder, autism spectrum disorder, and/or an emotional and behavioral disorder—that impedes their ability to learn. These students are commonly referred to as twice-exceptional or "2E" learners. As more students with disabilities are participating in gifted programs, it is important to shift the primary focus of instructional strategies away from remediation and social skills improvement for gifted students with disabilities and toward their strengths, talents, and interests to promote social, emotional, and academic gains, and also to expose these students to rich curricula. The CLEAR language arts units provide a structured model with instructional strategies directed toward developing student strengths (e.g., ability grouping, acceleration, formative assessment) that are recommended for both gifted students and students with disabilities. However, in recognition that these students will sometimes need additional support structures, the 2E icon supports teachers in their use of effective instructional strategies for twice-exceptional students.

## DISCIPLINE EXPLORATION

There are five icons used to explain how the discipline can be explored and where the teacher can focus student attention during instructional activities.

**Big Idea.** A big idea refers to an essential understanding about a topic or discipline that students should take away from the lesson or unit. It often helps to "unpack" or explain an important concept or the relationship between two or more concepts. Big ideas help students move beyond the facts and skills they are learning to focus on what is fundamentally important, enduring, and transferable about the topic. For example, in the poetry unit, students explore the big idea that poetry helps readers see the extraordinary in the ordinary. This is a big idea that guides the work of contemporary poets as they use concrete, sensory language and specific imagery to add layers of meaning to the description of everyday objects, events, and experiences. The big idea can be explored across different poems, poets, and periods of history. In this way, the big idea is a focal point that holds the unit together; students are gradually guided, through a range of learning activities, to arrive at a deep understanding of the big idea. The term *big idea* is sometimes used synonymously with principle, generalization, or understanding.

**Place-Based Pedagogy.** This task allows students to think critically about how this text (or context) relates to their own sense of place or local community.

**Language of the Discipline.** The task helps students achieve greater depth of understanding by coming to know and apply the vocabulary of professionals in the academic discipline.

**Tools of the Discipline.** The task helps students achieve greater depth of understanding by coming to know and apply the ways of thinking and working of professionals in the academic discipline.

**Real-World Application.** The task requires students to apply the language and tools of the discipline in an environment or activity similar to what an expert in the field would experience.

## SUBJECT ANALYSIS

There are three icons used to indicate how a task offers students depth and complexity of a particular topic.

**Details.** The task helps students achieve greater depth of understanding by studying the essential details relevant to what they are learning.

**Patterns.** The task helps students achieve greater depth of understanding by analyzing the patterns and trends that can be identified in what they are learning.

 **Over Time.** The task helps students achieve a more complex level of understanding by guiding them to consider what they are learning from a historical perspective.

## TIPS

 The tip icon indicates an important note for the teacher. The tip might refer to something to watch out for, such as potential classroom management issues or a particular type of talent potential during a learning activity.

# ASSESSMENTS IN THE UNITS

There are four types of assessments used throughout the units. Each unit begins with a preassessment to gauge students' initial interest and conceptual knowledge of the unit topic. For example, in poetry students are asked: *What do you know about poetry? What are some of the ways poets make their poems interesting? What would you like to learn about poetry in the next few weeks?* Teachers can use responses to understand students' prior knowledge about the subject and plan subsequent instruction accordingly.

The units also utilize formative assessments throughout. Formative assessments are used to inform next steps in the lesson. Directions are provided on how to use the assessment data to inform instruction in the activities or lessons that follow. For example, in the poetry unit, students take a poetry survey as a formative assessment after Lesson 5. Additionally, teachers are provided with the following instructions for utilizing the data:

> Use information from the assessment to determine whether there is any content you have taught so far that you need to review or reinforce. For example, you might find a group of students having trouble remembering the definition of an adjective or confusing concrete and abstract nouns, and you can plan to take these students aside for a "mini-lesson" at a convenient time. Students' responses to questions about what they would still like to learn might help you choose resources and try to incorporate opportunities to address students' individual interests in later lessons.

Other formative assessments might provide instructions for making decisions about how to group students.

The units also utilize performance and summative assessments. Students will be asked to produce authentic products throughout each of the units, and these final assessments will provide an opportunity for teachers and students to assess learning. For example, the poetry unit ends with a poetry reading and a collection of original works, along with a review of a canonical poem.

## GETTING STARTED

The lessons within each unit are clearly marked, along with the assessments, and icons will further direct your instruction. The two units for each grade level can be taught in whichever order you prefer. However, we found that third-grade teachers enjoyed teaching the poetry unit in the spring, as it coincides with National Poetry Month in April. We hope you and your students enjoy these CLEAR Curriculum units.

# Part II
# Unit Plans

# Unit 1
# The Magic of
# Everyday Things

## BACKGROUND

This is a unit designed to help students explore different forms of poetry as they expand their comprehension and writing skills. The title of the unit, The Magic of Everyday Things, reflects one of the big ideas of poetry: poetry helps readers see the extraordinary (the magic) in ordinary experiences. The Spanish poet García Lorca described the poet as "a professor of the senses," referring to the way the poet uses specific sensory detail to connect the reader with the bigger, more abstract ideas expressed in poetry. Along with the use of devices such as metaphor, sensory language and the use of concrete description are among the key ways that contemporary poets transform the ordinary into something extraordinary.

This unit encourages students to become explorers of their own experiences, and the experiences of others, as they read and write poems in which concrete detail links readers to larger, more abstract ideas. All students will have the opportunity to read and write a range of poetry related to their own experiences. The unit also gives students multiple opportunities for enhancing their word knowledge, comprehension strategies, and writing skills in line with state and national standards.

# OBJECTIVES/STANDARDS

This unit is designed to be consistent with common state third-grade reading and writing standards and national standards outlined by the National Council of Teachers of English (NCTE; NCTE & International Reading Association, 2012). It also aligns to the third-grade Common Core State Standards (CCSS; an alignment chart is provided on p. 309).

## STUDENTS WILL KNOW THE FOLLOWING TERMS

- *Imagery* is the expression of sensory detail—sight, sound, smell, touch, taste.
- *Sensory language* is that which describes imagery using the senses—sight, sound, smell, touch, taste.
- *Abstract language* is lacking physical detail. Poetry is concerned with the immediate, the specific, and the *concrete* (the opposite of abstract).
- *Metaphor* is a kind of figurative language in which two unlike nouns are compared.
- *Personification* is a kind of figurative language in which an inanimate object, animal, or other nonhuman is given human traits.
- *Rhythm* is a pattern of stressed and unstressed sounds.
- *Rhyme* is a repetition of identical or similar sounds in two or more different words.
- *Verse* is poetic writing that is usually metrical and conveys an idea.
- A *line* of poetry is the text written across a single row. Lines are numbered within stanzas.
- A *stanza* is a group of lines of verse that forms a section in a poem. Stanzas are numbered according to where the poem shows distinct breaks.
- A *couplet* is a pair of lines of verse, usually rhyming.
- A *cinquain* is a poem of five lines.

Other vocabulary:
- Noun
- Adjective
- Verb
- Synonym
- Antonym
- Prefix
- Suffix

## STUDENTS WILL UNDERSTAND THE
## FOLLOWING BIG IDEAS ABOUT POETRY

- ≫ Poetry helps readers see the extraordinary in the ordinary.
- ≫ Poets use concrete language and sensory detail to communicate abstract ideas, emotions, and truths.
- ≫ Poets use metaphors to connect readers to important ideas through imagery.
- ≫ The structure of a poem often contributes to its meaning.

## STUDENTS WILL DEMONSTRATE
## THE FOLLOWING SKILLS

- ≫ Generate ideas for writing.
- ≫ Develop an idea within a brief text.
- ≫ Know and use complex word families when writing (e.g., -ight).
- ≫ Learn and use the writing process (e.g., prewriting, drafting, revising, proofreading, and editing).
- ≫ Use literary devices in their own writing, including metaphors, personification, point of view, rhyme, rhythm and repetition.
- ≫ Build poetry vocabulary.
- ≫ Know and use complex word families when reading (e.g., -ight) to decode unfamiliar words.
- ≫ Identify the author's purpose in a simple text.
- ≫ Identify the main idea of a selection.
- ≫ Identify literary devices, including metaphors, personification, point of view, rhyme, rhythm, and repetition.
- ≫ Identify poetry structures.
- ≫ Develop the skills to participate as knowledgeable, reflective, creative, and critical members of a literary community.
- ≫ Respond to written and oral presentations as a reader, listener, and articulate speaker.

# UNIT 1 OUTLINE

|  | Big Idea(s) | Overview | Skills |
|---|---|---|---|
| **Unit 1 Preassessment** | | | |
| Lesson 1 | ≫ Poets use concrete language and sensory detail to communicate abstract ideas, emotions, and truths. | *Welcome to Poetry*<br>≫ Visualization activity.<br>≫ Introduction to key terms.<br>≫ Poetry for Appreciation: "The Fish" by Elizabeth Bishop. | ≫ Generate ideas for writing.<br>≫ Learn and use the writing process.<br>≫ Develop the skills to participate as knowledgeable, reflective, creative, and critical members of a literary community. |
| **Formative Assessment 1: Exit Card** | | | |
| Lesson 2 | ≫ Poets use concrete language and sensory detail to communicate abstract ideas, emotions, and truths.<br>≫ Poetry helps readers see the extraordinary in the ordinary. | *Concrete Versus Abstract*<br>≫ Distinguishing between concrete and abstract nouns.<br>≫ Introduction to "The Red Wheelbarrow."<br>≫ Poetry for Appreciation: "Baby Tortoise" by D. H. Lawrence; "The Red Wheelbarrow" by William Carlos Williams. | ≫ Build poetry vocabulary.<br>≫ Identify and use various parts of speech.<br>≫ Develop the skills to participate as knowledgeable, reflective, creative, and critical members of a literary community. |
| Lesson 3 | ≫ Poets use concrete language and sensory detail to communicate abstract ideas, emotions, and truths.<br>≫ Poetry helps readers see the extraordinary in the ordinary. | *"The Red Wheelbarrow" Returns*<br>≫ Develop original poems following a model.<br>≫ Poetry for Appreciation: "My First Memory (Of Librarians" by Nikki Giovanni. | ≫ Build poetry vocabulary.<br>≫ Identify and use various parts of speech.<br>≫ Generate ideas for writing.<br>≫ Identify author's purpose in a simple text.<br>≫ Develop the skills to participate as knowledgeable, reflective, creative, and critical members of a literary community. |
| Lesson 4 | ≫ Poets use concrete language and sensory detail to communicate abstract ideas, emotions, and truths.<br>≫ Poetry helps readers see the extraordinary in the ordinary. | *"The Magic Box"*<br>≫ Develop original poems following a model.<br>≫ Poetry for Appreciation: "A Nest Full of Stars" by James Berry; "The Magic Box" by Kit Wright. | ≫ Build poetry vocabulary.<br>≫ Identify and use various parts of speech.<br>≫ Develop ideas for writing.<br>≫ Develop the skills to participate as knowledgeable, reflective, creative, and critical members of a literary community. |

|  | Big Idea(s) | Overview | Skills |
|---|---|---|---|
| **Lesson 5** | ≫ Poets use concrete language and sensory detail to communicate abstract ideas, emotions, and truths.<br>≫ Poetry helps readers see the extraordinary in the ordinary. | *Poet's Workshop*<br>≫ Introduction to Poet's Workshop: How to give and receive feedback on poetry.<br>≫ Poetry for Appreciation: "Hand Shadows" by Mary Cornish. | ≫ Generate ideas for writing.<br>≫ Develop an idea within a brief text.<br>≫ Learn and use the writing process.<br>≫ Develop the skills to participate as knowledgeable, reflective, creative, and critical members of a literary community.<br>≫ Respond to written and oral presentations as a reader, listener, and articulate speaker. |
| **Formative Assessment 2** | | | |
| **Lesson 6** | ≫ Poets use concrete language and sensory detail to communicate abstract ideas, emotions, and truths.<br>≫ Poetry helps readers see the extraordinary in the ordinary. | *The Memory Box*<br>≫ Write original memory poems guided by a model.<br>≫ Poetry for Appreciation: "Combing" by Gladys Cardiff. | ≫ Generate ideas for writing.<br>≫ Develop an idea within a brief text.<br>≫ Learn and use the writing process.<br>≫ Identify and use parts of speech.<br>≫ Develop the skills to participate as knowledgeable, reflective, creative, and critical members of a literary community. |
| **Lesson 7 (Optional)** | ≫ Poets use concrete language and sensory detail to communicate abstract ideas, emotions, and truths.<br>≫ Poetry helps readers see the extraordinary in the ordinary. | *Postcards From My Life*<br>≫ Write postcards to practice clear, descriptive writing.<br>≫ Poetry for Appreciation: "The Serenity in Stones" by Simon J. Ortiz. | ≫ Generate ideas for writing.<br>≫ Develop an idea within a brief text.<br>≫ Learn and use the writing process.<br>≫ Identify and use parts of speech.<br>≫ Develop the skills to participate as knowledgeable, reflective, creative, and critical members of a literary community. |

| | Big Idea(s) | Overview | Skills |
|---|---|---|---|
| **Lesson 8** | ≫ Poets use concrete language and sensory detail to communicate abstract ideas, emotions, and truths.<br>≫ Poetry helps readers see the extraordinary in the ordinary. | *Workshop Day 2*<br>≫ Work on original poems and engage in poetry conferences.<br>≫ Poetry for Appreciation: "A Boy Juggling a Soccer Ball" by Christopher Merrill. | ≫ Generate ideas for writing.<br>≫ Develop an idea within a brief text.<br>≫ Learn and use the writing process.<br>≫ Develop the skills to participate as knowledgeable, reflective, creative, and critical members of a literary community.<br>≫ Respond to written and oral presentations as a reader, listener, and articulate speaker. |
| **Lesson 9** | ≫ Poets use metaphors to connect readers to important ideas through imagery. | *Meet Metaphor*<br>≫ Introduction to metaphors.<br>≫ Recognize metaphors in poetry.<br>≫ Poetry for Appreciation: "Dreams" by Langston Hughes. | ≫ Identify literary devices, including metaphors.<br>≫ Identify the main idea of a selection.<br>≫ Generate ideas for writing.<br>≫ Develop the skills to participate as knowledgeable, reflective, creative, and critical members of a literary community. |
| **Lesson 10** | ≫ Poets use metaphors to connect readers to important ideas through imagery.<br>≫ Poetry helps readers see the extraordinary in the ordinary. | *More Metaphor*<br>≫ Use metaphors in writing.<br>≫ Poetry for Appreciation: "Hope is the thing with feathers" by Emily Dickinson. | ≫ Identify literary devices, including metaphors.<br>≫ Generate ideas for writing<br>≫ Develop an idea within a brief text.<br>≫ Develop the skills to participate as knowledgeable, reflective, creative, and critical members of a literary community. |
| **Formative Assessment 3** | | | |
| **Lesson 11** | ≫ Poets use metaphors to connect readers to important ideas through imagery.<br>≫ Poetry helps readers see the extraordinary in the ordinary. | *Personification*<br>≫ Introduction to personification.<br>≫ Write short stories using personification.<br>≫ Poetry for Appreciation: "Playground" by Adrian Mitchell. | ≫ Identify literary devices, including metaphors and personification.<br>≫ Identify poetry structures.<br>≫ Generate ideas for writing.<br>≫ Develop an idea within a brief text.<br>≫ Develop the skills to participate as knowledgeable, reflective, creative, and critical members of a literary community. |

|  | Big Idea(s) | Overview | Skills |
|---|---|---|---|
| Lesson 12 | ≫ Poetry helps readers see the extraordinary in the ordinary. | *A Different Point of View* <br> ≫ Read and write poems using point of view in different ways. <br> ≫ Poetry for Appreciation: "Tiny" by Mandy Coe. | ≫ Identify literary devices, including point of view. <br> ≫ Generate ideas for writing. <br> ≫ Learn and use the writing process. <br> ≫ Develop the skills to participate as knowledgeable, reflective, creative, and critical members of a literary community. |
| Lesson 13 | ≫ Poets use concrete language and sensory detail to communicate abstract ideas, emotions, and truths. <br> ≫ Poets use metaphors to connect readers to important ideas through imagery. <br> ≫ Poetry helps readers see the extraordinary in the ordinary. | *Workshop Day 3* <br> ≫ Work on original poems from various models, and engage in the conference process. <br> ≫ Poetry for Appreciation: "Dream Deferred" by Langston Hughes. | ≫ Learn and use the writing process. <br> ≫ Develop an idea within a brief text. <br> ≫ Respond to written and oral presentations as a reader, listener, and articulate speaker. |
| **Formative Assessment 4** | | | |
| Lesson 14 | ≫ Poetry helps readers see the extraordinary in the ordinary. <br> ≫ The structure of a poem often contributes to its meaning. | *Time to Rhyme* <br> ≫ Introduction to rhyme and rhythm. <br> ≫ Create a rhyming dictionary for the classroom. <br> ≫ Poetry for Appreciation: "The Leaf's Lament" by Andrew Fusek Peters. | ≫ Identify literary devices, including rhyme and rhythm. <br> ≫ Identify poetry structures. <br> ≫ Know and use complex word families when writing (e.g., *-ight*). <br> ≫ Develop the skills to participate as knowledgeable, reflective, creative, and critical members of a literary community. |
| Lesson 15 | ≫ Poetry helps readers see the extraordinary in the ordinary. <br> ≫ The structure of a poem often contributes to its meaning. | *Rhythm and Repetition* <br> ≫ Read and write poems that employ rhythm and repetition. <br> ≫ Poetry for Appreciation: "Stopping by Woods on a Snowy Evening" by Robert Frost; "Granny Is" by Valerie Bloom; "Love That Boy" by Walter Dean Myers; "The Distant Talking Drum" by Isaac Olaleye. | ≫ Identify literary devices, including rhyme and rhythm. <br> ≫ Identify poetry structures. <br> ≫ Know and use complex word families when reading and writing (e.g., *-ight*). |

| | Big Idea(s) | Overview | Skills |
|---|---|---|---|
| **Lesson 16** | ≫ Poets use concrete language and sensory detail to communicate abstract ideas, emotions, and truths.<br>≫ Poets use metaphors to connect readers to important ideas through imagery.<br>≫ Poetry helps readers see the extraordinary in the ordinary.<br>≫ The structure of a poem often contributes to its meaning. | *How to Read a Poem*<br>≫ Develop a "how-to" guide for critically reading poetry.<br>≫ Poetry for Appreciation: "This Moment" by Eavan Boland. | ≫ Identify literary devices, including rhyme, rhythm, metaphors, personification, and point of view.<br>≫ Identify poetry structures.<br>≫ Develop the skills to participate as knowledgeable, reflective, creative, and critical members of a literary community. |
| **Lesson 17** | ≫ Poets use concrete language and sensory detail to communicate abstract ideas, emotions, and truths.<br>≫ Poets use metaphors to connect readers to important ideas through imagery.<br>≫ Poetry helps readers see the extraordinary in the ordinary.<br>≫ The structure of a poem often contributes to its meaning. | *Workshop Days 4 and 5*<br>≫ Complete an anthology of original poems and an analysis of a selected poem. | ≫ Identify literary devices.<br>≫ Identify poetry structures.<br>≫ Learn and use the writing process.<br>≫ Respond to written and oral presentations as a reader, listener, and articulate speaker. |
| **Lesson 18** | | *Class Poetry Reading*<br>≫ Conduct class poetry reading. | |
| **Performance Assessment**<br>**Summative Assessment** | | | |

# PREPARING TO TEACH THE UNIT

## RESOURCES AND MATERIALS

This unit features an organizing concept map (Handout 0.1). To help students grasp the big ideas in a visual way, the concept map builds upon components progressively in the unit. This can also be displayed as an image of a tree, called a "poetree," which be displayed in the classroom to help students see the

| Roots | |
|---|---|
| Language | Lesson 1 |
| Abstract/Concrete | Lesson 2 |
| Imagery | Lesson 3 |
| Sensory Details | Lesson 4 |
| **Trunk** | |
| Ideas | Lesson 6 |
| Details | Lesson 7 or 8 |
| Structure | Lesson 9 |
| Expression | Lesson 10 |
| **Limbs** | |
| Unique Ideas/Fresh View | Lesson 11 |
| Ordinary in the Extraordinary | Lesson 12 |
| Structure (Rhyme, Rhythm, Repetition) | Lessons 14 and 15 |
| How to Understand a Poem | Lesson 16 |

FIGURE 3. "POETREE" COMPONENTS.

connections in both their work and the elements of poetry they will experience throughout the unit. Figure 3 details the structure of the poetree.

Poems used in the unit are documented in each lesson plan. Internet links to the poems are included in each lesson and are also available on our website at http://www.prufrock.com/assets/clientpages/Poetry_FairyTales.aspx. An important goal for the unit is to help students explore a wide range of topics and types of poetry. Teachers are encouraged to have a collection of poetry books (e.g., borrowed from the school library) appropriate for a broad range of reading levels available in the classroom for students to peruse and borrow. Teachers are also encouraged to share some of their favorite poems with students, to invite students to share or bring in poems they enjoy, and to explore local opportunities for hearing live poetry readings (or even invite a real poet to visit the classroom).

In order to respond to student diversity, attention should be given to selecting poems that reflect a variety of cultures and backgrounds and tailoring instructional strategies and activities to address learners with disabilities in the gifted classroom.

Each student will require a composition book for the unit. The composition book will be a *workbook*, in which students can complete class writing activities, jot down ideas, and work on drafts of their poems. They should be encouraged to make mistakes in this book, since they should be experimenting with words and ideas. Students will also require a pocket folder, which will include what will become the student's *anthology book.* In the anthology, students will write out final copies of their best poems (i.e., poems that have been through idea development and draft processes and have been corrected for spelling).

## CLASSROOM ENVIRONMENT

The teacher is encouraged to set up a classroom environment that is conducive to the exploration and enjoyment of poetry. For example, the teacher might start a "Poetry Wall," which can be used to display (1) copies of the poems read in class; (2) copies of poems recommended by students; (3) information about the lives and work of specific poets; (4) poems written by students; or (5) interesting photos, pictures, postcards, or other objects and images that could inspire or provide ideas for writing poetry. It is also important to have areas of the classroom that work well for individual work, small-group work, and for whole-group discussions and activities (preferably apart from desks).

## CLASSROOM MANAGEMENT

This unit incorporates many different types of activities, from independent work to creative visualization to group work. Students will sometimes be grouped by readiness levels, sometimes by common interests, and sometimes by preferred ways of learning or working. In other words, there will be much movement and changing from one activity to another. Some students and some groups will manage this type of learning environment better than others. This means that the teacher might need to work with students on how to manage transitions and routines that could be unfamiliar. The lessons in this unit are structured so that there is some sense of routine built in. It is still likely that the teacher will have to help students adjust. The teacher might need to explain that because all students are different, there will be times when several different activities are going on at once, or that students will be working from different lists of words. It might also be helpful for students to practice moving (and perhaps rearranging the furniture) from small groups, to individual desks, to the space dedicated to group discussion.

## ONGOING ASSESSMENT

Ongoing assessments are administered to students throughout the unit in order to: (1) assess students' developing skills so that resources and activities can be tailored to each student; (2) assess what students already know about poetry, which will help tailor the activities and group students appropriately; and (3) provide a baseline for comparison at the end of the unit so that the teacher can assess the growth of each student throughout the course of the unit. Assessment tasks are included in the lessons in which they should be administered. A brief preassessment to be administered at the beginning of the unit and a summative assessment for the end of the unit are also provided.

## THE CLEAR CURRICULUM MODEL

This unit has been designed using the CLEAR Curriculum Model. The CLEAR (Challenge Leading to Engagement, Achievement and Results) Curriculum incorporates elements from three research-based curriculum models—differentiation, Depth and Complexity, and the Schoolwide Enrichment Model—by Carol Tomlinson, Sandra Kaplan, and Joseph Renzulli, respectively. These elements are applied to a curriculum framework that is consistent with state and national standards in reading, but build layers of challenge and opportunities for more in-depth study authentic to the work of professionals within a discipline, to better meet the needs of all students. Refer to page 15 for more information about the CLEAR Curriculum Model.

## ICONS EXPLAINED

Integrated throughout the lesson plans are a series of icons or symbols intended to draw your attention to the particular content focus, learning objective, or instructional configuration of each learning activity. Some of these icons are derived from Sandra Kaplan's Depth and Complexity curriculum model, while others have been developed specifically for the CLEAR Curriculum Model used in these units. Refer to page 16 for an explanation of each icon.

HANDOUT 0.1

# THE MAGIC OF EVERYDAY THINGS

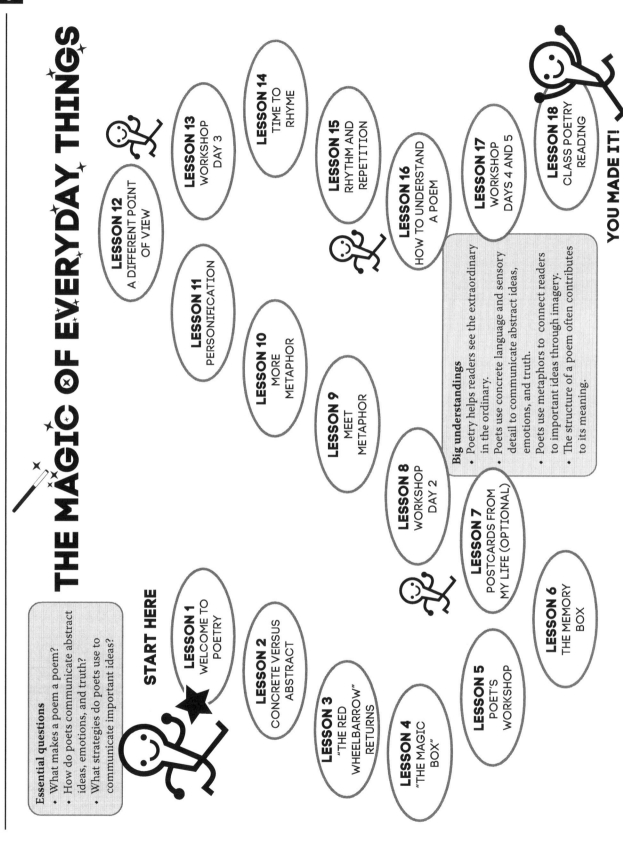

**Essential questions**
- What makes a poem a poem?
- How do poets communicate abstract ideas, emotions, and truth?
- What strategies do poets use to communicate important ideas?

**START HERE**

**LESSON 1**
WELCOME TO POETRY

**LESSON 2**
CONCRETE VERSUS ABSTRACT

**LESSON 3**
"THE RED WHEELBARROW" RETURNS

**LESSON 4**
"THE MAGIC BOX"

**LESSON 5**
POET'S WORKSHOP

**LESSON 6**
THE MEMORY BOX

**LESSON 7**
POSTCARDS FROM MY LIFE (OPTIONAL)

**LESSON 8**
WORKSHOP DAY 2

**LESSON 9**
MEET METAPHOR

**LESSON 10**
MORE METAPHOR

**LESSON 11**
PERSONIFICATION

**LESSON 12**
A DIFFERENT POINT OF VIEW

**LESSON 13**
WORKSHOP DAY 3

**LESSON 14**
TIME TO RHYME

**LESSON 15**
RHYTHM AND REPETITION

**LESSON 16**
HOW TO UNDERSTAND A POEM

**LESSON 17**
WORKSHOP DAYS 4 AND 5

**LESSON 18**
CLASS POETRY READING

**YOU MADE IT!**

**Big understandings**
- Poetry helps readers see the extraordinary in the ordinary.
- Poets use concrete language and sensory detail to communicate abstract ideas, emotions, and truth.
- Poets use metaphors to connect readers to important ideas through imagery.
- The structure of a poem often contributes to its meaning.

# LESSON 1

# Welcome to Poetry

## MATERIALS

- ✓ Student workbooks
- ✓ Teacher's copy of "The Fish" by Elizabeth Bishop (available at http://www.poemhunter.com/poem/the-fish)
- ✓ Handout 1.1: Unit Preassessment
- ✓ Handout 1.2: The Magic of Everyday Things Vocabulary Sheet
- ✓ Appendix A1: Grouping Plan Chart

 Poets use concrete language and sensory detail to communicate abstract ideas, emotions, and truths.

## OBJECTIVES

Students will:

- ✓ develop ideas for writing;
- ✓ learn and use the first step in the writing process; and
- ✓ develop the skills to participate as knowledgeable, reflective, creative, and critical members of a literary community.

- Imagery
- Abstract and concrete language

## SEQUENCE

## UNIT PREASSESSMENT

1. Administer the Unit Preassessment (Handout 1.1). Explain to students that this assessment is not for a grade. Rather, it is to find out how much they already know about poetry.

## WARM UP

2. Invite students to lie down, close their eyes, and relax by taking deep breaths (continue instructing students to breathe deeply until the room is quiet). Say: *I am going to say a word. I want you to concentrate on the first image or picture that comes into your mind when I say the word. Try to notice as many details as you can about the picture or scene that comes into your mind. I will say the word and then give you 30 seconds to quietly get a clear picture with lots of details in your mind. Ready. The word is:* excitement. Time students for 30 seconds.

3. After the 30 seconds are up, ask students to write (and draw), in their workbooks, some words, phrases, and pictures that describe what they imagined. Let students know that they only have a couple of minutes to get down as many details as they can.

- Some 2E students who struggle with the writing process might prefer to draw the images rather than write them.
- Make sure students have their workbooks and something to write with already out on their desks or next to them on the floor to make the transition as smooth as possible.
- Make sure students know that they will have a chance to share what they imagined with the group, but *not yet*. Their job at this stage is to get the details down quickly in their own notebooks in preparation for the next task.

4. Repeat steps 1 and 2 using a different abstract noun instead of *excitement*. You might try one of these: *truth, love, fear, rage, beauty.* If time permits, you might repeat steps 1 and 2 with a third word.

## DISCUSSION

5. Gather the whole group back together. Give each student a chance to share one of the images they experienced. Students should share what they imagined and some of the words they wrote down in their workbooks.

6. Ask students: *What did you notice about the responses?* Students might need some prompting but will probably notice that everyone came up with a different image.

This observation is important, because it can lead you to introduce a big idea about poetry: Poets use lots of sensory detail to communicate their ideas about something abstract like *beauty* or *truth*. That is, we don't experience beauty as a general category, but as we interact with specific people, events, and objects. This is the secret to writing good poetry—being able to communicate a very general, universal (abstract) idea using concrete words and images.

This is a good time to stop and explain the "Poetree." This was created to help students have a visual and conceptual understanding of the unit and how the essential components of a poem fit together. (See p. X for an example.)

7. Write the vocabulary words (*imagery*, *concrete*, and *abstract*) on the blackboard or whiteboard and explain what they mean in terms of the discussion you just had (see definitions and suggestions below). Students do not need to write these down. They will be seeing these words again later in the unit.

   ✓ *Imagery* in poetry is the expression of sensory detail (sight, sound, smell, touch, taste). This word originates from Latin and has the same root as words such as *image, imagine, imagination*, and *imitate*, which are all concerned with creating a picture, impression, or copy of something. A good way to introduce this term would be to ask students to suggest as many words as they know that might be related to *imagery*, to list these on the board, and then to have students think about what meaning these words have in common. After identifying that all the words have something to do with creating a picture or impression of something, introduce the meaning of imagery in poetry, which is what poets create by using details that connect readers to the poem through all of their senses (although mainly sight). Explain to students that in the earlier activity, when they created a picture in their minds of the word you gave them, they were using their *imaginations* to form *images*. When poets describe these images in detail, we call this *imagery*.

- When discussing words related to *imagery*, some students might suggest words like **im**possible or **im**mature. These are words in which the prefix *im-* (meaning "not" or the negative form of) changes the meaning of the base word. These words do not share the same root as *imagery*. It will be important to clarify this distinction for students to avoid confusion. You might do this by generating two lists with students—one for words sharing the same root as imagery and another for words in which the prefix *im-* is at work.
- When discussing the term *concrete*, ask students to think about the word *combine* and to generate other words they know that begin with the prefix *com-*, meaning "together." Examples include: *community, communication, commune, committee, commonwealth, computer*.

   ✓ *Concrete* originates from the Latin *concretus*, from *com-* ("together") and crescere ("to grow"). Originally it meant "to grow together," or "to combine," as in the building substance, concrete, which was used as far back as in Ancient Rome (although the art was "lost" for many years after that) and was made by combining water, gravel, sand, and some cement. When these ingredients are mixed together, they turn into a hard, rigid solid. Thus, when we use *concrete* as an adjective, especially when talking about language, it can mean "representing an actual substance or thing," as opposed to *abstract* ("expressing a quality or characteristic apart from any specific object or instance").

After explaining the origins and meaning of the word concrete and the meaning of the word abstract to students, ask them to identify what type of *-nym* is represented by this pair of words (antonyms = opposite in meaning). You might also ask students to suggest synonyms (similar in meaning) for *concrete* (examples might include: *solid, specific, actual, real, material, tangible*).

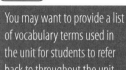

You may want to provide a list of vocabulary terms used in the unit for students to refer back to throughout the unit. See Handout 1.2: The Magic Of Everyday Things Vocabulary Sheet.

8.  Explain to or remind students that a *noun* (a "naming" word) is the name of a person, place, or thing. Explain that during this poetry unit, they will be interested in two special kinds of nouns. Tell students: *Some nouns are the names of things or people that you can point to, see, or touch: chair, pickle, book, bus, elephant, doctor. These are called* concrete nouns. *Some nouns refer to qualities and conditions we cannot point to or see or touch: anger, intelligence, fear. These are called* abstract nouns. Based on your earlier discussion, ask students to suggest which kind of nouns poets use most frequently to create imagery (concrete nouns). Students will have opportunities to reinforce their understanding of these terms throughout the unit, so it is fine if they do not seem to be entirely clear at this stage.

## POETRY FOR APPRECIATION

9.  Explain to students that each lesson for the next few weeks will begin with a poetry reading, where their job is to listen and appreciate what they hear. For today's poem, tell students they will listen to a famous poem called "The Fish" by Elizabeth Bishop. Ask students if any of them want to share what they wrote about in their preassessment. (You may want to return these to students prior to discussion.)

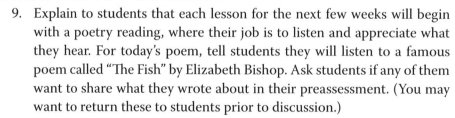

The type of poetry students will study in this unit is related to a movement in early 20th-century Anglo-American poetry known as "Imagism." Imagism emphasized precise imagery, and clear, specific language (the poet Ezra Pound famously described this in terms of "luminous details") to connect readers to bigger ideas. This approach was a significant shift from Romantic and Victorian poetry, which favored abstract, sentimental language over concrete details grounded in the physical world.

10.  Before reading, encourage students to listen for as many details as they can—not just visual details, but also those where the poet taps into the reader's other senses to create imagery. Point out to students that all poets have different perspectives about a topic. If 20 people wrote about a fish, you would have 20 different unique poems.

11.  Read "The Fish" aloud.

12. Afterward, have students turn to the person next to them and share one image or phrase that stuck in their minds while listening to the poem. If time permits, you might like to read this poem twice, since there is so much detail involved.

 Some students may have difficulty visualizing details in the poem. If you feel your students may struggle with this, consider starting by telling a story with rich visual imagery, and having students identify the imagery in the story before they listen to the poem.

## PREPARATION: FORMATIVE ASSESSMENT 1

13. Following Lesson 1, have students complete the following activity in their journals or as an exit card. An exit card is a simple strategy whereby you can keep track of students' understanding throughout a unit of study, rather than making assumptions about what students have understood.
    ✓ Ask students to fold a sheet of paper in half and copy the word concrete on one side, and the word abstract on the other.
    ✓ Now ask students to write at least two examples of nouns that fit the category on each side of paper. Encourage them to think of examples beyond the ones discussed in class.
    ✓ You should allow only a few minutes for this task (the goal is to check understanding of the terms, not to see how many examples each student can generate).

14. **Using the assessment data:** In this case, use the information gathered from having students complete the exit card to sort students into three readiness groups, as follows. A sorting chart is provided (Appendix A1).
    ✓ **Group A:** Students were able to demonstrate their understanding of concrete and abstract nouns by writing down multiple accurate examples of each category, including those not provided as examples during the lesson.
    ✓ **Group B:** Students correctly identified one or two examples from the class discussion, but could not identify their own examples and possibly included a couple of nonexamples.
    ✓ **Group C:** Students had trouble completing the task. They asked for significant help from the teacher, did not know the definitions of each term, or perhaps did not remember the definition of a noun.

 Keep in mind that the three readiness groups are suggested or potential groups, but for a given class of students, not all might be applicable. For example, all of your students might fall into Groups B and C, or all might fall into Groups A and B, etc. In that case, in Lesson 2, you may not need to use all three versions of the task.

## HANDOUT 1.1
# UNIT PREASSESSMENT

**Directions:** Answer the following questions about poetry. Use a separate sheet of paper if necessary.

1. What do you know about poetry?

2. Write the titles of some poems you know:

3. Write the names of some poets you know:

4. What are some of the ways poets make their poems interesting?

## HANDOUT 1.1, CONTINUED

5. Why do you think we read poetry?

6. What would you like to learn about poetry in the next few weeks?

7. On a separate sheet of paper, write a poem about a fish.

# THE MAGIC OF EVERYDAY THINGS VOCABULARY SHEET

| Word | Definition | Example |
|---|---|---|
| Imagery | Words that make you think about something you touch, see, taste, smell, or hear. | By October, the leaves of the tree had changed from dark green to shades of yellow, red, and orange. |
| Concrete Noun | A person, place, or thing that can be touched; an actual person, place, or thing. | Chair, bowl, food, ball, bat, doll, pickle, bus, doctor. |
| Abstract Noun | A person, place, or thing that cannot be touched or lacking physical detail. | Anger, intelligence, fear, love. |
| Cinquain | A poem of five lines. | Line 1: Title: 1 concrete noun. Line 2: Description: 2 adjectives describing the noun. Line 3: Action: 3 action verbs. Line 4: Descriptive phrase: 4 words. Line 5: Synonym for the title: 1 word. |
| Synonym | Word that has the same meaning as another word. | Shoes and sneakers. |
| Metaphor | When two unlike nouns are directly compared. | Time is money. |
| Personification | When you give a nonliving object human qualities. | The apple jumps. The car groans. The stop sign screams. |
| Rhyme | Repetition on identical or similar sounds in two or more different words. | Car, jar, and tar. Light, bite, kite, and night. |
| Rhythm | A pattern of stressed and unstressed sounds. | A poem that has a beat that you can clap along with. |
| Couplet | Two lines of a poem that usually rhyme. | *Humpty Dumpty sat on a wall. Humpty Dumpty had a great fall.* |
| Repetition | Saying the same words or group of words more than once in a poem. | In the poem "The River," the words "The River" begin each stanza of the poem. |

# LESSON

# 2 Concrete Versus Abstract

## MATERIALS

- ✓ Student workbooks
- ✓ Teacher's copy of "Baby Tortoise" by D. H. Lawrence (available at http://poets.org/poetsorg/poem/baby-tortoise)
- ✓ Teacher's copy of "The Red Wheelbarrow" by William Carlos Williams (available at http://www.poets.org/poetsorg/poem/red-wheelbarrow). If possible, write out this poem on sentence strips and place in a pocket chart or on the board.
- ✓ Teacher's copy of "The Fish" by Elizabeth Bishop (available at http://www.poemhunter.com/poem/the-fish)
- ✓ Handout 2.1A: Concrete Versus Abstract Activity (hardest)
- ✓ Handout 2.1B: Concrete Versus Abstract Activity (on-level)
- ✓ Handout 2.1C: Concrete Versus Abstract Activity (easiest)
- ✓ Appendix A2: Concrete Versus Abstract Activity Answer Keys

- • Poets use concrete language and sensory detail to communicate abstract ideas, emotions, and truths.
- • Poetry helps readers see the extraordinary in the ordinary.

## OBJECTIVES

Students will:
- ✓ build a vocabulary list;
- ✓ identify and use various parts of speech (concrete and abstract nouns, adjectives); and
- ✓ develop the skills to participate as knowledgeable, reflective, creative, and critical members of a literary community.

- Imagery
- Abstract and concrete language (Antonyms: abstract-concrete)

# SEQUENCE

## POETRY FOR APPRECIATION

1.  Invite students to find a comfortable place for listening (this could be at their desks or lying or sitting on the carpet with their eyes closed). Remind students that one very important purpose of reading is for personal enjoyment. Their job during this time is to listen to and enjoy the way the poem sounds, and they might also listen for some of the imagery and details used by the poet.

2.  Read "Baby Tortoise" by D. H. Lawrence aloud.

> You may wonder, *are these poems too difficult for my students to understand?*
>
> The goal of "Poetry for Appreciation" is simply to expose students to the sounds and rhythms of good poetry, which many students might not have encountered before. The poems selected are deliberately above the comprehension and independent reading level of most elementary school students. This allows students to concentrate on how the poems sound rather than analyzing every aspect of their meanings, as they will do with other poems used in the lesson activities. The poems have also been carefully selected because they each contain a lot of sensory detail and are, therefore, consistent with the imagist movement which forms the basis for the big ideas about poetry that are explored throughout this unit.

3.  Afterward, have students turn to the person next to them and share one image or phrase that stuck in their minds while listening to the poem. See if students can recall any of the specific words used in the poem.

4.  As you finish reading the "Poetry for Appreciation" poem each day, you might invite a student to come forward and pin or tape a copy of the poem to a class poetry wall or board, so that students can see the collection building over time and also look at them more closely if they wish. Some students might have favorite poems of their own that they wish to bring in and add to the poetry wall.

## ACTIVITY: CONCRETE VERSUS ABSTRACT

5.  In this independent activity, using Handouts 2.1A–C: Concrete Versus Abstract Activity, students will work with word lists appropriate to their readiness levels as they practice identifying the distinction between

concrete and abstract nouns. Some of the nouns students work with during this activity will be incorporated into a subsequent poetry-writing activity.

6. Ask students to think back to Lesson 1. Remind them that they were introduced to some new vocabulary words and see if any students can recall the words (*imagery, abstract, concrete*). Explain that for the next task, students will be working on different activities, but that they will all be working on recognizing the difference between concrete and abstract nouns to prepare them to write some of their own poems later in the lesson.

7. Display Lines 1–21 of "The Fish" by Elizabeth Bishop and distribute Handout 2.1A. Students will be assigned one of three versions of the task, based on their readiness as assessed through Formative Assessment 1.

As students finish, they can compare notes with a peer who has also completed the same task. At the end of the lesson, collect students' notebooks so that you can address any ongoing misunderstandings before the next lesson.

- Students in Group A will use Handout 2.1A to find as many concrete nouns and abstract nouns as they can in the excerpt from Elizabeth Bishop's poem "The Fish."
- Students in Group B will be provided with Handout 2.1B, which includes a set of vocabulary cards made by cutting out the words (to save time, these can be prepared ahead of time and handed to the students in baggies). Students will sort the words from their list into the two columns on Handout 2.1A.
- Students in Group C will be given Handout 2.1B and Handout 2.1C, which includes definitions and several examples to help students sort their words on Handout 2.1A.

Some twice-exceptional students have difficulty transferring words and ideas they read (from text, blackboard, etc.) to words and ideas they write down. They might also struggle with tasks requiring manual dexterity such as using scissors. You can allow these students to simply distinguish abstract and concrete nouns by highlighting or underlining each type of noun in a different color. Their poem copy or word lists can be kept in their poetry folders.

## DISCUSSION: "THE RED WHEELBARROW"

8. Before showing students "The Red Wheelbarrow" by William Carlos Williams, take a quick poll (by show of hands), asking: (1) *Does a poem have to rhyme?* and (2) *Could a poem be only one sentence long?* Inform students that the poem you are going to share is quite famous and was written in 1923 by a well-known poet from New York. Invite students to close their eyes and try to create a picture in their minds of the scene the poem describes. Gather students together somewhere where they can all see the pocket chart (or poem written on the board). Read the poem aloud.

Review adjectives prior to this activity, giving examples such as *the green string, the huge alligator,* and *the quiet child.* As a class, discuss how the adjective describes the noun, and review the directions for this lesson's activity, paying close attention to its request for the noun, not the adjective attached to it.

9. Give students a chance to share their initial impressions of the poem. Use the following questions to guide a discussion about the poem:

- Did you form a clear, vivid picture in your mind as you listened to the poem? (Some students might like to describe in more detail what they visualized.)
- How did the poet help his readers create a clear, vivid picture?
- What questions are you left with after hearing this poem? (Why does so much depend . . . ? Why did he choose something so ordinary to write about?)

In this discussion, focus students' attention on the imagery of the poem, created through sensory detail and concrete language. In the next lesson, students will revisit this poem and analyze it more closely by using background information and by using the form of the poem to plan their own poems. The introduction of "The Red Wheelbarrow" in this lesson is designed as a teaser to get students thinking about the poem and to share their initial thoughts.

10. Ask: *What do you notice about the punctuation in this poem? Why do you think the poet arranged the words in this way?*

Point out that this poem has stanzas, and indicate how each stanza is made up of lines. (You might rearrange the words in the pocket chart or write them out on the board so that they form a conventional sentence and ask students to reflect on which they like better.) In this poem, the structure helps to create a sense of suspense or a feeling that the poet is walking you through the scene.

11. After the discussion, give students an opportunity to revisit their initial impressions about poetry by asking again (by show of hands): (1) *Does a poem have to rhyme?* and (2) *Could a poem be only one sentence long?* This closure activity will help students realize that poets use many forms and that poems can come in different lengths with and without rhyming. The introduction of "The Red Wheelbarrow" in this lesson is designed as a teaser to get students thinking about the poem and to share their initial thoughts. Let students know that they will be seeing this poem again in the next lesson.

## HANDOUT 2.1A
# CONCRETE VERSUS ABSTRACT ACTIVITY

**Directions:** Find as many concrete nouns and as many abstract nouns as you can in the excerpt from Elizabeth Bishop's poem "The Fish."

| Concrete Nouns | Abstract Nouns |
|---|---|
| | |

## HANDOUT 2.1B
# CONCRETE VERSUS ABSTRACT ACTIVITY

**Directions:** Sort the vocabulary cards into the two columns—*concrete* and *abstract*—on Handout 2.1A.

| | | |
|---|---|---|
| HOOK | BLOOD | HOPE |
| LIBRARY | WISDOM | SCHOOL |
| LADDER | BONE | WATER |
| TRUST | MEMORY | PEACE |
| MOUTH | CHILDREN | HONESTY |
| BOAT | FISH | POOL |
| POWER | ENGINE | RAINBOW |
| VICTORY | OIL | JAW |
| GUNNELS | THREAD | RIBBON |
| FREEDOM | WISH | FAITH |

## HANDOUT 2.1C
# CONCRETE VERSUS ABSTRACT ACTIVITY

**Directions:** Sort the vocabulary cards (Handout 2.1B) into the two columns—*concrete* and *abstract*—on Handout 2.1A. An example chart is provided below.

| Concrete Nouns | Abstract Nouns |
|---|---|
| A *noun* is a *naming* word. It names a person, place, or thing. A *concrete* noun names something you can see, hear, touch, smell, or feel. | An *abstract* noun names a feeling or quality that you *cannot* see, hear, touch, smell, or feel. |
| HOOK | WISDOM |
| BLOOD | VICTORY |

# LESSON 3

# "The Red Wheelbarrow" Returns

## MATERIALS:

- ✓ Student workbooks
- ✓ Student anthology books
- ✓ Teacher's copy of "My First Memory (of Librarians)" by Nikki Giovanni (available at http://www.poets.org/viewmedia.php/prmMID/19505)
- ✓ Thesauruses for student reference
- ✓ Index cards (1–2 per group)
- ✓ Handout 3.1: "The Red Wheelbarrow" Ideas Sheet
- ✓ Handout 3.2: Words for "Glazed" (one per small group cut into separate cards, plus boxes/containers for the cards)
- ✓ Handout 3.3: Sample Words (for students having difficulty)
- ✓ Appendix A3: Focus on the Rubric, Part 1

- Poets use concrete language and sensory detail to communicate abstract ideas, emotions, and truths.
- Poetry helps readers see the extraordinary in the ordinary.

## OBJECTIVES

Students will:

- ✓ build a vocabulary list,
- ✓ identify and use various parts of speech (concrete and abstract nouns, adjectives),
- ✓ develop ideas for writing,
- ✓ identify the author's purpose in a simple text, and
- ✓ develop the skills to participate as knowledgeable, reflective, creative and critical members of a literary community.

- Abstract and concrete nouns
- Adjective
- Imagery

# SEQUENCE

## POETRY FOR APPRECIATION

1. Invite students to find a comfortable place for listening (this could be at their desks or lying or sitting on the carpet with their eyes closed). Remind students that one very important purpose of reading is for personal enjoyment. Their job during this time is to listen to and enjoy the way the poem sounds, and they might also listen for some of the imagery and details used by the poet.

Ask students to focus on the place this poem describes. Remind them that this is called the setting.

2. Read "My First Memory (of Librarians)" by Nikki Giovanni aloud.

3. Afterward, have students turn to the person next to them and share one image or phrase that stuck in their minds while listening to the poem. See if students can recall any of the specific words or details (imagery) used in the poem.

Rather than distributing different parts of the rubric, project the resource (Appendix A3) for your students (or use a document camera). The idea is to expose students to the rubric part by part so they will understand it for their process later in the unit.

- **Focus on the rubric:** On the SmartBoard or overhead, show the students the first part of the Poem Review Student Rubric (Appendix A3: Focus on the Rubric, Part 1).
- As a class, decide how the poem, "First Memory (of Librarians)," fits into this rubric.

## DISCUSSION: "THE RED WHEELBARROW" RETURNS

4. Ask students to think back to the previous lesson and share what they learned. If necessary, remind students that they read "The Red Wheelbarrow" and worked on identifying concrete and abstract nouns. Refer to the poem (on the board or pocket chart).

5. Now explain to students that one of the things really good readers do when they read is to think about the author's purpose in writing. Sometimes, a poet has a hidden message in a poem, and to find out what this might be, it is sometimes necessary to gather more information about the author by doing some research. Explain that, in later lessons, they will have a chance to research some information about different poets, but in the meantime they could think about the author's purpose whenever they read a poem. Now share the background information about this poem in a way that makes sense to your students.

There are different accounts of how and why Williams wrote "The Red Wheelbarrow." It has been commonly reported that the poet, who was a physician, saw the wheelbarrow scene when he looked out the window of a hospital room, in which he was sitting by the bedside of a seriously ill child he was treating. The intense emotion of the moment made the specific details of the scene extraordinarily vivid. One interpretation is that "so much depends" on the specifics of time, place, and people because that is what matters to us as we experience life. It is not "loss" as a general, abstract category that we experience, but the loss of an intensely personal nature. In considering the imagism movement that Williams belonged to, this poem is also interpreted as highlighting what is important in poetry—not the general, abstract sentiments of the Romantic and Victorian poets, but the vivid imagery of actual experience, conveyed by clear, specific language as in this deliberately sparse text. Williams uses language in a way that makes the ordinary seem extraordinary to the reader. In this way, helping students connect with, question, and analyze this short poem can help them engage with some of the big ideas of this unit.

6. Draw students' attention to the words in "The Red Wheelbarrow." With input from students, identify and underline the concrete nouns in the poem (wheelbarrow, water, chickens). Ask how many abstract nouns are in the poem (none). Ask what would happen if you took out those three concrete nouns and substituted different ones. Try this out with a few different combinations of nouns generated by you and/or your students (e.g., *So much depends on a red backpack glazed with syrup beside the white bicycle.*).

7. Ask students if they can identify what kind of word (part of speech) comes right before each concrete noun (adjective). You might need to remind students that an adjective is a describing word—the part of speech that describes a noun. (This definition will be reinforced in subsequent lessons. On the board, make a list with students of other adjectives they know to generate ideas for the upcoming activity.

## ACTIVITY: CONCRETE POEM STARTERS

8. During this activity, students will work in small groups of 2–3 and will use Handout 3.1: "The Red Wheelbarrow" Idea Sheet to generate ideas for poems they will write modeled on Williams's poem. First, have students select an interesting concrete noun they might want to use in a poem. They can select the noun from the list they generated in the Concrete Versus Abstract Activity in Lesson 2, or choose a new one of their own. Each student should write the noun in his or her workbook. Then, students will choose a second concrete noun. Allow 5–10 minutes for students to decide on a selection of interesting concrete nouns to use in writing their own poems.

For this activity, group students in the same groups as they were in for the concrete versus abstract activity in Lesson 2. Students who completed the same task will have a common list of nouns to choose from.

It will be helpful for students to have at least one thesaurus per group available to help them generate adjectives. If your students are not familiar with how to use a thesaurus, you might want to conduct a "mini-lesson" either during or prior to this poetry lesson to familiarize your students with the thesaurus.

9. Next, instruct each group to work together to generate a list of interesting adjectives that modify or describe the concrete nouns they chose. These should be written on separate sheets of paper or on index cards, so that they can later be displayed in the classroom. Each group should be assigned one of the following categories:
   ✓ Colors
   ✓ Size (e.g., tiny, enormous, giant)
   ✓ Time or age (e.g., young, old, early, late)
   ✓ Emotions (e.g., happy, sad, frightened, joyful)
   ✓ Personality characteristics (e.g., kind, rude, helpful)
   ✓ Sounds (e.g., loud, quiet, noisy)
   ✓ Feel (e.g., rough, smooth, soft, slippery)
   ✓ Smell (e.g., pungent, horrible, sweet)

When assigning categories for the adjective task, keep in mind that some categories may be suitable for higher readiness groups. For example, the color and size categories might be suitable for your lower readiness groups, because students might be familiar with more words to describe color and size characteristics, while higher readiness groups might enjoy the challenge of generating adjectives to describe the way objects feel or smell. Use Handout 3.3: Sample Words for students who are having trouble generating words of their own.

10. Allow 15–20 minutes for groups to work on this task, and spend time moving between the groups to monitor their work, help with spelling, etc.

11. Allow each group time to share some of the adjectives from their list. Explain to students that the adjectives they came up with will be on display in the classroom, so that they can refer to these whenever they are writing poems and want to use strong and descriptive adjectives. Encourage students to add to these lists.

12. Now distribute Handout 3.1: "The Red Wheelbarrow" Ideas Sheet to each student. Instruct students to work together in their groups to write the first concrete noun they selected in the appropriate box, together with an interesting adjective to describe it. (Discuss what makes an adjective "strong." For example, which words give the most vivid picture? Start with examples they know: a red sweater versus one that is scarlet, fiery, candy apple, and so forth.)

13. Next, a representative from each group should select from the box or container one of the words to go in place of *glazed* (Handout 3.2). With this word in place, they will then discuss the next adjective-noun combination. If students are having trouble and wish to select an alternative word from the box or container, they may do so. Students should continue to fill in the boxes on the sheet until they have created a full poem.

 **Focus on the rubric:** Ask the students to look again at the section of the rubric presented today (Appendix A3), and encourage them to work toward mastery in their language.

14. Once you have reviewed their work to ensure that students have placed the right part of speech in the right box, instruct each group member to copy out the poem on a sheet of paper to place in their anthology books. (Have students keep a designated folder or notebook for anthologies.) You might need to take a few minutes to remind students that their best, finished poems will be copied into their anthology books, while notes, ideas, and drafts go in the workbook.

15. Find a way of displaying each group's finished poems in the classroom (e.g., on the Poetry Wall). Once the Poetree is constructed, poems can be added to the limbs as leaves. If time permits, allow a representative of each group to read their poem aloud to the group.

 If students finish early, invite them to begin working on a second poem, either independently or with a partner, also following "The Red Wheelbarrow" model. Students might want to use another ideas sheet to develop a poem, or some students might want to write a draft straight into their workbooks by following the model.

**HANDOUT 3.1**
# "THE RED WHEELBARROW" IDEAS SHEET

so much depends

upon

a [_____]
*adjective (describing word)*

[_____]
*concrete noun*

[_____]  with  [_____]
*choose a word from the box!\**        *adjective*

[_____]
*concrete noun*

[_____]  the  [_____]
*choose a direction word*                    *adjective*
*beside, under, behind, above, next to*

[_____].
*concrete noun*

## HANDOUT 3.2
# WORDS FOR "GLAZED"

**Directions:** Cut along the lines and place the individual words in a box or container. As students complete the Red Wheelbarrow Ideas Sheet, they can select a word from the box, and copy the word into the appropriate box on their sheet. Students can replace the word they select with another if the word does not fit their poem.

| | | |
|---|---|---|
| WET | HEAVY | COVERED |
| DRENCHED | ERUPTING | BURSTING |
| BOILING | VISITING | COLLAPSING |
| BRIMMING | PERFORMING | COMFORTABLE |
| SHINY | SPARKLING | SITTING |
| STANDING | CONTAGIOUS | PLAYING |
| DANCING | WATCHING | SLIMY |
| SLIPPERY | HUMMING | MOVING |
| GROWING | STICKY | BRIGHT |
| BURNING | GLOWING | DARK |

## HANDOUT 3.3
# SAMPLE WORDS

## EXAMPLES OF CONCRETE NOUNS

| | | |
|---|---|---|
| Bowl | Car | Watch |
| Teacher | Ball | Bat |
| Pickle | Dress | Pencil |
| Frog | Book | Truck |
| Cow | Flower | Tree |

## EXAMPLES OF ABSTRACT NOUNS

| | | |
|---|---|---|
| Love | Anger | Happiness |
| Fun | Fear | Sadness |
| Intelligence | Excitement | Rage |

## EXAMPLES OF ADJECTIVES

| | | |
|---|---|---|
| Red | Blue | Tiny |
| Giant | Young | Old |
| Happy | Sad | Kind |
| Loud | Noisy | Rough |
| Smooth | Sweet | Spicy |
| Pungent | Slippery | Cold |

## EXAMPLES OF ACTION VERBS

| | | |
|---|---|---|
| Running | Talking | Smiling |
| Shimmering | Glowing | Eating |
| Leaping | Jumping | Dodging |
| Galloping | Exploding | Hiding |

# LESSON 4

# "The Magic Box"

## MATERIALS

- ✓ Student workbooks
- ✓ Teacher's copy of "A Nest Full of Stars" by James Berry (available at http://www.poets.org/viewmedia.php/prmMID/16734)
- ✓ Teacher's copy of "The Magic Box" by Kit Wright (from *The Magic Box: Poems for Children* by Kit Wright [2009, Macmillan])
- ✓ "Pocket Poetry" notepads (1 per student)—small, easy-to-carry note-pads
- ✓ Handout 4.1: "My Magic Box" Ideas Web
- ✓ Handouts 4.2A–D: Station Instruction Sheets (to be placed at each of 4 stations)
- ✓ Appendix A4: Focus on the Rubric, Part 2
- ✓ Appendix A5: Station Rotation Manager Sheet

- Students understand that poets use concrete language and sensory detail to communicate abstract ideas, emotions, and truths.
- Poetry helps readers see the extraordinary in the ordinary.

## OBJECTIVES

Students will:

- ✓ build a sight word vocabulary,
- ✓ identify and use various parts of speech (concrete and abstract nouns, adjectives),
- ✓ develop ideas for writing, and
- ✓ develop the skills to participate as knowledgeable, reflective, creative, and critical members of a literary community.

- Abstract and concrete nouns
- Adjective
- Imagery

# SEQUENCE

## POETRY FOR APPRECIATION

1. Invite students to find a comfortable place for listening. Remind students to listen to and enjoy the way the poem sounds, and they might also listen for some of the imagery and details used by the poet.
2. Read "A Nest Full of Stars" by James Berry aloud.
3. Afterward, have students turn to the person next to them and share one image or phrase that stuck in their minds while listening to the poem.

- **Focus on the rubric:** On the SmartBoard or overhead, show the students the second part of the Poem Review Student Rubric (Appendix A4).
- As a class, decide how the poem "A Nest Full of Stars" fits into this rubric. Show the children the poem, and again, point out stanzas and lines.

## INSTRUCTION: THE "POCKET POETRY" NOTEPAD

Remind students about the observations William Carlos Williams made about the red wheelbarrow. Poets must be careful and deliberate observers of their environment.

The Pocket Poetry notepad can be any small, easy-to-carry notebook. Encourage students to write their names on the outside cover and to keep it wherever they are most likely to use it in a moment's notice.

4. Encourage students to get in the habit of carrying Pocket Poetry notepads to observe the everyday magic all around them. As they collect observations, sounds, images, smells, etc., they will find that they become more attuned to the world around them.

## ACTIVITY: "THE MAGIC BOX"

5. Read "The Magic Box" twice aloud to the whole class. Ask students what they notice about the imagery of the poem. Try to guide students to recognize that the poet has used many different images in the poem to help create different pictures in the reader's mind.

6. Ask students to return to their desks with their workbooks and a pencil, ready to write down some ideas. Allow students 5–7 minutes of free writing time to write down some things they might put in their own "Magic Box." This is a good opportunity for students to get down some of their initial ideas.

 As the poetry unit advances, students will be increasingly asked to write for extended periods of time. Some 2E students might benefit from the use of assistive technologies such as laptops or keyboards to use during the writing process.

7. Now, set up four different stations, clearly labeled 1–4, in different parts of the classroom. At each station, place the appropriate instruction sheet (Handouts 4.2A–D). Assign each student a specific order of rotation through the stations, using Appendix A5: Station Rotation Manager Sheet.

8. Before students move to their first station, make sure they have:
   ✓ Handout 4.1: "My Magic Box" Ideas Web
   ✓ Their individual order of rotation (Appendix A5)

 The organizational demand of the stations activity might challenge some 2E students. You should be prepared to assist those students in getting from station to station, following the instructions sheet, and labeling their sheets. You should also be prepared to help students who struggle with organization to make sure these materials are placed in a spot where the students will easily access them again.

If you do not have sufficient time to complete all stations in one day, you can carry one or more over to the following day.

9. Allow 8–10 minutes at each station (adjust as needed for class size). Move among the students and stations to provide scaffolding as needed.

## CLOSE

10. When students finish the fourth station, make sure they keep their resources together and store these in a place they can access during the next lesson. Gather the group back together to close the lesson. Allow students to turn to the person next to them, and in 30 seconds, tell each other one thing they decided to put in their magic box. Inform students that they will use their ideas to write a poem about their magic box in the next lesson. In the meantime, suggest that as they are on their way home, or getting ready to go to sleep tonight, they can be thinking about the following question: *What would my magic box be made out of?*

 Encourage students to think of items/artifacts from their community to include in their magic box. Or, perhaps there is a common type of tree or material in the community. Could the magic box be made of that material?

**Poetry**

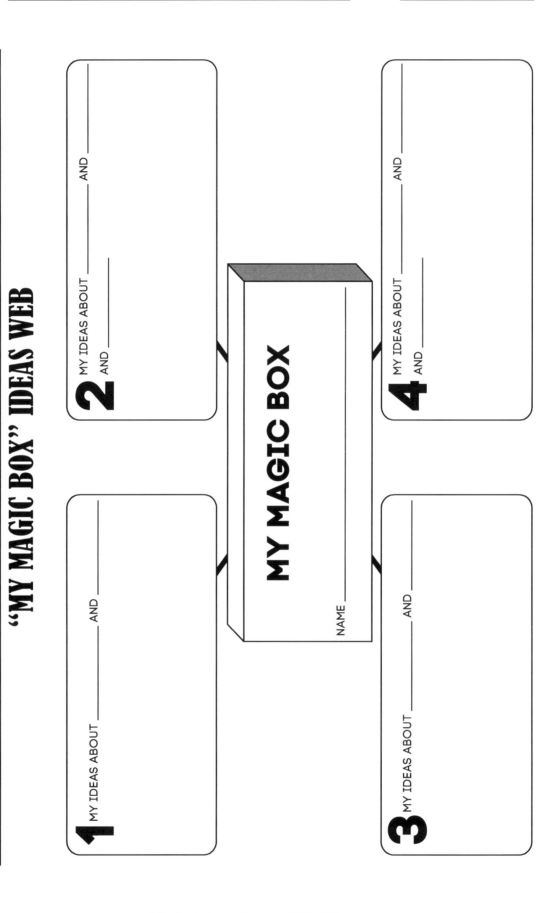

HANDOUT 4.1

## "MY MAGIC BOX" IDEAS WEB

**2** MY IDEAS ABOUT _____ AND _____ AND _____

**4** MY IDEAS ABOUT _____ AND _____ AND _____

### MY MAGIC BOX

NAME _____

**1** MY IDEAS ABOUT _____ AND _____

**3** MY IDEAS ABOUT _____ AND _____

**HANDOUT 4.2A**

# STATION 1 INSTRUCTION SHEET

LOOK AT YOUR IDEAS WEB. ONE OF THE BOXES HAS A NUMBER "1" IN THE CORNER. IN THE BOX WITH THE NUMBER 1 IN THE CORNER, WRITE YOUR IDEAS ABOUT:

- <u>SIGHTS</u> THAT WOULD GO IN YOUR MAGIC BOX.

- <u>COLORS</u> THAT WOULD GO IN YOUR MAGIC BOX.

## HANDOUT 4.2B

# STATION 2 INSTRUCTION SHEET

LOOK AT YOUR IDEAS WEB. ONE OF THE BOXES HAS A NUMBER "2" IN THE CORNER. IN THE BOX WITH THE NUMBER 2 IN THE CORNER, WRITE YOUR IDEAS ABOUT:

- <u>SMELLS</u> THAT WOULD GO IN YOUR MAGIC BOX.

- <u>SOUNDS</u> THAT WOULD GO IN YOUR MAGIC BOX.

- <u>TEXTURES</u> (THE WAY OBJECTS AND SURFACES FEEL) THAT WOULD GO IN YOUR MAGIC BOX.

HANDOUT 4.2C
# STATION 3 INSTRUCTION SHEET

LOOK AT YOUR IDEAS WEB. ONE OF THE BOXES HAS A NUMBER "3" IN THE CORNER. IN THE BOX WITH THE NUMBER 3 IN THE CORNER, WRITE YOUR IDEAS ABOUT:

- <u>ANIMALS OR CREATURES</u> THAT WOULD GO IN YOUR MAGIC BOX.

- <u>THINGS FROM NATURE</u> THAT WOULD GO IN YOUR MAGIC BOX.

Name: _____ Date: _____

### HANDOUT 4.2D
# STATION 4 INSTRUCTION SHEET

LOOK AT YOUR IDEAS WEB. ONE OF THE BOXES HAS A NUMBER "4" IN THE CORNER. IN THE BOX WITH THE NUMBER 4 IN THE CORNER, WRITE YOUR IDEAS ABOUT:

- **THINGS TO EAT AND DRINK** THAT WOULD GO IN YOUR MAGIC BOX.

- **THINGS YOU LIKE TO DO** THAT WOULD GO IN YOUR MAGIC BOX.

- **FEELINGS, HOPES AND DREAMS** THAT WOULD GO IN YOUR MAGIC BOX.

# LESSON 5
# Poet's Workshop

## MATERIALS
- ✓ Student workbooks
- ✓ Student anthology books
- ✓ Teacher's copy of "Hand Shadows" by Mary Cornish (available at http://www.loc.gov/poetry/180)
- ✓ Collection of poems/poetry books from school library or teacher's collection
- ✓ Handout 5.1: Poet's Workshop Conversation Sheet
- ✓ Handout 5.2: Workshop Rubric Guide
- ✓ Handout 5.3: "The Magic Box" Poem Guide
- ✓ Handout 5.4: Formative Assessment 2: Poetry Survey
- ✓ Appendix A6: Poet's Workshop Conference Notes

- Poets use concrete language and sensory detail to communicate abstract ideas, emotions and truths.
- Poetry helps readers see the extraordinary in the ordinary.

## OBJECTIVES
Students will:
- ✓ develop ideas for writing;
- ✓ develop an idea within a brief text;
- ✓ learn and use the writing process (e.g., prewriting, drafting, revising, proofreading, and editing);
- ✓ develop the skills to participate as knowledgeable, reflective, creative, and critical members of a literary community; and
- ✓ respond to written and oral presentations as a reader, listener, and articulate speaker.

- Abstract and concrete nouns
- Sensory language
- Imagery

# SEQUENCE

## POETRY FOR APPRECIATION

1. Invite students to find a comfortable place for listening. Remind students to listen to and enjoy the way the poem sounds, and they might also listen for some of the imagery and details used by the poet.
2. Read "Hand Shadows" by Mary Cornish aloud.
3. Afterward, ask students to think about the four animals mentioned in the poem. Tell students: *With a partner, discuss how the qualities of the animals might represent the father in the poem. What animal might represent one of their parents or family members?*

 Allow students to think about the underlying message of the poem while connecting personally to its topic.

## POET'S WORKSHOP

4. Explain to students that they will be writing more of their own poems over the next couple of weeks. One of the things poets do is to show their work to other poets to give and receive feedback on drafts of their work. Some poets meet in small groups to share their work with each other. Explain to students that, in this lesson, they will learn to give and receive feedback on poems.

 **2E** You may also photocopy poems for 2E students for whom copying selected poems in their workbooks would be difficult.

5. Before students use their own poems for giving and receiving feedback, they will practice on other poems that they enjoy.
6. Invite students to look through the poetry books and copies of poems you have assembled, and select a poem they might enjoy. Allow students to have access to the rubric for this lesson to help them evaluate the poems they've selected. Students should copy their selected poems into their workbooks.

Rather than allowing students to freely select their own poems, there are several ways you can make this process run more efficiently and effectively:

- Organize the books and poems available into categories to help students choose. For example, labeling groups of poems by their subject matter or by author can help students choose poems that match their interests.
- Select poems at a variety of different topics, reading levels or levels of complexity, and encourage students to select from a particular pile (you could color code these) based on your knowledge of students' readiness and interests.

7. Once students have selected their own poems, gather the group together again. Choose a student to help you role play a Poet's Workshop conversation:

   ✓ Ask the student to read his or her selected poem aloud.
   ✓ Use Handout 5.1: Poet's Workshop Conversation Sheet to provide brief feedback on the poem.
   ✓ Allow the other students to make comments or ask questions about the process.
   ✓ Now switch roles with the student, so that you read a poem and allow the student to use Handout 5.1 to provide you feedback.

8. After the demonstration, have students break into pairs. They should use Handout 5.1 and follow the feedback process you just modeled.

9. Explain to students that each time they finish writing a poem that they would like to include in their poetry anthology, they should:

   ✓ Sign up for a poet's workshop conversation and use Handout 5.1 to give feedback to a partner who has also signed up. You should allocate a place in the room where students can sign up for workshop conversations (e.g., names on the whiteboard or Velcro name tags that can be attached to a list).
   ✓ Arrange a conference with you (determine the sign-up procedure for this with your students). During these short conferences, focus your feedback to students on: (1) use of concrete, descriptive language; (2) use of multiple senses in choice of sensory language; and (3) use of imagery.
   ✓ Revise and submit for a review by the teacher for spelling and writing mechanics.
   ✓ Write the final copy of the poem on a sheet of paper to place in their anthology books.

- Encourage students to reference Handout 5.2: Workshop Rubric Guide. This ongoing use of the rubric will help students to become more comfortable in understanding the criteria that will later be used to assess their own poems.
- Make use of Appendix A6: Poet's Workshop Conference Notes during teacher-student conferences to record feedback that the student can use to strengthen his or her poems.

## ACTIVITY: MAGIC BOX POEMS

10.  Use Handout 5.3: "The Magic Box Poem Guide" to have students turn the notes they took during stations in the previous lesson into poems following the format of "The Magic Box" by Kit Wright. Once students have finished working on the guide, they should sign up for peer conferences and teacher conferences using the procedures you have arranged. If students do not get to this stage by the end of the lesson, they will have time to keep working on this poem in the next and future lessons.

As students choose items, encourage them to use their Pocket Poetry notepads to record ideas and memories.

## PREPARATION: FOR NEXT LESSON

11.  Ask students to bring in a small object from home that is special to them because it reminds them of a particular memory. A three-dimensional object rather than a photograph is likely to work better for the activity.

## PREPARATION: FORMATIVE ASSESSMENT 2

12.  Distribute Handout 5.4: Formative Assessment 2: Poetry Survey. Read the questions on the sheet aloud to students and instruct them to write something in each box on the first page and to complete the sentences on the following pages.

13.  **Using the assessment data:** Use information from the assessment to determine whether there is any content you have taught so far that you need to review or reinforce. For example, you might find a group of students having trouble remembering the definition for an adjective or confusing concrete and abstract nouns, and you can plan to take these students aside for a "mini-lesson" at a convenient time.

**HANDOUT 5.1**

# POET'S WORKSHOP CONVERSATION SHEET

Name of poem: _____

Name of poet: _____

Name of person giving feedback: _____

1.  Something I like about this poem is . . .

2.  An image I like in this poem is . . .

3.  Some sensory language I noticed in this poem is . . .

4.  A suggestion I have for you about this poem is . . .

5.  A question I have for you about this poem is . . .

**HANDOUT 5.2**

# WORKSHOP RUBRIC GUIDE

| | Master | Journeyman | Apprentice |
|---|---|---|---|
| **Choice of language** | ≫ Language is clear and descriptive.<br>≫ Most language is concrete rather than abstract.<br>≫ Choice of words is interesting and surprising to the reader. | ≫ Language is clear and descriptive in most sections of the poem.<br>≫ Most language is concrete rather than abstract. | ≫ Language is unclear and does not help paint a picture of the specific scene in the reader's mind.<br>≫ Most language is abstract. |
| **Imagery** | ≫ Imagery is used to create a picture in the reader's mind that is unique and surprising; imagery helps the reader see something in a new way.<br>≫ Imagery is used effectively to connect with more than one of the reader's senses.<br>≫ Tools such as metaphor, personification, and point of view are used effectively to connect with the reader through imagery. | ≫ Imagery is used to create a clear picture in the reader's mind.<br>≫ Imagery is used effectively to connect with at least one of the reader's senses.<br>≫ Tools such as metaphor, personification, and point of view are attempted, but are used inconsistently or are confusing to the reader. | ≫ Imagery does not create a clear picture in the reader's mind.<br>≫ Imagery does not connect with the reader's senses.<br>≫ Tools such as metaphor, personification, and point of view are not attempted or are confusing to the reader. |

## HANDOUT 5.3
# "THE MAGIC BOX" POEM GUIDE

Use this guide to organize your notes into a poem following the format of "The Magic Box" by Kit Wright.

I will put into the box

_____

_____

_____

I will put into the box

_____

_____

_____

I will put into the box

_____

_____

_____

I will put into the box

_____

_____

_____

**Poetry**

# FORMATIVE ASSESSMENT 2: POETRY SURVEY

| Things I have learned about poetry so far: | Things I would still like to learn about poetry: |
|---|---|
| | |
| **Questions I still have about poetry:** | **I hope I get the chance to read poems about:** |
| | |

## HANDOUT 5.4, CONTINUED

**Directions:** Finish each sentence to show what you have learned so far. Use a separate sheet of paper if necessary.

1. A noun is:

2. Types of nouns I have learned about are

3. A word used to describe a noun is

4. Some examples are

5. What do adjectives do?

6. Give three examples of an adjective

7. Imagery is

**Now answer this:**

8. Give several examples of how poets use language in special ways.

# LESSON 6

# The Memory Box

## MATERIALS

- ✓ Student workbooks
- ✓ Student anthology books
- ✓ Teacher's copy of "Combing" by Gladys Cardiff (available at http://aam. govst.edu/projects/cmietlicki/student_page4.html along with a short biography of the author)
- ✓ Handout 5.1: Poet's Workshop Conversation Sheet (copies available in a designated location in the classroom)
- ✓ Collection of poems/poetry books from school library and/or teacher's collection
- ✓ Handout 6.1: "The Memory Box" Poem Guide
- ✓ Appendix A7: Focus on the Rubric, Part 3

- Poets use concrete language and sensory detail to communicate abstract ideas, emotions, and truths.
- Poetry helps readers see the extraordinary in the ordinary.

## OBJECTIVES

Students will:

- ✓ identify and use various parts of speech (concrete and abstract nouns, adjectives);
- ✓ develop ideas for writing;
- ✓ develop an idea within a brief written text;
- ✓ learn and use the writing process (e.g., prewriting, drafting, revising, proofreading, and editing); and
- ✓ develop the skills to participate as knowledgeable, reflective, creative, and critical members of a literary community.

- Abstract and concrete language
- Sensory language
- Imagery

# SEQUENCE

## POETRY FOR APPRECIATION

1. Invite students to find a comfortable place for listening. Remind students to listen to and enjoy the way the poem sounds, and they might also listen for some of the imagery and details used by the poet.
2. Read "Combing" by Gladys Cardiff aloud.
3. Afterward, have students turn to the person next to them and share one image or phrase that stuck in their minds while listening to the poem.

**Focus on the rubric:** On the SmartBoard or overhead, show the students Appendix A7: Focus on the Rubric, Part 3. As a class, decide how "Combing" fits into this rubric.

Because this poem is about memories (a theme of this lesson), draw students' attention to the fact that the poet is writing about a memory that she cherishes, using distinctive imagery. Cardiff uses this simple image of combing hair to communicate an important idea; that is, everyday rituals are one of the important means through which wisdom is passed down through generations.

## ACTIVITY: MEMORY POEMS

4. Remind students that for the last two days they have worked on "Magic Box" poems. This week, suppose they have a "Memory Box" into which they can put special memories. Perhaps the object they brought into class this week reminds them of a special time, person, or event they might want to put into their memory box.
5. Ask students to sit with their object in front of them and their workbooks open. If they do not have their object, have them write what their object is on the top of the page. One by one, ask the following questions, and give students a small amount of time to write responses in their workbooks.
   ✓ What is your object?
   ✓ What color is it?
   ✓ What is an adjective you could use to describe its size?
   ✓ Describe the shape of your object.

  ✓   Run your hands over the object. What are some adjectives you could use to describe how it feels to touch?

  ✓   Does your object have a particular smell?

  ✓   How long have you had the object?

  ✓   How and where did you get it?

  ✓   Where do you usually keep the object?

  ✓   What special memory does it remind you of? Close your eyes and think of that memory. Now open your eyes and write a little bit about the memory. Use as many details as you can.

Because this is the prewriting stage, in which students are encouraged to freely generate ideas, emphasize that spelling mistakes are allowed and full sentences are not necessary. Poets very rarely sit down and write a poem from beginning to end. The process of generating ideas and jotting down brief notes in the form of single words, short phrases, and images is fundamental to the writing of poetry.

6.   To write poems about their memories, offer students the following choices or help guide students based on readiness:

  •   Students can use Handout 6.1: "The Memory Box" Poem Guide, a graphic organizer that is modeled after "The Magic Box" poems students wrote in the last lesson.

  •   Students can use the "Red Wheelbarrow" model to write their poems. That is, they can use the graphic organizer that begins "So much depends upon . . ." from Lesson 3 using the object they brought from home as the subject of the poem.

  •   Students can choose to determine their own poetic form for the memory poem. This is a more open-ended version of the task, but may be appropriate for students who are ready for a greater challenge.

## POET'S WORKSHOP

Students have now been introduced to the following poem models:

  ✓   "So much depends upon . . . "

  ✓   "The Magic Box"

  ✓   "The Memory Box"

7.   As students are introduced to more models or poetry ideas, begin to keep copies of these prompt sheets/graphic organizers in a designated part of the room. In future lessons, there will be time for Poet's Workshop, in which students can choose one of these models to write about, finish poems they have started in other lessons, read poetry in books to get ideas, or engage in poet's workshop conferences. Sometimes, you might allow students to work with a partner on a poem. All of these activities

While students are working independently in Poet's Workshop, this is a great opportunity for you to (a) hold individual conferences with students or offer individual help, or (b) collect a group of students for a "mini-lesson" on a particular concept or model if they need additional explanation, practice, or extension.

will contribute to the development of their own poetry anthologies. In some lessons, Poet's Workshop can be used as an anchor activity as students finish their other work.

8. In this lesson, remind students how Poet's Workshop operates, and make sure students know what to do and where to find materials.

## HANDOUT 6.1
# "THE MEMORY BOX" POEM GUIDE

I will put into the box

_____

_____

_____

I will put into the box

_____

_____

_____

I will put into the box

_____

_____

_____

I will put into the box

_____

_____

My box is fashioned from_____

_____

_____

_____

I shall _____ in my box

_____

_____

*The Magic Box* is a poem by Kit Wright.

# LESSON 7

# Postcards From My Life

**Teacher's Note:** Please note that this lesson is an optional one. This lesson provides an opportunity to illustrate the importance of clear, descriptive language in poetry by having students choose their words carefully in a postcard format. However, depending on students' depth of understanding, this lesson may not be necessary.

## MATERIALS

- ✓ Student workbooks
- ✓ Student anthology books
- ✓ Teacher's copy of "The Serenity in Stones" by Simon J. Ortiz (available at http://iamthelizardqueen.wordpress.com/2008/04/16/simon-j-ortiz-the-serenity-in-stones)
- ✓ Blank cards (about three per student) cut to approximately the size of postcards (or postcards made with Handout 6.1: Postcard Template)
- ✓ Either assorted postcards that have not been written on or a variety of pictures that can be used to make postcards, such as old copies of National Geographic or travel magazines. To save time, have an assortment of precut pictures from which students can choose.
- ✓ Collection of poems/poetry books from school library and/or teacher's collection
- ✓ Handout 5.1: Poet's Workshop Conversation Sheet (copies available in a designated location in the classroom)

- Poets use concrete language and sensory detail to communicate abstract ideas, emotions, and truths.
- Poetry helps readers see the extraordinary in the ordinary.

## OBJECTIVES

Students will:

- ✓ identify and use various parts of speech (concrete and abstract nouns, adjectives);
- ✓ generate topics and develop ideas for a variety of writing and speaking purposes;
- ✓ develop an idea within a brief text;
- ✓ learn and use the writing process (e.g., prewriting, drafting, revising, proofreading, and editing); and
- ✓ develop the skills to participate as knowledgeable, reflective, creative, and critical members of a literary community.

- • Abstract and concrete nouns
- • Sensory language
- • Imagery

## POETRY FOR APPRECIATION

1. Invite students to find a comfortable place for listening. Remind students to listen to and enjoy the way the poem sounds, and they might also listen for some of the imagery and details used by the poet.
2. Read "The Serenity in Stones" by Samuel J. Ortiz aloud.
3. Afterward, have students turn to the person next to them and share one image or phrase that stuck in their minds as making an ordinary object extraordinary.

Remind students that during the last lesson they described an object that was special to them as they worked on memory poems. Tell them that the poem you are about to read is about a special object, and the poet makes the ordinary object seem extraordinarily special. Ask students to pay particular attention as they listen to the way the poet uses language to create imagery that makes the object extra special.

## ACTIVITY: POSTCARDS

*Note:* Elements of this activity were adapted from *Postcards Home* by Paul Hyland, 2012, retrieved from http://www.poetryclass.poetrysociety.org.uk.

4. Ask students:
   - ✓ What is a postcard?
   - ✓ Have you ever received a postcard? If so, who sent it and from where?
   - ✓ Does a postcard have a lot of room for writing or little room?

✓ How is the way language is used on a postcard like the way language is used in a poem? (Discuss that because there is not much room to write on a postcard, it is important to choose words carefully. In the same way, poets must choose the most clear, descriptive language, since every word counts).

5. Explain to students that in this lesson they will be practicing writing with clear, descriptive language by writing postcards.

6. The first postcard that students write will be written from their own perspective to a family member.

✓ Students should describe their experience in rich, interesting detail (e.g., what they are doing, what the classroom looks like, what they can hear, what they can see, the texture of the chair/desk/carpet, the smells of the classroom, etc).

✓ Encourage students to notice details they might not usually notice.

✓ Students can decorate the flip side of their postcards with a drawing once they are finished.

> Remind students how to address a letter (Dear . . . ) and ways to sign off in a friendly letter.

7. For a second postcard, students should either select a picture postcard that has not been written on or cut out a picture from a magazine and paste it to one side of a blank card. This time, students can choose to write from their own perspective, or they can choose to take on the persona of someone else—an imaginary person, a character from a book they have read, a historical figure, or even an animal or inanimate object, and write from (or to) that perspective.

8. For each postcard, the student should first draft the text in his or her workbook and then write the good copy onto the postcard. The postcards would make a great classroom display!

9. Debrief with students by discussing whether it was difficult to choose the right words without much space, and how they went about deciding which were the most important or interesting details to include.

Keep in mind that writing from a perspective other than their own is likely to be more challenging for students than writing from their own perspective to someone they actually know. If you have students who would benefit from additional challenge, encourage them to choose an unfamiliar perspective.

Poet's Workshop can be used as an anchor activity in this lesson, or alternatively students who finish their second postcard might choose to work on a third, or to turn one of their postcard messages into a poem.

**Name:** _____ **Date:** _____

## HANDOUT 7.1
# POSTCARD TEMPLATE

## MATERIALS

- ✓ Student workbooks
- ✓ Student anthology books
- ✓ Teacher's copy of "A Boy Juggling a Soccer Ball" by Christopher Merrill (available at http://www.poets.org/viewmedia.php/prmMID/15951)
- ✓ Copies of graphic organizers/poem models introduced in previous lessons
- ✓ Collection of poems/poetry books from school library or teacher's collection
- ✓ Handout 3.3: Sample Words (for students who have difficulty)
- ✓ Handout 5.1: Poet's Workshop Conversation Sheet (copies available in a designated location in the classroom)
- ✓ Handout 8.1: Cinquain Poems
- ✓ Handout 8.2: Cinquain Graphic Organizer (one per student plus extras for group poem activity)
- ✓ Handout 8.3: Workshop Rubric Guide

- Poets use concrete language and sensory detail to communicate abstract ideas, emotions, and truths.
- Poetry helps readers see the extraordinary in the ordinary.

## OBJECTIVES

Students will:

- ✓ develop an idea within a brief text;
- ✓ learn and use the writing process (e.g., prewriting, drafting, revising, proofreading, and editing);
- ✓ identify and use various parts of speech (concrete and abstract nouns, verbs, adjectives);

✓ develop the skills to participate as knowledgeable, reflective, creative, and critical members of a literary community; and

✓ respond to written and oral presentations as a reader, listener, and articulate speaker.

Sensory language
- Imagery
- Cinquain
- Synonym

# SEQUENCE

## POETRY FOR APPRECIATION

1. Invite students to find a comfortable place for listening. Remind students to listen to and enjoy the way the poem sounds, and they might also listen for some of the imagery and details used by the poet.
2. Read "A Boy Juggling a Soccer Ball" by Christopher Merrill aloud.
3. Afterward, have students turn to the person next to them and share a phrase that stuck in their minds while listening to the poem that made them really hear the sound the poet was trying to convey.

## INSTRUCTION: INTRODUCING CINQUAIN

4. Introduce students to the cinquain form by using Handout 8.1: Cinquain Poems. Read the poems aloud (or have students volunteer to read them), and challenge students to see if they can figure out the pattern by identifying the parts of speech used in each of the five lines:
   ✓ Line 1: One concrete noun
   ✓ Line 2: Two adjectives describing the noun
   ✓ Line 3: Three verbs giving action to the noun in the gerundive "ing" form.
   ✓ Line 4: A descriptive phrase in four words
   ✓ Line 5: A synonym for the noun in Line 1

5. Construct several cinquains as a class by having different students select words for the poem (this is a good chance to use the nouns and adjectives you have displayed on the walls from earlier lessons).
6. Provide students with Handout 8.2: Cinquain Graphic Organizer so that they can create their own poem in this form if they wish during poet's workshop.

Cinquain actually means "group of five." It is related to the Spanish "cinco" for five, so if you have students whose first language is Spanish, or who are learning Spanish, give them an opportunity to point this out. This is a good chance to ask students what other prefix they know that means "five" (pent-) and to discuss other number prefixes (uni-1, bi-2, tri-3, quad-4, dec-10, cent-100, etc.).

## POET'S WORKSHOP

7. Because Poet's Workshop has been used predominantly as an anchor activity in the unit so far, it is likely at this point that students have spent varying amounts of time working on poems for their anthologies, and some students might not have had much time to work on their own poetry. This lesson should be used as a catch-up day, so that students can work in poet's workshop for the lesson and so that the teacher has a chance to work with students who need assistance or extension. After the cinquain form has been introduced, use all but the last 10 minutes of class in Poet's Workshop. Distribute Handout 8.3: Workshop Rubric Guide and encourage students to use this tool to help them improve their writing. Students have now been introduced to the following poem models:
   - ✓ So much depends upon . . .
   - ✓ The Magic Box
   - ✓ The Memory Box
   - ✓ Postcards (optional)
   - ✓ Cinquain

   Students can also consult the classroom collection of poems and poetry books to gather additional ideas and to try modeling a poem after one they like from a book.

 While students are working independently in Poet's Workshop, this is a great opportunity for you to (a) hold individual conferences with students or offer individual help, or (b) collect a group of students for a "mini-lesson" on a particular concept or model if they need additional explanation, practice, or extension.

 **2E** You'll notice on the rubric that there is a section called "Mechanics." Many 2E students have difficulty in the areas of spelling and grammar. You may need to target the mechanics of writing and work with 2E students to support their success in these areas.

## CLOSE: COLLECTIVE CINQUAIN CHALLENGE

8. For the last 10 minutes of class, engage students in writing an interactive group cinquain:
   - ✓ Break students into small groups of 3–4 (it would be appropriate for students to select their own groups for this activity).
   - ✓ Give each group a copy of Handout 8.2: Cinquain Graphic Organizer and give groups 1 minute to write down a concrete noun on the first line of the organizer.

- ✓ Have groups pass their sheet to another group and give groups 1 minute to come up with two adjectives and write these down on Line 2 of the sheet they just received from another group.
- ✓ Have groups pass their sheet to the same group they passed to in the last round (so that each sheet rotates through five different groups).
- ✓ Give groups 90 seconds to come up with Line 3 of the poem on the new sheet they have just received.
- ✓ Have groups pass their sheet once again and give groups 2 minutes to come up with Line 4 of the poem and to write this on their new sheet.
- ✓ Have students pass their sheets once again and give groups 1 minute to come up with the last line of the poem.
- ✓ Give each group the opportunity to read aloud the finished poem they now have in front of them.

You can provide some groups with Handout 3.3: Sample Words to prompt them if they are having difficulty generating words for this activity.

## HANDOUT 8.1
# CINQUAIN POEMS

## YOUNG TREE
seedling
young, wispy
growing, arching, stretching
reaching toward the sun
sapling

## SNEAKERS
shoe
canvas, striped
sprinting, dodging, leaping
part of my foot
sneaker

## BRACELET
bracelet
silver, engraved
shimmering, shining, turning
memory encircling my wrist
keepsake

## HANDOUT 8.2
# CINQUAIN GRAPHIC ORGANIZER

Line 1 (one word):

|  |
|---|

*concrete noun*

Line 2 (two words):

|  |  |
|---|---|

*adjective*                            *adjective*

Line 3 (three words):

|  |  |  |
|---|---|---|

*verb*            *verb*            *verb*

Line 4 (four words):

|  |  |  |  |
|---|---|---|---|

*related phrase*

Line 5 (one word):

|  |
|---|

*synonym*

# HANDOUT 8.3
# WORKSHOP RUBRIC GUIDE

| | Master | Journeyman | Apprentice |
|---|---|---|---|
| **Choice of language** | ⋙ Language is clear and descriptive.<br>⋙ Most language is concrete rather than abstract.<br>⋙ Choice of words is interesting and surprising to the reader. | ⋙ Language is clear and descriptive in most sections of the poem.<br>⋙ Most language is concrete rather than abstract. | ⋙ Language is unclear and does not help paint a picture of the specific scene in the reader's mind.<br>⋙ Most language is abstract. |
| **Imagery** | ⋙ Imagery is used to create a picture in the reader's mind that is unique and surprising; imagery helps the reader see something in a new way.<br>⋙ Imagery is used effectively to connect with more than one of the reader's senses.<br>⋙ Tools such as metaphor, personification, and point of view are used effectively to connect with the reader through imagery. | ⋙ Imagery is used to create a clear picture in the reader's mind.<br>⋙ Imagery is used effectively to connect with at least one of the reader's senses.<br>⋙ Tools such as metaphor, personification, and point of view are attempted, but are used inconsistently or are confusing to the reader. | ⋙ Imagery does not create a clear picture in the reader's mind.<br>⋙ Imagery does not connect with the reader's senses.<br>⋙ Tools such as metaphor, personification, and point of view are not attempted or are confusing to the reader. |
| **Mechanics** | ⋙ Few or no mistakes are evident in the spelling and mechanics of the poem. | ⋙ Minor mistakes are evident in the spelling and mechanics of the poem, but these do not detract from the work. | ⋙ Mistakes are evident in the spelling and mechanics of the poem to an extent that they detract from the work. |

# LESSON 9

# Meet Metaphor

## MATERIALS

- ✓ Student workbooks
- ✓ Teacher's copy of "Dreams" by Langston Hughes (available at http://www.poets.org/viewmedia.php/prmMID/16075)
- ✓ Handout 9.1: What's the Metaphor?
- ✓ Handout 9.2: Animal Metaphor Prompt Sheet (for students who have difficulty)

- • Poets use metaphor to connect readers to important ideas through imagery.
- • Poetry helps readers see the extraordinary in the ordinary.

## OBJECTIVES

Students will:
- ✓ identify literary devices, including metaphor;
- ✓ identify the main idea of a selection;
- ✓ generate ideas for writing; and
- ✓ develop the skills to participate as knowledgeable, reflective, creative, and critical members of a literary community.

- • Imagery
- • Metaphor

# SEQUENCE

## POETRY FOR APPRECIATION

1. Invite students to find a comfortable place for listening. Remind students to listen to and enjoy the way the poem sounds, and they might also listen for some of the imagery and details used by the poet.
2. Read "Dreams" by Langston Hughes aloud.
3. Afterward, have students turn to the person next to them and share one image or phrase that stuck in their minds while listening to the poem.

Biographical information about Langston Hughes, who remains one of the best-loved American and African American poets, is available at http://www.poets.org, along with several of his other poems.

## INSTRUCTION: INTRODUCING METAPHOR

4. Read "Dreams" again, this time asking students to think about the two images the poet uses to describe life ("Life is a broken-winged bird/That cannot fly;" "Life is a barren field/Frozen with snow"). Discuss unknown words as needed.
5. Ask: *Is life actually a bird? A field? Why do you think the poet described life in that way? What is he trying to communicate about what life is like if we let go of our dreams?*

During Lessons 9 and 10, you might wish to refer to online resources for additional materials for teaching metaphor. These resources may be helpful for struggling students as well as those needing an anchor activity.

 Explain that the kind of images Hughes uses in "Dreams" are called *metaphors*.

6. Have students copy the word and definition for *metaphor* into their workbooks: A *metaphor* is a comparison between two unlike nouns (people, places, or things).
7. Give some other examples of metaphors in everyday language (e.g., Time is money; I am in a sea of trouble; My friend was a rock during my time of trouble), and see if students can suggest some others. Be sure students understand the meaning of each one.
8. Explain that metaphor is a powerful tool used by poets to connect readers to important ideas. Poets don't usually use common, everyday metaphors like the ones discussed above. Instead, they create their own metaphors so that they can help readers see something in a surprising way that they have never before considered.

 Consider "Dreams" without the metaphors for life: *Hold fast to dreams/For if dreams die/Life is really bad/Hold fast to dreams/For when dreams go/ Life is terrible.* In this version, the poet is telling readers straight out what he wants to say. But what good poets do is *show*, through the use of strong imagery, instead of *tell*. A good image sticks in the reader's mind, so the important message also sticks.

## ACTIVITY: RECOGNIZING METAPHOR

9. Distribute Handout 9.1: What's the Metaphor? Work through the first one or two examples as a whole class by reading the excerpts aloud and discussing the metaphors that are used by each poet. Students should write these in the spaces provided on the sheet: (1) The sea is a hungry dog; (2) Hope is a bird; (3) Life is a staircase; (4) Life is a play; (5) The brook is a sheet of paper.

 Offer students the choice of working in small groups or individually on this task.

10. Allow students to work individually or in small groups of 2–3 to identify one or more metaphors used by the poet in each example.

11. Spend some time as a whole group discussing each example. Ask students to describe the image that the metaphor makes for them.

## ACTIVITY: IF I WERE AN ANIMAL . . .

12. Invite students to close their eyes and try to imagine that they have turned into an animal. Give them a minute or two to imagine which animal they have turned into and what it would be like to be that animal.

 • Provide Handout 8.2: Animal Metaphor Prompt Sheet to students who have difficulty generating ideas for characteristics and actions.

 • It would be helpful and enjoyable for the students if the teacher also generates a metaphor animal to represent him- or herself.

13. Ask students to open their workbooks. Students should write down or draw some of the characteristics and actions of the animal they imagined. How would that animal be similar to or different from how students think they act or behave?

14. Ask several students to share their animal with the class and to say whether the animal would make a good metaphor for them in a poem. That is, do the characteristics or actions of the animal tell us something important about that student?

Suggest to students that they might like to use their animal metaphor in a future poem.

## HANDOUT 9.1
# WHAT'S THE METAPHOR?

**Directions:** See if you can find the metaphors in these short poetic examples.


The sea is a hungry dog,
Giant and grey.
He rolls on the beach all day.
With his clashing teeth and shaggy jaws

_James Reeves_


_____ is a _____.


Hope is the thing with feathers
That perches in the soul,
And sings the tune – without the words,
And never stops at all,

_Emily Dickinson_


_____ is a _____.


Well, son, I'll tell you:
Life for me ain't been no crystal stair.
It's had tacks in it,
And splinters,
And boards torn up,
And places with no carpet on the floor—
Bare.

_Langston Hughes_


_____ is a _____.

## HANDOUT 9.1, CONTINUED

All the world's a stage,
And all the men and women merely players;
They have their exits and their entrances,
And one man in his time plays many parts

*William Shakespeare*

_____ is a _____.

Its bed is left a faded paper sheet
Of dead leaves stuck together by the heat—
A brook to none but who remember long.

*Robert Frost*

_____ is a _____.

**Name:** _____ **Date:** _____

HANDOUT 9.2
# ANIMAL METAPHOR PROMPT SHEET

## CHARACTERISTICS

| STRONG | LOVABLE | FURRY |
|--------|---------|-------|
| WILD | WILY | SHY |

## ACTION

| CRAWLING | SPRINTING | SWIMMING |
|----------|-----------|----------|
| STALKING | HIDING | CACKLING |

# LESSON 10

# More Metaphor

## MATERIALS
- ✓ Student workbooks
- ✓ Student anthology books
- ✓ Teacher's copy of "Hope is the thing with feathers" by Emily Dickinson (available at http://www.poets.org/viewmedia.php/prmMID/19729)
- ✓ If needed, paper bags and slips of paper showing concrete and abstract nouns
- ✓ Collection of poems/poetry books from school library or teacher's collection
- ✓ Handout 3.3: Sample Words (available for students who have difficulty generating words)
- ✓ Handout 5.1: Poet's Workshop Conversation Sheet (have copies available in a designated location in the classroom)
- ✓ Handout 10.1: Metaphor Prompt Sheet
- ✓ Handout 10.2: Formative Assessment 3

- • Poets use metaphor to connect readers to important ideas through imagery.
- • Poetry helps readers see the extraordinary in the ordinary.

## OBJECTIVES
Students will:
- ✓ identify literary devices, including metaphor;
- ✓ develop ideas for writing;
- ✓ develop an idea within a brief text; and
- ✓ develop the skills to participate as knowledgeable, reflective, creative, and critical members of a literary community.

• Imagery
• Metaphor

# SEQUENCE

## POETRY FOR APPRECIATION

1. Invite students to find a comfortable place for listening. Remind students to listen to and enjoy the way the poem sounds, and they might also listen for some of the imagery and details used by the poet.
2. Read "Hope is the thing with feathers" by Emily Dickinson.

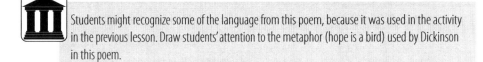

Students might recognize some of the language from this poem, because it was used in the activity in the previous lesson. Draw students' attention to the metaphor (hope is a bird) used by Dickinson in this poem.

3. Afterward, have students turn to the person next to them and share one image or phrase that stuck in their minds while listening to the poem.

## INSTRUCTION: RECOGNIZING METAPHOR

4. Take a few minutes to review the last lesson. Restate the definition of *metaphor*, and ask students to recall some of the examples they encountered in the previous lesson.
5. Discuss with students that "good" metaphors avoid cliché. To help them see this, draw a large heart or another symbol that would elicit many clichés, such as an American flag. Ask students to say every word they can think of related to the symbol on the board (e.g., *love* or *freedom*), and put those words inside your drawing. After compiling a sizeable list, ask students to write a metaphor (or even a poem) about the symbolized concept without using any of the words within the drawing. (Pretty tough, right?) This brief activity will illustrate that anyone can quickly think of an association for an idea but that poets must see beyond the "ordinary" to express a familiar and abstract idea (such as love) in an innovative and extraordinary way.

The word cliché literally means "stencil." Explain to students that when they use a stencil, they get the same image over and over. To use a cliché is to say something in a way that is not fresh and new—just as a stencil always leads to the same image.

You might allow 2E students who struggle with the writing process to state their metaphor(s) and you can be their scribe by writing the metaphor(s) in their workbooks.

## ACTIVITY: MAKING METAPHOR

6. Explain to students that in this lesson, they will be creating their own interesting metaphors, and that they might use some of these in their own poetry. Distribute Handout 10.1: Metaphor Prompt Sheet.

 Remind students that in Lesson 1 they were given abstract nouns (such as emotions) and invited to imagine a scene or image that represented each noun to them. Link this lesson to the big idea that metaphor is one tool poets use to connect readers to abstract, important ideas through more concrete imagery.

7. Instruct students to use these sheets to develop unusual metaphors for each of the nouns provided. Remind students that they should write a noun (usually a concrete noun) on the line, since a metaphor is a comparison between two unlike nouns. Provide the Handout 3.3: Sample Words for students who are having difficulty generating words for this activity.

8. As a group, do "Holidays are . . ."

9. Check in with students as they work and have students check in with you when they have completed the prompts.

10. Instruct students to select several (3–4) of the metaphors they have developed. For each of these, they should rewrite the metaphor into their workbooks, and then write 1–2 sentences explaining how X is Y. For example: *Hope is a bicycle. It helps you get through difficult stretches of road, it takes you to places you never imagined, and it makes you feel free.*

 For students who are not able to come up with their metaphors using the materials provided, offer the following activity: Using two bags, place slips of paper showing concrete nouns in one bag and slips of paper showing abstract nouns in the second bag. Ask students to draw a slip of paper from each bag. How are the two nouns (one should be concrete and the other abstract) alike? What do they have in common? How can one be the same as the other? Provide as many bags and slips of paper as needed to provide ample practice time for these students.

## POET'S WORKSHOP

11. As students complete the metaphor task, invite them to work independently on a poem in any form that includes a metaphor. They could

use the animal image they generated in the previous lesson, or any of the metaphors they came up with during this lesson.

## PREPARATION: FORMATIVE ASSESSMENT 3

12. Administer Handout 10.2: Formative Assessment 3. Check for understanding of metaphor at the end of this lesson.

13. **Using the assessment data:** Plan time during Poet's Workshop to run a "mini-lesson" for students who are still having trouble understanding the concept of metaphor. Choose some sample poems from the classroom collection to help illustrate the concept.

## HANDOUT 10.1
# METAPHOR PROMPT SHEET

**Directions:** For each of the following, complete the metaphor with a concrete noun. Then explain the meaning behind the metaphor you created. An example is given.

Holidays are *icing*_____ because *they make life sweeter* .

**Now you try:**

Holidays are _____ because _____ .

Love is _____ because _____ .

School is _____ because _____ .

Freedom is _____ because _____ .

Pain is _____ because _____ .

My family is _____ because _____ .

Fear is _____ because _____ .

**Now come up with some of your own metaphors:**

_____ is _____ .

_____ is _____ .

_____ is _____ .

_____ is _____ .

_____ is _____ .

## HANDOUT 10.2
# FORMATIVE ASSESSMENT 3

**Directions:** Answer the following questions about metaphor. Use a separate sheet of paper if necessary.

1.  What is a metaphor?

2.  Give an example of a metaphor used in everyday language.

3.  Give an example of a metaphor from a poem you have heard or read.

# LESSON 11

# Personification

## MATERIALS

- ✓ Student workbooks
- ✓ Loose leaf paper
- ✓ Teacher's copy of "Bodyweight" by Matthew Schwartz (available at http://www.poets.org/poetsorg/poem/bodyweight)
- ✓ Handout 3.3: Sample Words (for students who have difficulty)
- ✓ Handout 5.1: Poet's Workshop Conversation Sheet (available in a designated location in the classroom)

- Poets use metaphor to connect readers to important ideas through imagery.
- Poetry helps readers see the extraordinary in the ordinary.

## OBJECTIVES

Students will:

- ✓ identify literary devices, including personification and metaphor;
- ✓ identify poetry structures;
- ✓ develop ideas for writing;
- ✓ develop an idea within a brief text; and
- ✓ develop the skills to participate as knowledgeable, reflective, creative, and critical members of a literary community.

- Imagery
- Metaphor
- Personification
- Verb

109

# SEQUENCE

## POETRY FOR APPRECIATION

1. Invite students to find a comfortable place for listening. Remind students to listen to and enjoy the way the poem sounds, and they might also listen for some of the imagery and details used by the poet.
2. Read "Bodyweight" by Matthew Schwartz aloud.

## INSTRUCTION: INTRODUCING PERSONIFICATION

3. Ask students to listen carefully and try to figure out what all of these metaphors have in common:
   - ✓ The oak is a wise old man.
   - ✓ Happy flowers dance in the breeze.
   - ✓ The math test stares up at me, willing me to fail.

   (*Note:* All of these metaphors imply that the noun is a person or has human characteristics or actions.)

4. Explain that personification is a special type of metaphor, in which the noun is likened to a person (note the word "person" in the word personification). Ask: *What about these sentences suggests that the nouns are like people?* Explain that it is not always easy to tell straightaway when the poet is using personification, because he or she will not come straight out and say "The tree is a person," for example.
5. Explain that personification and metaphor are used not only in poetry, but in other types of writing and communication as well.
6. Next, review the parts of speech covered so far in this unit (concrete and abstract nouns, adjectives), and make sure students remember how these words function. Ask if any students know what part of speech is an "action" or "doing" word (verb). Tell students that verbs can be written in many ways. Have them look at some of the poems they have read and list verbs. Note that verbs can often be written with the suffix "-ing" (such as running, jumping, thinking). Invite students to generate a list of examples of verbs, and post this list for all to see.
7. Ask: *Why do you think verbs are important in personification?* Discuss that by giving an object a particular action a poet or writer can make that object appear human.

## ACTIVITY: HOW TO PERSONIFY A . . .

8. Explain to students that in this activity, they will write a short description or story using personification.

9.  To warm up, students should generate a list of at least 10 interesting verbs on a loose sheet of paper labeled "verbs." Next, they should write a list of 10 common objects (e.g., apple, chair, bus) on a separate sheet of paper labeled "objects."

 2E students who struggle with the writing process may use assistive technologies such as laptops for this activity. If you would like to see their revisions, ask students using assistive technologies to save each draft of their poem separately.

10. Have students give each of their lists to a different student in the class. In return, each student should receive a list of verbs from another student and a list of objects from a second student.

11. Students should now "match" each object on their list with an action on the other list, and write these pairs of words into their workbooks, even if these seem nonsensical (e.g., car groans; apple jumps; time flies).

12. Now ask students to decide which of these word pairs could work well in a story or poem.

13. Invite students to generate additional ways of personifying the object. This can be done by (a) giving the object additional human-like actions; (b) asking questions such as: Who? What? Why? Where? When? How? (e.g., Why does the car groan? Where does the time fly?); or (c) giving the object some personality characteristics (Is the car grumpy? Friendly? Adventurous?). You can write some of these prompt questions on the board.

14. Once students have generated ideas, they should write a short description, poem, or story about the object in which the object is personified.

## CLOSE

15. Allow students to work on their writing for the remainder of the lesson. They should go through the usual workshop procedure (peer review; teacher conference) as they work toward a final copy.

- One way to display students' finished personification stories could be to cut out colored paper in the shape of the object in each story, and write the stories on these shapes to display around the classroom.
- Encourage students to use their Pocket Poetry notepads to personify some of the usual sights on their way to or from school. Who does the old tree on the corner remind you of? What would the traffic light sound like if it could talk? Prompt students to extend these lessons from class into their everyday activities.

# LESSON 12

# A Different Point of View

## MATERIALS

✓ Student workbooks
✓ Student anthology books
✓ Teacher's copy of "Tiny" by Mandy Coe (available at http://www.tes.com/teaching-resource/tiny-by-mandy-coe-6376102)
✓ Collection of poems/poetry books from school library or teacher's collection
✓ Handout 5.1: Poet's Workshop Conversation Sheet (copies available in a designated location in the classroom)

 Poetry helps readers see the extraordinary in the ordinary.

## OBJECTIVES

Students will:
✓ identify literary devices, including point of view;
✓ generate ideas for writing;
✓ learn and use the writing process (e.g., prewriting, drafting, revising, proofreading, and editing); and
✓ develop the skills to participate as knowledgeable, reflective, creative, and critical members of a literary community.

- Imagery
- Point of view

# SEQUENCE

## POETRY FOR APPRECIATION

1. Invite students to find a comfortable place for listening. Remind students to listen to and enjoy the way the poem sounds, and they might also listen for some of the imagery and details used by the poet.
2. Read "Tiny" by Mandy Coe aloud.
3. Afterward, have students turn to the person next to them and share one image or phrase that stuck in their minds while listening to the poem.

Ask: *If you were suddenly tiny like the person in this poem, how would the world look different? How would your everyday experience be different?* This question asks students to consider the context in which a text is being read.

In your discussion of the poem, draw students' attention to the poet's use of an unusual way of looking at the world (from the point of view of a tiny person or creature), which gets readers thinking about ordinary things in a different way. Explain that during this lesson, students will have a chance to experiment with this idea in their own writing.

## ACTIVITY: SEEING THE CLASSROOM FROM . . .

4. Invite students to sit underneath their desks with their workbooks and a pencil. Give students time to settle down and then a couple of minutes of quiet in which they should observe everything they can. Encourage students to look out for details of the classroom they would not usually notice. *What looks different? Does it sound different? Smell different? Feel different?*
5. Ask students to share some of the details they recorded. Now introduce the term "point of view," and explain that this is one of the tools poets and other writers use to make their work interesting and to help readers see ordinary things in a new way. Ask: *How did the poet use point of view in "Tiny" to help readers think about ordinary things differently?*

When introducing point of view, make sure you explain to students that point of view can refer to (1) a physical (or spatial) viewpoint, such as the point of view one has from under the table, or (2) the viewpoint of the narrator of a story or poem. That is, a scene or story could be told differently from the points of view of different characters.

You can also ask students to think about their local community. What do locals or insiders know that tourists or visitors do not?

6.  Give students the opportunity to write a short poem describing the classroom. They can choose to write from the under-the-desk perspective or choose a new one, such as a bird's eye view of the room, or even write from the point of view of an object in the room (e.g., the wall clock, a book on the shelf, or even the class pet).

Students should work on point of view poems in today's Poet's Workshop.

# LESSON 13

# Workshop Day 3

## MATERIALS

- ✓ Student workbooks
- ✓ Student anthology books
- ✓ Teacher's copy of "A Dream Deferred" by Langston Hughes (available at http://www.americanpoems.com/poets/Langston-Hughes/2381)
- ✓ Collection of poems/poetry books from school library or teacher's collection
- ✓ Handout 13.1: Poet's Workshop Conversation Sheet II
- ✓ Handout 13.2: Workshop Rubric Guide
- ✓ Handout 13.3: Formative Assessment 4
- ✓ Appendix A8: Focus on the Rubric, Part 4
- ✓ Appendix A9: Formative Assessment 4 Answer Key

- • Poetry helps readers see the extraordinary in the ordinary.
- • Poets use concrete language and sensory detail to communicate abstract ideas, emotions and truths.
- • Poets use metaphor to connect readers to important ideas through imagery.

## OBJECTIVES

Students will:

- ✓ develop an idea within a brief text;
- ✓ learn and use the writing process (e.g., prewriting, drafting, revising, proofreading, and editing);
- ✓ develop the skills to participate as knowledgeable, reflective, creative, and critical members of a literary community; and
- ✓ respond to written and oral presentations as a reader, listener, and articulate speaker.

- Imagery
- Sensory language
- Metaphor
- Personification

# SEQUENCE

## POETRY FOR APPRECIATION

1. Invite students to find a comfortable place for listening. Remind students to enjoy the way the poem sounds, and to listen for some of the imagery and details used by the poet.
2. Read "A Dream Deferred" by Langston Hughes aloud. Remind students that they have heard poems by this author in previous lessons.
3. Afterward, have students turn to the person next to them and share one example of personification or metaphor or other image(s) that stuck in their minds while listening to the poem.

**Focus on the rubric:** On the SmartBoard or overhead, show the students the fourth part of the rubric (Appendix A8). As a class, decide how the poem "A Dream Deferred" fits into this rubric.

## POET'S WORKSHOP

4. Today's lesson is a chance for students to process the many models and concepts to which they have been introduced by allowing extended time for Poet's Workshop.

Before you allow students to start work, introduce them to the updated Poet's Workshop Conversation Sheet II (Handout 13.1). This sheet includes reference to metaphor, personification, and point of view. For students who struggle with writing, explain that a word or two is sufficient, and that they can provide oral feedback to classmates.

While students are working independently in Poet's Workshop, this is a great opportunity for you to (a) hold individual conferences with students or offer individual help, or (b) collect a group of students for a "mini-lesson" on a particular concept or model if they need additional explanation, practice, or extension.

5. Remind students that they have now been introduced to the following forms, models, and devices:
   - ✓ So much depends . . .
   - ✓ The Magic Box
   - ✓ The Memory Box
   - ✓ Postcards (optional)
   - ✓ Cinquain
   - ✓ Metaphor
   - ✓ Personification
   - ✓ Point of view

6. Explain to students that they may work on any poem using these models and devices, on an unfinished poem from another lesson, or on a new poem. Distribute Handout 13.2: Workshop Rubric Guide to help them focus on key areas. Remind students that they have already seen

the various parts of this rubric and should now be quite familiar with the criteria.

7. Remind students that they should write final copies of their poems (after the prewriting, drafting, and conference process) in their anthology books, which is their final collection of poetry.

 As you are working with individual students on their anthologies, you might alert some students to the notion that many poets use a theme to unite different poems in an anthology. Some students might be ready to think about developing their work around a coherent theme, such as poems about family or poems about the experience of feeling like an outsider.

 Make sure that students who have been using assistive technology have access to a printer so they can add revised and final poems to their anthology books.

## ACTIVITY: READING POETRY

8. Toward the end of the lesson, allow students to freely explore the poetry books and poems available in the classroom. Encourage students to find several different poems they might enjoy reading. Invite students to pay particular attention to poems that include interesting imagery and speak to their different senses and to poems that employ unusual forms or structures. Encourage students to read some of these poems aloud or to a friend, so that they can hear how the poems sound.

## PREPARATION: FORMATIVE ASSESSMENT 4

9. Administer Handout 13.3: Formative Assessment 4 in preparation for the next lesson, which introduces rhyme. In the following lesson, students will create a rhyming dictionary for the classroom. They will receive words based on this assessment. This assessment is a quick test of students' facility with different rhyming patterns. An answer key is provided (Appendix A9).

 Some students with specific learning disabilities have difficulty with spelling patterns. For those students, you can sit beside the student and read the word aloud while pointing at the word. Discuss with these students the different spelling patterns and brainstorm other words in that pattern.

10. **Using the assessment data:** Use the assessment data to plan which words you will assign to particular students. Try to match each student to two or more words that are challenging for him or her (i.e., not too easy or too difficult given current readiness level).

**Name:** _____ **Date:** _____

## HANDOUT 13.1

# POET'S WORKSHOP CONVERSATION SHEET II

Name of poem: _____

Name of poet: _____

Name of critic: _____

1. Something I like about your poem is . . .

2. An image that stands out in your poem is . . .

3. Some sensory language I like from your poem is . . .

4. A metaphor I noticed in your poem is . . .

5. You have created a sense of rhythm in your poem by . . .

6. A suggestion I have for you about your poem is . . .

7. A question I have for you about your poem is . . .

# HANDOUT 13.2
# WORKSHOP RUBRIC GUIDE

| | Master | Journeyman | Apprentice |
|---|---|---|---|
| **Discussion of language** | ⟫ Language is clear and descriptive. <br> ⟫ Most language is concrete rather than abstract. <br> ⟫ Choice of words is interesting and surprising to the reader. | ⟫ Language is clear and descriptive in most sections of the poem. <br> ⟫ Most language is concrete rather than abstract. | ⟫ Language is unclear and does not help paint a picture of the specific scene in the reader's mind. <br> ⟫ Most language is abstract. |
| **Imagery** | ⟫ Imagery is used to create a picture in the reader's mind that is unique and surprising; imagery helps the reader see something in a new way. <br> ⟫ Imagery is used effectively to connect with more than one of the reader's senses. <br> ⟫ Tools such as metaphor, personification, and point of view are used effectively to connect with the reader through imagery. | ⟫ Imagery is used to create a clear picture in the reader's mind. <br> ⟫ Imagery is used effectively to connect with at least one of the reader's senses. <br> ⟫ Tools such as metaphor, personification, and point of view are attempted, but are used inconsistently or are confusing to the reader. | ⟫ Imagery does not create a clear picture in the reader's mind. <br> ⟫ Imagery does not connect with the reader's senses. <br> ⟫ Tools such as metaphor, personification, and point of view are not attempted, or are confusing to the reader. |
| **Mechanics** | ⟫ Few or no mistakes are evident in the spelling and mechanics of the poem. | ⟫ Minor mistakes are evident in the spelling and mechanics of the poem, but these do not detract from the work. | ⟫ Mistakes are evident in the spelling and mechanics of the poem to an extent that they detract from the work. |
| **Poetic Devices** | ⟫ The use of tools such as metaphor, personification, point of view, rhythm, and rhyme are used. | ⟫ Tools such as metaphor, personification, point of view, rhythm, and rhyme are used some. | ⟫ Poetic devices, such as metaphor, personification, point of view, rhythm, and rhyme are not used. |

## HANDOUT 13.3

# FORMATIVE ASSESSMENT 4

**Directions:** In each group of words, circle the one that does <u>not</u> rhyme with the others.

| | | | |
|---|---|---|---|
| 1. bright | bite | high | height |
| 2. pale | gray | stay | bay |
| 3. shoe | through | though | two |
| 4. secret | meat | meet | secrete |
| 5. high | under | cry | untie |
| 6. eight | undulate | commiserate | community |
| 7. steak | stake | create | shake |
| 8. towel | show | stow | toe |
| 9. dream | unclean | serene | machine |
| 10. soap | hope | heliotrope | throat |
| 11. goad | odor | unload | ode |
| 12. mud | blood | food | stud |
| 13. scare | scar | prepare | unfair |
| 14. instant | bled | bread | instead |

# LESSON 14

# Time To Rhyme

## MATERIALS

- ✓ Student workbooks
- ✓ Teacher's copy of "The Leaf's Lament" by Andrew Fusek Peters (available in text and audio at http://www.poetryarchive.org/poem/leafs-lament)
- ✓ A rhyming dictionary from the school library (visit http://www.poetry4kids.com/rhymes if your school library does not have a dictionary available)
- ✓ Collection of poems/poetry books from school library or teacher's collection
- ✓ Handout 14.1: Rhyming Dictionary
- ✓ Handout 14.2: Rhyming Pattern Examples

 Poetry helps readers see the extraordinary in the ordinary.

## OBJECTIVES

Students will:
- ✓ identify literary devices, including rhyme and rhythm;
- ✓ identify poetry structures;
- ✓ know and use complex word families when reading (e.g., *-ight*) to decode unfamiliar words; and
- ✓ develop the skills to participate as knowledgeable, reflective, creative and critical members of a literary community.

- Rhyme
- Rhythm
- Couplet

123

# SEQUENCE

## POETRY FOR APPRECIATION

1. Invite students to find a comfortable place for listening. Remind students to enjoy the way the poem sounds and to listen for some of the imagery and details used by the poet.
2. Read "The Leaf's Lament" by Andrew Fusek Peters aloud.
3. Afterward, have students turn to the person next to them and share one image or phrase that stuck in their minds while listening to the poem.

## INSTRUCTION: TIME TO RHYME

4. Read "The Leaf's Lament" for a second time, and ask students to identify the pattern at the end of each pair of lines (rhyme).
5. Explain to students than when two words have the same sound in their final syllable, we say that they rhyme. Provide students with examples and write these on the board. For example, write a student's name on the board, and see if students can come up with real words that rhyme with that name (e.g., Jane, Train). Or, reference nursery rhymes that many students know
6. Ask students to identify any poems they have read so far that rhyme. Recall that not all poems rhyme, but that poets often use rhyme to create a rhythm in the way the poem sounds as it is read. You might select some other poems from the collection and read (or have students read) a few rhyming lines. You might also alert students to the fact that songwriters (lyricists) often incorporate rhyme in a way that works with the rhythm of the music.

## ACTIVITY: MAKING RHYMING DICTIONARY PAGES

7. Show students the rhyming dictionary (or the online version). Explain that some poets use such a dictionary as a reference when they are writing rhyming poems. Show how it works by looking up some words that students suggest.
8. Explain to students that in this lesson, they will be making some rhyming dictionary pages (Handout 14.1) for a game called "Pass the Rhyme." This handout can also be used to create a classroom rhyming dictionary if you choose. Explain that each student will initially be assigned two words. Once students have their two words, their job will be to write their words at the top of the handout and then write as many rhyming words as they know in the space provided.
9. Display Handout 14.1 and show students an example. In the spaces provided, write the word *boo*. As a group, generate several rhyming words

for *boo*. Use this demonstration to draw students' attention to the fact that while the final sound of each word ("oo") is identical, the spelling can be different (as in *shoe/blue/new/do*). Students must consider whether there are different spellings that make the same final sound as their target word and not to fall into the trap of writing only words that look the same.

10. Based on the information from Formative Assessment 4, use the groupings in Table 2 to assign words to students.

11. Encourage students to begin by (1) thinking about different ways of spelling the final sound in their target word, and (2) writing down in their workbooks the consonants and some common consonant blends (such as br/tr/str/bl/sw/cl) and other beginning sounds (sh/ch) that they can "test out" with the ending sound. You might need to assist some students by writing these prompts for them.

12. Allow students to work independently on their dictionary pages; keep in mind that speaking the sounds and potential words aloud will be an important part of this process. As students finish each page, help them correct spelling errors as necessary. If students exhaust their list, offer them a second page to work with.

## ACTIVITY: PASS THE RHYME

13. Invite students to stand in a large circle.

14. Select several students' copies of Handout 14.1. Choose one to begin with (preferably one that contains many familiar words).

15. Explain that you are going to say a line that ends with one of the words on the page. You will then pass the page to someone else in the circle (you may walk across the circle if you wish, or pass to someone within arms reach). The person to whom you pass the page must come up with a second line that is related to yours, and which ends in another word on the same page. For example, you might say, "I am visiting the sea." The next person might say, "What a lovely place to be." That person will then pass the page to a third person in the circle, who must also come up with a rhyming line to continue the poem.

16. Continue to "pass the rhyme" around the circle until the lines become harder to create, or until someone comes up with a good line to end the poem. Then, select another student's handout, and begin another group poem.

17. After you have tried a couple of poems using the handouts as prompts, try one with no safety net, in which students have to generate rhymes without visual prompts.

18. Continue playing "Pass the Rhyme" until all students have had a chance to participate.

## TABLE 2
## RHYMING DICTIONARY WORD GROUPS

### GROUP 1: LEAST CHALLENGING

| Pie | Bay | Hill | Hat | Too |
|-----|-----|------|-----|-----|
| Boat | Cry | Late | Hit | Pan |
| Go | Road | Line | Game | Win |
| Dog | Soap | Dish | Hot | |

### GROUP 2: MORE CHALLENGING

| Best | Dream | Steak | Dark | Less |
|------|-------|-------|------|------|
| Meet | Pain | Tack | Red | Leave |
| Scare | Small | Shell | | |

### GROUP 3: MOST CHALLENGING

| Faint | Dance | Good | Light |
|-------|-------|------|-------|
| Ring | Power | Mouse | |

### GROUP 4: A BIGGER CHALLENGE

| Sugar | Conflict | Rotten | Student |
|-------|----------|--------|---------|
| Amaze | Cereal | Quiet | Brilliant |

## CLOSE: PRACTICE WITH WRITING RHYMES

19. Explain to students that, in their workbooks, they are going to practice rhyming by writing:
    - ✓ A rhyming couplet (2 lines)
    - ✓ A verse of 4 lines with 2 rhyming couplets (a-a-b-b)
    - ✓ A verse of 4 lines in the pattern a-b-a-b

20. Encourage students to use the rhyming dictionary to stimulate their thinking. If they are stuck for topics to write about, encourage students to look back through their workbooks (or Pocket Poetry notepads) at the ideas they have previously generated. Alternatively, they could use some of the rhymes that were generated during the "Pass the Rhyme" activity. As they finish, students can either work on extending one of these exercises into a full poem, or they can begin writing a new rhyming poem.

Provide Handout 14.2 Rhyming Pattern Examples sheet to students who require additional structure/prompting to complete this task.

**HANDOUT 14.1**

# RHYMING DICTIONARY

| Word: |
|---|
|  |
|  |
|  |
|  |
|  |
|  |
|  |
|  |
|  |
|  |

| Word: |
|---|
|  |
|  |
|  |
|  |
|  |
|  |
|  |
|  |
|  |
|  |

## HANDOUT 14.2
# RHYMING PATTERN EXAMPLES

1. A rhyming couplet

| Example: | Your turn: |
|---|---|
| Humpty Dumpty sat on a wall. (a) | (a) |
| Humpty Dumpty had a great fall. (a) | (a) |

2. Four lines with two rhyming couplets

| Example: | Your turn: |
|---|---|
| **"Bed in Summer"** **Robert Louis Stevenson** | |
| In Winter I get up at night (a) | (a) |
| And dress by yellow candle light. (a) | (a) |
| In Summer, quite the other way, (b) | (b) |
| I have to go to bed by day. (b) | (b) |

3. Four lines in the pattern of a-b-a-b

| Example: | Your turn: |
|---|---|
| **"The Cow"** **Robert Louis Stevenson** | |
| The friendly cow, all red and white, (a) | (a) |
| I love with all my heart: (b) | (b) |
| She gives me cream with all her might, (a) | (a) |
| To eat with apple tart. (b) | (b) |

# LESSON 15

# Rhythm and Repetition

## MATERIALS

- ✓ Student workbooks
- ✓ Student anthology books
- ✓ Teacher's copy of "Stopping By Woods on a Snowy Evening" by Robert Frost (available at http://www.sparknotes.com/poetry/frost/section10.rhtml)
- ✓ Teacher's copy of "Love That Boy" by Walter Dean Myers (available at http://www.poemhunter.com/poem/love-that-boy)
- ✓ Teacher's copy of "Granny Is" by Valerie Bloom (available in text and audio at http://www.poetryarchive.org/poem/granny)
- ✓ Student copies of "The Distant Talking Drum" by Isaac Olaleye (available at http://ncpublicschools.org/docs/accountability/testing/eog/reading/20080122gr4set4.pdf)
- ✓ Collection of poems/poetry books from school library or teacher's collection

- • Poetry helps readers see the extraordinary in the ordinary.
- • The structure of a poem often contributes to its meaning.

## OBJECTIVES

Students will:
- ✓ identify literary devices, including rhyme and rhythm;
- ✓ identify poetry structures; and
- ✓ know and use complex word families when reading (e.g., *-ight*) to decode unfamiliar words.

- Rhyme
- Rhythm
- Repetition

# SEQUENCE

## POETRY FOR APPRECIATION

1. Invite students to find a comfortable place for listening. Remind students to enjoy the way the poem sounds and to listen for some of the imagery and details used by the poet.
2. Read "Stopping By Woods on a Snowy Evening" by Robert Frost aloud.
3. Afterward, have students turn to the person next to them and share one image or phrase that stuck in their minds while listening to the poem.

## INSTRUCTION: FINDING RHYTHM

4. Ask: *Did the poem by Robert Frost rhyme?* (Yes.)
5. Tell students you will read "Stopping By Woods on a Snowy Evening" for a second time. This time, you want them to listen not to the words, but to the sound of the poem. You want them to listen for its rhythm or beat. Read the poem again.

Ask: *Do you think you could clap along to the poem? Do you know where you would put the claps?* Read the poem for a third time, and invite students to clap along. (They should clap at the stressed syllables; there are four in every line.)

6. Tell students that they can figure out where to clap along in Frost's poem because the author has created a rhythm. *Rhythm* is the pattern of sound or the beat of a poem. It is important in both poetry and music. Ask whether you have any students who have taken dance or music lessons who can explain more about beat.
7. Now ask: *What did you notice about the last two lines of Frost's poem?* (Repetition.) *Why do you think he repeated the last line?* Discuss that, like rhyme, repetition is a way that poets create rhythm in their work. Repetition is also related to the meaning of a poem; i.e., poets don't repeat lines that are unimportant, but they do repeat lines that tell the reader something important that they don't want the reader to miss. Introduce the idea that the structure of a poem, including its rhythm, contributes to its meaning.

8.  Now read "Love That Boy" by Walter Dean Myers, and ask students to listen for rhythm and repetition. Read the poem a second time and invite students to clap along. Now ask: *Which words are repeated in the first verse?* ("Love that boy . . .") *Why do you think the poet has chosen to repeat these words?* Reinforce the idea that structure, or the way the poem is put together (including its rhyme, rhythm, and repetition), often contributes to the meaning of the poem (and therefore the author's purpose).

9.  Now read "Granny Is" by Valerie Worth. Ask: *What words are repeated in this poem?* (The poet begins each of the first four stanzas with "Granny Is.") Ask why the poet might have structured the poem in this way (perhaps to emphasize that Granny is so many different things to the speaker). It is also worth commenting on the imagery in this poem.

There is a terrific book for children by Sharon Creech, titled *Love That Dog*, which follows one boy's introduction to poetry. This book includes a poem titled "Love That Dog" that is modeled after Walter Dean Myers's poem, and also contains other great poems for this age group. Well worth a look!

## ACTIVITY: THE TALKING DRUM

10. Distribute copies of "The Distant Talking Drum" by Isaac Olaleye. Ask students whether they have ever heard of "talking drums" before. If not, explain that the talking drum is an instrument from West Africa that has been used for thousands of years, and it got its name because skilled players can use it to reproduce the sounds and rhythms of speech; they can pass messages across many miles.

11. Instruct students to read the poem silently and to underline repeated words or phrases.

12. Now read the poem aloud once so that students get an idea of its rhythm. Invite students to read along.

Discuss the use of rhythm and repetition in this poem. Ask: *How do these contribute to the meaning of the poem?* Emphasize the way the poet has used the sounds and rhythms of drums in the poem. That is, the poet has made the poem sound like what it is about.

13. Give students time to construct their own poetry incorporating a strong rhythm and repetition to emphasize meaning. Write the following options on the board and discuss them with students before they make their choices and begin working:

- Continue working on your rhyming poem (started in the previous lesson) and incorporate rhythm and repetition into this poem.
- Start a new poem with rhythm and repetition.
- Write a "Love that . . ." poem (modeled after "Love That Boy" but choosing a different subject).
- Write a "Granny Is . . ." poem using something or someone other than Granny as the subject of the poem.
- Write a poem that sounds like its subject, like the "Distant Talking Drum" poem (e.g., a poem about thunder, dancing, marching, basketball, or a different musical instrument).

14. As students work on their poems, encourage them to clap out the rhythm and to read their work aloud to determine its rhythm.

Some students with attention and/or sensory difficulties may find this clapping activity to be distracting or overwhelming due to the noise from so many students clapping. If possible, provide those students with earphones or ask the class to clap out their rhythm using only their index fingers.

# LESSON 16
# How to Read and Understand a Poem

## MATERIALS

✓ Student workbooks

✓ Student anthology books

✓ Teacher's copy of "This Moment" by Eavan Boland (available at http://www.loc.gov/poetry/180/138.html)

✓ Collection of poems/poetry books from school library or teacher's collection

✓ Handout 16.1: How to Understand a Poem

- Poetry helps readers see the extraordinary in the ordinary.
- Poets use concrete language and sensory detail to communicate abstract ideas, emotions and truths.
- Poets use metaphor to connect readers to important ideas through imagery.
- The structure of a poem often contributes to its meaning.

## OBJECTIVES

Students will:

✓ identify literary devices, including metaphor, personification, rhyme, and rhythm;

✓ identify poetry structures; and

✓ develop the skills to participate as knowledgeable, reflective, creative, and critical members of a literary community.

- Metaphor
- Personification
- Rhyme
- Rhythm
- Imagery
- Sensory language

133

# SEQUENCE

## POETRY FOR APPRECIATION

In this poem, the poet tries to capture a single moment in time and describe that moment in terms of brief, concrete images. You might ask students to think about the moment in time they are currently experiencing. If they were to capture this exact moment in poetic images, what would they describe?

1. Invite students to find a comfortable place for listening. Remind students to enjoy the way the poem sounds and to listen for some of the imagery and details used by the poet.
2. Read "This Moment" by Eavan Boland.
3. Afterward, have students turn to the person next to them and share their idea about what the moment in time is for this poem and what images let them to that conclusion.

## INSTRUCTION: HOW TO UNDERSTAND A POEM

4. This lesson is designed to bring together the big ideas and vocabulary of the unit as students create a how-to guide for understanding a poem. Students will then use that guide to critically analyze a poem of their choice. Say: *Think back to all of the poems we have read and written, and the discussions we have had about poetry over the past few weeks. What are some of the most important things you have learned about poetry?* Write students' responses on the board. Try to steer the discussion toward the big ideas of the unit.
5. Say: *Suppose you were going to write a how-to guide for third-grade students that would explain how to understand a poem. Your guide would include tips about what to look for in a poem that would help a student understand the important ideas in the poem. What advice would your guide include?* Have a discussion about what could be included in the guide and write students' responses on the board. Encourage students to consider what kinds of questions a student should ask about a poem (e.g., Does the poem rhyme? Does the language in the poem speak to all five senses?).

 Consider allowing students to work with a partner on this task.

6. If needed, use Handout 16.1: How to Understand a Poem for generating ideas for the guide.
7. Students will write a how-to guide for reading and understanding a poem for third graders. Explain that they will write a draft first and then engage in a peer conference and a teacher conference (teacher conferences can be conducted with small groups of students as they finish their drafts). Final copies should be written on colored paper or cards so that they can eventually be displayed in the classroom.

Some 2E students might struggle with this activity, not because they haven't learned how to understand a poem or acquired solid comprehension of the concepts of the unit, but because they struggle with the writing process. In this case, be sure to partner a 2E student with a student of a similar readiness level who can be a positive peer mentor/tutor. Alternatively, you can act as a scribe for the student in creating the how-to guide and help him or her synthesize and demonstrate understanding.

## ACTIVITY: HOW TO READ A POEM . . . IN ACTION!

8.  If students finish their guide during this lesson, they should work on selecting a poem they would like to analyze (from the classroom collection or one of the model poems used in earlier lessons) to test their guide.

9.  Students will have time to work on their review during the next lessons, so they do not need to finish the whole project in this lesson. If students finish the task, they may return to writing and revising their own poems in progress.

## PREPARATION: FOR NEXT LESSON

10.  Before the next lesson, read over each student's how-to guide. If students are missing key information, be sure to include this for them since they will use their guide to analyze a poem during the unit's formal assessment. Refer to the formal assessment rubric (p. 143) as a guide to the elements students should include, but ensure that the how-to guide includes these elements in language that students can easily understand.

**Name:** _____ **Date:** _____

## HANDOUT 16.1
# HOW TO UNDERSTAND A POEM

| | |
|---|---|
| **Choice of language** | What is important to know about this? |
| **Imagery** | How does it help us understand the meaning? |
| **Poetic devices** | What tools help us connect to the meaning? |
| **Main idea** | How can we figure out the purpose of a poem? |
| **Mechanics** | Why is it important to have correct spelling and organization? |
| **Other** | |
| **Other** | |

# LESSON 17

# Workshop Days 4 and 5

## MATERIALS

- ✓ Student workbooks
- ✓ Student anthology books
- ✓ Rhyming dictionary created by students
- ✓ Collection of poems/poetry books from school library or teacher's collection
- ✓ Graphic organizers/models of previous poems used in lessons and workshop
- ✓ Handout 13.1: Poet's Workshop Conversation Sheet II
- ✓ Handout 17.1: Final Assessment Tracking Sheet
- ✓ Handout 17.2: Summative Assessment Rubric
- ✓ Handout 17.3: Performance Assessment Rubric

## SEQUENCE

### POETRY FOR APPRECIATION

1. During this 2-day lesson, invite students to select favorite poems from the unit. You might put this to a vote through a show of hands to select two poems to read each day.

### POET'S WORKSHOP

2. Explain to students that they are nearing the end of the poetry unit. The last lesson (Lesson 18) will be a class poetry reading, in which each student will have a chance to share some of his or her own work. In preparation for the final poetry reading, this 2-day workshop will give students a chance to finish the poems they have been working on, to

place these in their anthologies, and to choose one (or two, depending on your class size) poems to read aloud on the final day.

3.  Although students have written different numbers and types of poems throughout the unit, tell them you are expecting to see final copies of at least four poems in the anthology and at least one of these should be a rhyming poem. Distribute Handout 17.1: Final Assessment Tracking Sheet. Explain that by the end of the first day of this lesson, students should turn in this handout with the titles of four poems written on it. They should mark (e.g., with an asterisk or by underlining) which of these are rhyming poems.

4.  Explain that you will be selecting two poems by each student for inclusion in a class poetry anthology. Each student in the class will receive a copy of this book.

5.  Distribute Handout 17.2: Summative Assessment Rubric. This is the rubric you will use to assess their poems. Discuss the quality indicators you will look for. Students should be familiar with the various features on the rubric.

6.  Remind students of the conferencing process required for each poem and explain that you will need to see drafts and records of peer conferences for each poem they submit (i.e., in their folders they have been keeping throughout the unit).

7.  Explain to students that in addition to submitting their anthologies, each student must complete a one-page review of any poem of their choice using the how-to guide they created in the previous lesson. They should write this review on a loose sheet of paper with their name and the name of the poem and poet at the top of the page.

8.  Distribute Handout 17.3: Performance Assessment Rubric and discuss the quality indicators that you will be looking for in their reviews.

9.  For rest of this 2-day lesson, students should work independently on finalizing their anthologies and writing their poem reviews. The teacher should conduct conferences with students as they complete drafts of their poems and monitor students' progress.

## PREPARATION: FOR NEXT LESSON

10. At the end of the first day of Lesson 17, the teacher should collect Handout 17.1 and check students' progress by looking in their workbooks and anthologies. Any students who appear to be making insufficient progress toward these final projects should be targeted for extra assistance at the beginning of the second day.

11. At the end of the second day, gather the group together and make sure students have selected one of their original poems to be shared at the class poetry reading. Talk with students about how to read a poem to an

audience by introducing themselves and the title of their poem, explaining a little bit about the poem, reading in a loud, clear voice, and pausing where necessary. Invite several students to practice in front of the class and have other students offer constructive feedback.

12. If time permits, you could allow students (either alone in front of a mirror or in pairs) time to practice reading through their poems and/or also have students listen to audio recordings of poetry readings.

- Your school library might have some poetry books on tape, or you can access poetry readings online at the Academy of American Poets website (http://www.poets.org) or from a number of other sources.
- If you have the opportunity to invite a poet to your classroom or school at some point during the unit, it would be a wonderful experience for your students to hear a practicing poet share his or her work and to ask questions of the poet. Your school librarian might be able to help you investigate this option.

**Name:** _____ **Date:** _____

**Poetry**

# FINAL ASSESSMENT TRACKING SHEET

| Title | Draft | Peer Edit | Final Copy | Rhyming (You must have at least ONE that rhymes.) |
|---|---|---|---|---|
| Poem #1 | ☐ Yes ☐ No | ☐ Yes ☐ No | ☐ Yes ☐ No | ☐ Yes ☐ No |
| Poem #2 | ☐ Yes ☐ No | ☐ Yes ☐ No | ☐ Yes ☐ No | ☐ Yes ☐ No |
| Poem #3 | ☐ Yes ☐ No | ☐ Yes ☐ No | ☐ Yes ☐ No | ☐ Yes ☐ No |
| Poem #4 | ☐ Yes ☐ No | ☐ Yes ☐ No | ☐ Yes ☐ No | ☐ Yes ☐ No |

Did you complete a one-page review of a poem? ☐ Yes ☐ No

Title and author of poem you reviewed: _____

# HANDOUT 17.2
# SUMMATIVE ASSESSMENT RUBRIC

| | Master | Journeyman | Apprentice | Teacher's comments: |
|---|---|---|---|---|
| **Choice of language** | ⩘ Language is clear and descriptive.<br>⩘ Most language is concrete rather than abstract.<br>⩘ Choice of words is interesting and surprising to the reader. | ⩘ Language is clear and descriptive in most sections of the poem.<br>⩘ Most language is concrete rather than abstract. | ⩘ Language is unclear and does not help paint a picture of the specific scene in the reader's mind.<br>⩘ Most language is abstract. | |
| **Imagery** | ⩘ Imagery is used to create a picture in the reader's mind that is unique and surprising; imagery helps the reader see something in a new way.<br>⩘ Imagery is used effectively to connect with more than one of the reader's senses.<br>⩘ Tools such as metaphor, personification, and point of view are used effectively to connect with the reader through imagery. | ⩘ Imagery is used to create a clear picture in the reader's mind.<br>⩘ Imagery is used effectively to connect with at least one of the reader's senses.<br>⩘ Tools such as metaphor, personification, and point of view are attempted, but are used inconsistently or are confusing to the reader. | ⩘ Imagery does not create a clear picture in the reader's mind.<br>⩘ Imagery does not connect with the reader's senses.<br>⩘ Tools such as metaphor, personification, and point of view are not attempted, or are confusing to the reader. | |

**HANDOUT 17.2, CONTINUED**

| | Master | Journeyman | Apprentice | Teacher's comments: |
|---|---|---|---|---|
| **Rhythm** | ⚐ The poem has a consistent sense of rhythm throughout.<br>⚐ If applicable, rhyme is used effectively to contribute to rhythm.<br>⚐ If applicable, repetition is used effectively to contribute to rhythm.<br>⚐ The rhythm of the poem is used to help connect readers to its meaning. | ⚐ The poem has a reasonably consistent sense of rhythm throughout.<br>⚐ If applicable, rhyme is used to contribute to rhythm.<br>⚐ If applicable, repetition is used to contribute to rhythm. | ⚐ The sense of rhythm in the poem is inconsistent.<br>⚐ If applicable, rhyme is used inconsistently or interrupts the rhythm of the poem. | |
| **Mechanics** | ⚐ Few or no mistakes are evident in the spelling and mechanics of the poem. | ⚐ Minor mistakes are evident in the spelling and mechanics of the poem, but these do not detract from the work. | ⚐ Mistakes are evident in the spelling and mechanics of the poem to an extent that they detract from the work. | |
| **Writing process** | ⚐ There is evidence of the effective use of the writing process; prewriting notes, conference records and several drafts are included. | ⚐ There is evidence that some steps of the writing process have been used. | ⚐ There is no evidence of the effective use of the writing process; prewriting notes, conference records and several drafts are not included. | |

# HANDOUT 17.3
# PERFORMANCE ASSESSMENT RUBRIC

|  | Master | Journeyman | Apprentice | Teacher's comments: |
|---|---|---|---|---|
| **Discussion of language** | ⩘ Language is described as concrete or abstract, with specific examples provided.<br>⩘ The contribution of language choice to the meaning of the poem is discussed. | ⩘ Language choice is described in a general way, but is not linked to the meaning of the poem. | ⩘ The poet's choice of language is not discussed in the review. |  |
| **Discussion of Imagery** | ⩘ Specific examples of effective imagery are provided.<br>⩘ Imagery is discussed in terms of sensory language.<br>⩘ The contribution of imagery to the meaning of the poem is discussed. | ⩘ Imagery is discussed in a general way, but no links are made to sensory language or the meaning of the poem, and no specific examples are provided. | ⩘ The poet's use of imagery is not discussed in the review. |  |
| **Discussion of main idea** | ⩘ The main idea is stated clearly and evidence from the poem is used to support this claim. | ⩘ The main idea is unclear and evidence from the poem is not used to support this claim. | ⩘ The main idea of the poem is not discussed in the review. |  |

144    **Name:** _____    **Date:** _____

**Poetry**

**HANDOUT 17.3, CONTINUED**

| | | |
|---|---|---|
| **Discussion of poetic devices** | » The use of tools such as metaphor, personification, point of view, rhythm, and rhyme is discussed with appropriate examples from the text. | » The use of tools such as metaphor, personification, point of view, rhythm, and rhyme is discussed in a general way, but without appropriate examples from the text. | » The use of poetic devices is not discussed in the review. |
| **Mechanics** | » Few or no mistakes are evident in the spelling and mechanics of the review. <br> » The review is clearly organized and easy to follow. | » Minor mistakes are evident in the spelling and mechanics of the review, but these do not detract from the work. | » Mistakes are evident in the spelling and mechanics of the review to an extent that they detract from the work. <br> » The review is disorganized and difficult to follow. |

© Prufrock Press • *Poetry and Fairy Tales*

# LESSON 18

# Class Poetry Reading

## MATERIALS

- ✓ Class anthology
- ✓ Student anthologies
- ✓ Handout 17.2: Summative Assessment Rubric (teacher copies)
- ✓ Handout 17.3: Performance Assessment Rubric (teacher copies)
- ✓ Handout 18.1: Performance Assessment

## SEQUENCE

1. Conduct a class poetry reading day. This should be a celebration of all the great work students have done throughout the unit and a chance for students to share their work with a real audience. The following guidelines might help the day run smoothly:
   - ✓ Make sure each student has a chance to share at least one original poem.
   - ✓ Allow other students the opportunity to make comments and ask questions.
   - ✓ Encourage the audience to applaud each poet.
   - ✓ Display students' work around the room.
   - ✓ Make the classroom as inviting as possible. You might consider rearranging the furniture for the day to emphasize that this is a special occasion.
   - ✓ Encourage students to dress neatly and take extra care with their appearance for the event.
   - ✓ Invite additional audience members, such as family and friends, other class groups, and/or the principal.
   - ✓ If possible, have bound or stapled copies of the class poetry anthology/collection available for visitors to peruse or take.

For students needing extra preparation, notify parents/guardians that a reading will take place and encourage extra practice at home to reduce performance anxiety.

2. At the end of the unit, make sure each student gets a copy of the class poetry anthology to take home.

3. **Summative Assessment:** Collect students' poetry anthologies. Use the rubric provided (Handout 17.2) to assess and offer feedback on students' poems.

## PREPARATION: PERFORMANCE ASSESSMENT

4. Administer the Unit 1 Performance Assessment (Handout 18.1) during the next lesson or soon after the poetry reading day. Provide students with a copy of the assessment, loose-leaf paper, and up to one hour to complete their task. Use the information from the performance assessment to assess students' growth through the unit (i.e., compare performance on this task to responses on the unit preassessment). Use the Performance Assessment Rubric (Handout 17.3) to assess students' work.

## HANDOUT 18.1
# PERFORMANCE ASSESSMENT

**Directions:** Below is a poem titled "The Wind" by Robert Louis Stevenson. Imagine that you want to tell a friend about the poem. Read "The Wind" and then, on a separate sheet of paper, write a review, explaining the poem to your friend.

Tell your friend:
> ≫ about the *main idea* or message that you think the poet is trying to communicate;
> ≫ about the poet's *choice of language* and how the kinds of words chosen contribute to the poem;
> ≫ about the *imagery* used in the poem;
> ≫ about the poet's use of any tools such as *metaphor, personification, point of view, rhyme, rhythm,* and *repetition*;
> ≫ about how the *structure* of the poem might contribute to its *meaning*;
> ≫ anything else you think it is important to know in order to understand this poem.

**Remember:** Use examples from the poem to support your points. You may make notes on scrap paper or on the poem itself before you begin to write. You may write one or more drafts of your review if you wish. You should hand all notes and drafts in with your finished review.

## THE WIND
By Robert Louis Stevenson

I saw you toss the kites on high          I saw the different things you did,
And blow the birds about the sky;        But always you yourself you hid,
And all around I heard you pass,         I felt you push, I heard you call,
Like ladies' skirts across the grass.    I could not see yourself at all.
    O wind, a-blowing all day long,              O wind, a-blowing all day long,
    O wind, that sings so long a song!           O wind, that sings so long a song!

# Unit 2
# Fairy Tales, Fables, and Folklore
## The Art of Storytelling

## BACKGROUND

> Stories are powerful. They are a journey and a joining. In a tale
> we meet new places, new people, new ideas. And they become
> our places, our people, our ideas.
> —Jane Yolen (1998, p.8)

This is a unit designed to help students explore folklore and fairy tales as an act of storytelling and communicating societal norms and cultural mores. Students will explore these ideas as professionals in the field of Folkloristics. Acting as scholarly folklorists, dynamic storytellers, and creators of literary tales, students will experience a variety of folktales while practicing reading skills and strategies, reinforcing narrative elements, and writing for various purposes.

Through this unit, students are encouraged to become more empathic thinkers as they recognize the universality of people, places, and motifs in folktales. Students will experience the power of folktales that foster compassion for others' misfortunes and celebration of their triumphs. Students will also see the limitations of tales that sometimes promote stereotypes and superficiality.

Students will demonstrate their learning in a culminating class project—a folklore festival. After exploring three professions stemming from an interest in folklore, students will choose the one that most interests them and suits their learning preferences. As a class, they will plan and execute a festival for an appropriate audience.

# OBJECTIVES

This unit is designed to be consistent with common state third-grade reading and writing standards, and national standards outlined by the National Council of Teachers of English (NCTE; NCTE & International Reading Association, 2012). It also aligns to the third-grade Common Core State Standards (CCSS; an alignment chart is provided on p. 309). This unit addresses the following objectives:

## STUDENTS WILL KNOW THE FOLLOWING TERMS

- *Oral folklore* is information communicated from person to person and from generation to generation by word of mouth and through personal demonstration.
- *Folk* are the "regular" people of a society.
- *Folktale* is a form of oral narrative.
- *Fairy tale/wondertale/magic tales* are a complex type of folktale.
- *Fables* are simple type of folktale with an explicit moral.
- *Variants* are different versions of one folktale as recorded by different people and/or in different countries.
- *Types* are numbers assigned by folklorists to tales with a dominant motif.
- *Type indexes* catalogue folktales using different criteria.
- The *ATU system* was created by prominent folklorists (and altered over a span of many years) to universally categorize folktales by number.
- *Folklorists* are scholars who study folklore, the customs, traditions, art, and stories of a culture.
- *Culture* is the collective way of life of a people, passed down by generations.
- A *literary folktale* is a fictional story written by an author imitating the traditional fairy or "magic" tales of folklore, also called "art fairy tales."
- *Purpose* is the author's reason for writing—to entertain or to instruct.
- *Setting* is the time and place of a story; in folktales, they are imaginary and in the "unspecified distant past." In legends, these are real places.
- *Characters* are the people (and animals!) in stories; in folktales they are usually simple "types."
- *Plot* is the sequence of events that tell a story.

> ≫ *Motif* is a narrative element used in constructing a story; they are found repeatedly in folktales.
> ≫ *Stereotypes* are formulaic, oversimplified characters or conceptions.
> ≫ *Empathy* is the feeling people have toward characters in stories when they have experienced something similar.
> ≫ *Adjectives* describe nouns (such as settings or characters) and can be limiting or evocative.

## STUDENTS WILL UNDERSTAND THE FOLLOWING BIG IDEAS ABOUT FAIRY TALES, FABLES, AND FOLKLORE

> ≫ Fairy tales, myths, legends, and fables are all categorized as oral folklore.
> ≫ Folktales have had different purposes in different eras or times—to instruct and/or to entertain.
> ≫ Folktales can help us feel empathy for others.
> ≫ Folktales can be recognized by their formulaic elements.
> ≫ Fairy tales are marked by a consistent structure.
> ≫ One folktale can be found all over the world in many different cultures with many variations.
> ≫ Folktales aren't authored; they are collected from "the people."
> ≫ Folklores can be sorted into one system, although folklorists don't always agree on how to sort them.
> ≫ Storytellers are revered in cultures around the world and throughout history.
> ≫ Storytellers "deliver" tales with specific audiences in mind and choose their words accordingly.
> ≫ Folktales change when they are written down.
> ≫ "Re-tellers" change folktales from the original source—sometimes slightly, sometimes dramatically.
> ≫ Some folktale writers are not "re-tellers" at all, but creators of brand new tales, "literary tellers."
> ≫ When a folktale is altered and embellished, it becomes a "literary folktale," usually more stylishly written than traditional folktales.
> ≫ Professionals work as colleagues.

## STUDENTS WILL DEMONSTRATE THE FOLLOWING SKILLS

> ≫ Appreciate a read a wide range of literature from many periods in many genres to build an understanding of the many dimensions (e.g., philosophical, ethical, aesthetic) of human experience.

> Develop an understanding of and respect for diversity in language use, patterns, and dialects across cultures, ethnic groups, geographic regions, and social roles.

> Apply a wide range of strategies to comprehend, interpret, evaluate, and appreciate texts. They draw on their prior experience, their interactions with other readers and writers, their knowledge of word meaning and of other texts, their word identification strategies, and their understanding of textual features (e.g., sound-letter correspondence, sentence structure, context, graphics).

> Develop the skills to participate as knowledgeable, reflective, creative, and critical members of a variety of a literary community.

> Apply knowledge of language structure, language conventions (e.g., spelling and punctuation), media techniques, figurative language, and genre to create, critique, and discuss print and nonprint texts.

> Adjust their use of spoken, written, and visual language (e.g., conventions, style, vocabulary) to communicate effectively with a variety of audiences and for different purposes.

> Employ a wide range of strategies as they write and use different writing process elements appropriately to communicate with different audiences for a variety of purposes.

> Use spoken language to accomplish their own purposes.

## UNIT 2 OUTLINE

| | Big Idea(s) | Overview | Skills |
|---|---|---|---|
| **Unit Preassessment** | | | |
| Lesson 1 | > Fairy tales, myths, legend, and fables are all categorized as oral folklore. | *Welcome to Fairy Tales, Fables, and Folklore* <br> > Word work. <br> > Folklore flow chart. <br> > Read Aloud: "The Crocodile and the Monkey." | > Read a wide range of literature to build an understanding of human experience. <br> > Apply a wide range of strategies to comprehend, interpret, evaluate, and appreciate texts. <br> > Apply knowledge of language structure, language conventions, and genre to create, critique, and discuss print and nonprint texts. |
| Lesson 2 | > Folktales have different purposes—to instruct and/or to entertain. <br> > Folktales can help us feel empathy for others. | *Folktales: What and Why?* <br> > Introduce plot. <br> > Discuss fables versus fairy tales. <br> > Read Aloud: "The Boys and the Frogs." | > Read a wide range of literature to build an understanding of human experience. <br> > Apply a wide range of strategies to comprehend, interpret, evaluate, and appreciate texts. <br> > Apply knowledge of language structure, language conventions, and genre to create, critique, and discuss print and nonprint texts. |

| | Big Idea(s) | Overview | Skills |
|---|---|---|---|
| **Formative Assessment 1** | | | |
| **Lesson 3** | » Folktales can help us feel empathy.<br>» Folktales have formulaic elements. | *Magic Tales*<br>» Word work.<br>» Word splash activity.<br>» Discuss fairy tales.<br>» Read Aloud: "The Little Match Girl." | » Read a wide range of literature to build an understanding of human experience.<br>» Apply a wide range of strategies to comprehend, interpret, evaluate, and appreciate texts.<br>» Apply knowledge of language structure, language conventions, and genre to create, critique, and discuss print and nonprint texts. |
| **Lesson 4** | » Folktales can be recognized by their formulaic elements. They have:<br>   • stock or set openings and closings,<br>   • generic, unspecified settings, and<br>   • stereotyped characters. | *Once Upon a Time . . .*<br>» Fairy tale openings.<br>» Settings and character types.<br>» Word work. | » Read a wide range of literature to build an understanding of human experience.<br>» Apply a wide range of strategies to comprehend, interpret, evaluate, and appreciate texts.<br>» Apply knowledge of language structure, language conventions, and genre to create, critique, and discuss print and nonprint texts. |
| **Lesson 5** | » Fairy tales, myths, legends, and fables are all categorized as oral folklore.<br>» Folktales have different purposes—to instruct and/or to entertain.<br>» Folktales can help us feel empathy for others. | *Understanding Culture*<br>» What is culture?<br>» Introduce character.<br>» Review.<br>» Read Aloud: "The Ant and the Grasshopper." | » Read a wide range of literature to build an understanding of human experience.<br>» Apply a wide range of strategies to comprehend, interpret, evaluate, and appreciate texts. |
| **Formative Assessment 2** | | | |
| **Lesson 6** | » Folktales come from many different countries.<br>» One tale can "come from" many places. | *Variants*<br>» Folktales are universal.<br>» Can You Guess the Tale? activity.<br>» Word work.<br>» Read Aloud: "Cinderella." | » Read a wide range of literature to build an understanding of human experience.<br>» Apply a wide range of strategies to comprehend, interpret, evaluate, and appreciate texts.<br>» Apply knowledge of language structure, language conventions, and genre to create, critique, and discuss print and nonprint texts.<br>» Develop an understanding of and respect for diversity in language use, patterns, and dialects across cultures, ethnic groups, geographic regions, and social roles. |

| | Big Idea(s) | Overview | Skills |
|---|---|---|---|
| **Lesson 7** | ≫ Folktales don't have authors—they are collected by scholars from the people.<br>≫ Variants are different versions of one folktale as recorded by different people and/or in different countries. | *Collectors of Tales*<br>≫ Journal response.<br>≫ Introduce folklorists as collectors.<br>≫ Read Aloud: "Puss in Boots." | ≫ Read a wide range of literature to build an understanding of human experience.<br>≫ Apply a wide range of strategies to comprehend, interpret, evaluate, and appreciate texts.<br>≫ Apply knowledge of language structure, language conventions, and genre to create, critique, and discuss print and nonprint texts.<br>≫ Develop an understanding of and respect for diversity in language use, patterns, and dialects across cultures, ethnic groups, geographic regions, and social roles. |
| **Lesson 8** | ≫ Variants are different versions of one folktale as recorded by different people and/or in different countries.<br>≫ Types are numbers assigned by folklorists to tales with a dominant motif.<br>≫ Folklorists created (and altered over a span of many years) the ATU system to universally categorize folktales by number. | *Type Index*<br>≫ Introduce types and type index.<br>≫ Word work.<br>≫ Interest/strength of analysis activity.<br>≫ Read Aloud: "The Silkie Wife." | ≫ Read a wide range of literature to build an understanding of human experience.<br>≫ Apply a wide range of strategies to comprehend, interpret, evaluate, and appreciate texts.<br>≫ Apply knowledge of language structure, language conventions, and genre to create, critique, and discuss print and nonprint texts.<br>≫ Develop the skills to participate as knowledgeable, reflective, creative, and critical members of a variety of a literary community. |
| **Lesson 9** | ≫ Storytellers are revered in cultures around the world and throughout history.<br>≫ Storytellers "deliver" tales with specific audiences in mind and choose their words accordingly. | *Storytellers Carry Culture*<br>≫ Word work.<br>≫ "Get that Culture Off My Back" activity.<br>≫ Introduce topic bags.<br>≫ Read Aloud: "Why Tigers Never Attack Men Unless They Are Provoked." | ≫ Develop an understanding of and respect for diversity in language use, patterns, and dialects across cultures, ethnic groups, geographic regions, and social roles.<br>≫ Develop the skills to participate as knowledgeable, reflective, creative, and critical members of a variety of a literary community. |
| **Lesson 10** | ≫ Storytellers must tell their stories with their audiences in mind and choose their words accordingly. | *Delivering Stories*<br>≫ Word work.<br>≫ Introduce delivery.<br>≫ Choosing storytelling details activity.<br>≫ Read Aloud: "Little Red-Cap." | ≫ Develop an understanding of and respect for diversity in language use, patterns, and dialects across cultures, ethnic groups, geographic regions, and social roles. |

| | Big Idea(s) | Overview | Skills |
|---|---|---|---|
| **Lesson 11** | ≫ Characters are usually stereotypes with "set" descriptions.<br>≫ Characters are usually described using a single adjective.<br>≫ Storytellers use adjectives that are evocative not limiting. (We want the story to take place in the readers mind.)<br>≫ Folktales have stock or set openings and closings (to help storytellers remember). | *Storytellers*<br>≫ Limiting versus evocative adjectives activity.<br>≫ Telling a group story activity.<br>≫ Read Aloud: "The Little Mermaid" opening paragraphs. | ≫ Read a wide range of literature to build an understanding of human experience.<br>≫ Apply a wide range of strategies to comprehend, interpret, evaluate, and appreciate texts.<br>≫ Develop the skills to participate as knowledgeable, reflective, creative, and critical members of a variety of a literary community.<br>≫ Apply knowledge of language structure, language conventions, and genre to create, critique, and discuss print and nonprint texts. |
| **Formative Assessment 3** | | | |
| **Lesson 12** | ≫ Characters in folktales are usually stereotypes with "set" descriptions.<br>≫ Characters in folktales are usually described using a single adjective.<br>≫ Folktales have stock or set openings and closings (to help storytellers remember). | *Storytellers*<br>*Mini-Product*<br>≫ Group storytelling—practice, perform, and discuss. | ≫ Use spoken language to accomplish their own purposes (e.g., for learning, enjoyment, persuasion, and the exchange of information).<br>≫ Develop the skills to participate as knowledgeable, reflective, creative, and critical members of a variety of a literary community. |
| **Lesson 13** | ≫ Folktales change when they are written down. | *Re-Tellers*<br>≫ Comparing tales.<br>≫ Reread with purpose.<br>≫ Introduce retellings.<br>≫ Read Aloud: Grimms' "Snow White." | ≫ Read a wide range of literature to build an understanding of human experience.<br>≫ Apply a wide range of strategies to comprehend, interpret, evaluate, and appreciate texts.<br>≫ Apply knowledge of language structure, language conventions, and genre to create, critique, and discuss print and nonprint texts. |
| **Lesson 14** | ≫ When a folktale is altered and embellished, it becomes a "literary folktale," usually more stylishly written than traditional folktales.<br>≫ Some folktale writers are not re-tellers at all, but creators of brand new tales, "literary tellers." | *Literary Tellers*<br>≫ Introduce literary fairy tales and fairy tale structure.<br>≫ Prewriting activity.<br>≫ Read Aloud: Lang's ending of "Sleeping Beauty." | ≫ Read a wide range of literature to build an understanding of human experience.<br>≫ Apply a wide range of strategies to comprehend, interpret, evaluate, and appreciate texts.<br>≫ Employ a wide range of strategies as they write to communicate with different audiences for a variety of purposes. |

| | Big Idea(s) | Overview | Skills |
|---|---|---|---|
| **Lesson 14, continued** | | | ≫ Apply knowledge of language structure, language conventions, and genre to create, critique, and discuss print and nonprint texts.<br>≫ Adjust their use of spoken, written, and visual language (e.g., conventions, style, vocabulary) to communicate effectively with a variety of audiences and for different purposes. |
| **Lesson 15** | ≫ Projects require planning and having clear goals and strategies can help you work efficiently. | *Literary Tellers 2*<br>≫ Write a tale.<br>≫ Prepare for folklore festival. | ≫ Employ a wide range of strategies as they write to communicate with different audiences for a variety of purposes.<br>≫ Apply knowledge of language structure, language conventions, and genre to create, critique, and discuss print and nonprint texts. |
| **Lesson 16** | ≫ Professionals meet with colleagues. | *Festival Prework*<br>≫ Professional folklore work rotations.<br>≫ Planning card. | ≫ Students will assume the roles of professionals in the field by:<br>▪ sorting tales,<br>▪ prewriting a folk tale, or<br>▪ selecting a tale to perform. |
| **Lesson 17** | ≫ Professionals work as colleagues. | *Festival Prework, Seminars*<br>≫ Professional folklore work rotations.<br>≫ Review rubrics.<br>≫ Planning card. | ≫ Develop the skills to participate as knowledgeable, reflective, creative, and critical members of a variety of a literary community. |
| **Lesson 18** | | *Festival Prework, Final Prep*<br>≫ Professional folklore work rotations.<br>≫ Planning card. | ≫ Employ a wide range of strategies as they write to communicate with different audiences for a variety of purposes.<br>≫ Apply knowledge of language structure, language conventions, and genre to create, critique, and discuss print and nonprint texts.<br>≫ Develop the skills to participate as knowledgeable, reflective, creative, and critical members of a variety of a literary community. |
| **Lesson 19** | | *Folklore Festival and Assessment*<br>≫ Present their folklore festival and complete the unit's summative assessment. | ≫ Use spoken language to accomplish their own purposes (e.g., for learning, enjoyment, persuasion, and the exchange of information).<br>≫ Develop the skills to participate as knowledgeable, reflective, creative, and critical members of a variety of a literary community. |
| **Summative Assessment**<br>**Performance Assessment** | | | |

# PREPARING TO TEACH THE UNIT

## BEGINNING AT THE END

The unit culminates in a Folklore Festival. This can be as simple as sharing stories within your classroom or as grand as hosting a festival after school hours and inviting people from the community. Depending on the time of year and your school, you may invite another class, parents, or principals. These logistics should be considered before Lesson 15, in order to reserve a location (auditorium, library) and to coordinate with other teachers' schedules. However, teachers should be ready to scale up or back based on the students' final selection of product: If you don't have any storytellers, you will have a quiet festival. If you have 10, you'll need a longer program!

## ROUTINES

Each lesson opens with a read-aloud opportunity. It is crucial that teachers model fluency on a daily basis, just as it is crucial students have an opportunity to reread for fluency at some point in the lesson.

Although it would be ideal for children to "discover" the big ideas of the unit, out of respect for the teacher's time and deadlines, direct instruction is also used to impart some concepts. Whenever possible, however, the goal of the classroom is for children to construct their own knowledge.

Word work incorporates structural analysis and vocabulary instruction on content area words students might encounter as professionals in the field. These "professional" words are not intended to become a part of student's productive vocabulary—words they are expected to use and write—but their receptive or "listening" vocabulary—words they should recognize and understand when read or heard. Accordingly these words will be placed on a "professional" section of the folklore wall with which students will interact during the unit. Word work also includes word origins, word roots, prefixes, and suffixes. Spelling words will be tied to an element of word work. *Caution:* The spelling in the unit is challenging. Teachers are encouraged to supplement with words appropriate to their on- and below-level students. Story vocabulary suggestions are supplied, but teachers are also encouraged to select appropriate story vocabulary for their students.

## ASSESSMENT

A variety of assessment opportunities are provided for teachers to gather information about their students. A preassessment at the outset of the unit reveals students' prior knowledge of folktales both with a formal and informal assessment. This will help teachers group students appropriately. Continual formative assessments occur daily with journal prompts and responses, exit cards, and/or homework assignments. These allow teachers to track students' understanding of concepts as they unfold. Further, the accumulation of this data of the first several lessons will help teachers guide students into their final product choices.

## RESOURCES AND MATERIALS

Create a portfolio folder for each student (e.g., a file folder in which index cards can be taped to the inside cover as they are collected). This folder provides teachers with a central place to put assessments—both formal and informal—as well as a store of data on the students' strengths and weaknesses. Refer to the portfolio during planning conferences with students for their final project. This information will be especially helpful in guiding students toward the "right" profession for them (in the final project), if they are unsure. These assessments will help inform your instruction.

The tales provided in the unit have been rewritten from other sources (either the original tale or a retelling). Some of the texts have been informally leveled. Questionable language and details have been edited from the examples provided. Links to web-based lesson materials are provided in each lesson plan and on the book's webpage at http://www.prufrock.com/assets/clientpages/ Poetry_FairyTales.aspx.

Teachers can access an endless number of other folktales online, including hundreds of variants in their original forms. In many cases, the website gives educators permission to print them.

> ➢ **SurLaLune Fairy Tales:** http://www.surlalunefairytales.com/introduction/resteachers.html
> ➢ **Main Lesson:** http://www.mainlesson.com/displaystoriesbygenre.php
> ➢ **Andersen Stories:** http://www.andersenstories.com/en/andersen_fairy-tales/index
> ➢ **Grimm Stories:** http://www.grimmstories.com/en/grimm_fairy-tales/index
> ➢ **Folklore and Mythology Electronic Texts;** http://www.pitt.edu/~dash/folktexts.html
> ➢ **Arts Reformation:** http://www.artsreformation.com/records

## TEACHER CAUTIONS

**Value of and debate about fairy tales.** Much has been written about gender roles and stereotypes in fairy tales. This unit, written for 9- and 10-year-olds, touches upon the idea of folktale characters as stereotypes and the historical context of the tales, but does not dwell on the gender politics (i.e., girls identifying with weak heroines instead of strong male characters, powerful women portrayed as witches or evil, etc). A balance of tales has been selected from different cultures; however, the most popular Indo-European tales have been strongly embedded. Teachers should feel free to substitute and supplement the exemplars provided with tales they feel best reflect their student and community needs.

**About content.** Teachers should exercise caution in letting students peruse any of the sites provided as sources for online research. Part of fairy tale scholarship delves into the Jungian or psycho/sexual metaphors and motifs in tales. Students could encounter inappropriate content if allowed to freely search the web, including the sites provided for teacher reference. Hence, teachers' safest option is to provide access to anthologies, reviewed printed versions from the Internet, and picture books.

In fact, it is crucial for children's exploration to provide a variety of folktales on a cart in the room. Work with your librarian. Check in libraries from basal programs.

Teachers should also be aware that many tales in their original form are violent and not just a little gruesome—hearts being cut out and eaten, children freezing to death, etc. Too, bear in mind that religious themes and content appear in many tales, especially those of Hans Christian Andersen.

**Folkloristics: Where do folktales really come from?** Although students will operate as mini-professionals in the field, their level of operation is greatly simplified. The history of Folkloristics harbors a long argument about the origin of tales. Our goal at this age is not to walk down that slippery and many-forked path. Instead we focus on the universality of tales children know and love, stressing simply that variants occur around the world in many cultures. Were we to function solely as folklorists during the unit, we would limit product options and risk squeezing the wonder out of the very magical tales.

As for the classification system used (the ATU catalogue from *The Types of International Folktales*), the goal is not that the children memorize the numbers or types, only that they understand that "types" exist—that patterns or repeated motifs/plots occur in folktales from all over the world. Folktales are universal. For students, being universal means that people they don't even know—who lived at a different time or in a different county—have listened to and enjoyed similar stories that engendered similar feelings. Children can learn empathic thinking through this notion.

In order to differentiate for interest and learning style, the unit gives options beyond the folklorist profession. Students also learn to be storytellers and literary folktale writers with the option of pursuing those "professions" in their final product. Should a particularly advanced or single-minded student express a strong interest in one profession—folklorist, storyteller, literary "reteller"— teachers should consider a Renzulli-type independent study. For example, a student may take an interest in:

> ≫ finding tales from their own culture and cataloging them,

> finding one specific tale and pursuing all of the variants (entire dissertations, websites are built around them!),
> studying the tales of one writer (e.g., Hans Christian Andersen) as an independent folklorist study, or
> creating an anthology of their own tales.

## THE CLEAR CURRICULUM MODEL

This unit has been designed using the CLEAR Curriculum Model. The CLEAR (Challenge Leading to Engagement, Achievement and Results) Curriculum incorporates elements from three research-based curriculum models—differentiation, Depth and Complexity, and the Schoolwide Enrichment Model—by Carol Tomlinson, Sandra Kaplan, and Joseph Renzulli, respectively. These elements are applied to a curriculum framework that is consistent with state and national standards in reading, but build layers of challenge and opportunities for more in-depth study authentic to the work of professionals within a discipline, to better meet the needs of all students. Refer to p. 15 for more information about the CLEAR Curriculum Model.

## ICONS EXPLAINED

Integrated throughout the lesson plans are a series of icons or symbols intended to draw your attention to the particular content focus, learning objective, or instructional configuration of each learning activity. Some of these icons are derived from Sandra Kaplan's Depth and Complexity curriculum model, while others have been developed specifically for the CLEAR Curriculum Model used in these units. Refer to p. 16 for an explanation of each icon.

# LESSON 1
# Welcome To Fairy Tales, Fables, and Folklore

## MATERIALS

- ✓ Students' Folklorist journals
- ✓ Index cards
- ✓ Teacher's copy of "The Crocodile and the Monkey" (available at http://www.gutenberg.org/files/36039/36039-h/36039-h.htm#ch3)
- ✓ Student copies of examples of oral folklore
  - ▪ Fable: "The Turtle Who Couldn't Stop Talking" (available at http://www.sacred-texts.com/bud/jt/jt06.htm)
  - ▪ Fairy Tale: "Toads and Diamonds" (available at http://www.sacred-texts.com/neu/lfb/bl/blfb28.htm)
  - ▪ Legend: "Paul Bunyan and Babe the Blue Ox" (available at http://americanfolklore.net/folklore/2010/07/babe_the_blue_ox.html)
  - ▪ Myth: "Perseus and Medusa" (available at http://www.astro.wisc.edu/~dolan/constellations/extra/PerseusStory.html)
  - ▪ Riddles:
    - » "I have a little sister . . . " (available at http://www3.amherst.edu/~rjyanco94/literature/mothergoose/rhymes/ihavealittlesistertheycallherpeeppeep.html)
    - » "As round as an apple . . . " (available at http://www3.amherst.edu/~rjyanco94/literature/mothergoose/rhymes/asroundasanapple.html)
    - » "Two brothers we are . . . " (available at http://www.braingle.com/brainteasers/4348/two-brothers.html)

- ✓ Handout 1.1: Unit Preassessment
- ✓ Handout 1.2: Folktale Recording Chart
- ✓ Handout 1.3: Homework
- ✓ Appendix B1: Folkloristics Concept Map

Fairy tales, myths, legends, and fables are all categorized as oral folklore.

## OBJECTIVES

Students will:

- ✓ read a wide range of literature to build an understanding of human experience;
- ✓ apply a wide range of strategies to comprehend, interpret, evaluate, and appreciate texts; and
- ✓ apply knowledge of language structure, language conventions, and genre to create, critique, and discuss print and nonprint texts.

- Folk
- Folklore
- Folktale
- Fairy tale

- Oral
- Legend
- Myth

- The preassessment will provide data to inform your instruction and fairy tale groups, which will be based on prior knowledge of folktales. Keep the assessment in students' portfolios.
- Consider taping off a section of the board for activities for early finishers, so students know where to look autonomously.

# SEQUENCE

## UNIT PREASSESSMENT

1. Administer the Unit Preassessment (Handout 1.1). Explain to students that this assessment is not for a grade. Rather, it is to find out how much they already know about different kinds of stories and words.

 For students who finish early, write the following journal prompt on the board: *If you had to explain to a kindergartener what a fairy tale is, what might you tell them?*

Students can grade their own work or exchange with a peer. Having students grade the multiple-choice section will save time. The answers are: 1. D; 2. B; 3. A; 4. A; 5. B; 6. B; 7. B.

2. Grade responses to Sections A–C on the preassessment as a class. Students do not need to mark answers wrong with a big "X." Instead they should underline the correct answer. Discuss the answers as you collectively grade the paper.
3. Record responses from Section D on chart paper or the SmartBoard. (You may want to save this list to refer to later.) Ask students which of the Disney movies they think are fairy tales and why they think that. This will begin the dialogue, *What exactly is a fairy tale?*

## READ ALOUD

4. Read "The Crocodile and the Monkey" aloud.
5. On Handout 1.2: Folktale Recording Chart, tell students to record the story title and to put an X in the appropriate box.
6. Explain to students that they just heard a special kind of story. Ask: *Does anyone have a suggestion of what it's called?* Record ideas on the board.

## INFORMAL ASSESSMENT

7. Write the terms *fairy tale*, *myth*, *legend*, and *fable* on the board. Pass out index cards to the students.
8. Tell students they have just encountered these story types on the first assessment, and you would like to know if they can name another example of each type. On an index card, students should write the term for which they can think of an example. On the backside, they should write the example. If they can name an example of more than one type, they should raise their hand to get another index card.
9. Collect cards from students as they finish them. Be sure they write their name very small on the "term" side, as you will use these cards to take a quick informal assessment of students' prior knowledge of the various types of oral narratives.

Always write the Read Aloud title on the board and have students record it in their folktale chart (Handout 1.2). Share its country of origin.

- If students are unable to think of an example of any of the story types, they can just write their name on a card and turn it in blank.
- Depending on student responses, you might want to work toward consensus on criteria before students generate examples.

- Sort the cards into readiness piles as they are turned in. For example: (1) students who turn in multiple cards with unique/sophisticated examples, (2) students who turn in at least one correct example, (3) students who turn in no correct examples, or (4) students who leave them blank. (Note: Even scholars debate the difference between myths and legends. It is fine if students interchange these.)
- After you have made your readiness groups, consider taping the cards on the wall in groups, with the example facing forward. This is the beginning of your folklore wall. You will return to these later as a bank of tales. (Students can change, remove, and add to these cards later).

Assign the following task to students who finish early: *Pull a book from the folktales cart that interests you. Record the title in your journal and begin to read.*

## WORD WORK

10. Write the word *folklorisitics* on the board. Students can copy it into their personal word wall page in their Folklorist Journal.

Base words are words from which many other words are formed.
- *Folk* (noun): "The common people of a society or region considered as the representatives of a traditional way of life and especially as the originators or carriers of the customs, beliefs, and arts that make up a distinctive culture."
- *-ist*: Indicates one who does or believes in or studies something.
- *Folklore*, 1846: Germans use *Volkskunde*—the lore of the people. The French used folklore in addition to the term *traditions populaires*.

11. Explain that we can sometimes break down big words into smaller words. Have students emulate the next steps you take to deconstruct the word.

- Underline the base word *folk* and share what it means.
  > **Kid-Friendly Definition:** *Folk* are the regular people in the community—not the presidents, or kings and queens, or the famous people—the "common" people. *Folklorisitics*, then, has something to do with "common people."

- Tell students: *We can also look at the ending or suffixes of words to find meaning. If we erase the -ics, we find folklorist.* Circle the *-ist*. Explain that *-ist* at the end of a word means someone who works with something. Write the following words on the board: *dentist, florist, zoologist,* and ask students what each work with.
- Erase *-ist*, and write it separately. Tell students: *A folklorist works with or studies folklore. If we still don't know what the word means, we can break it down further. When a word can be broken into two smaller words, it is called a compound word.* Draw a line between folk and lore. Define *lore*.
  > **Kid-Friendly Definition:** *Lore* is knowledge, usually that is handed down from grandmothers to children, and so on. *So, folklore is the "lore" of the "people."*

- Display Appendix B1: Folkloristics Concept Map. Tell students: *There are many kinds of information that can be passed down from generation to generation—family recipes, ways to celebrate a holiday, songs, prayers, etc.*
- Highlight the path to *oral folklore*. Tell students: *We will be folklorists who study oral folklore.* Ask students for suggestions about what *oral* means.

## ACTIVITY: FOLKLORE FLOWCHART
12. Draw a flowchart on the board that starts with oral narratives and branches into legends, myths, and folktales.
13. Distribute examples of oral folklore (fable, fairy tale, myth, legend, riddle). Assign students to groups based on the cards you sorted in the informal assessment. These are their "fairy tale groups." After reading the folklore, group members will decide where to tape the cards on the flowchart.

Give students with less knowledge of folktales the obvious examples, and those with more knowledge trickier or more complex examples. If you prefer to group by reading level, give struggling readers simpler forms (riddle/song) and the advanced readers more abstract/subtle forms (legend/myth).

## CLOSE

14. Review the lesson's key terms with students, asking for kid-friendly definitions. Add the terms to the word wall.

15. Discuss how students placed their cards. Ask what all of the examples have in common. Possible answers: *They are passed down. They are told to somebody. They have animals that talk (some).*

At this point in the unit, create a unified word wall. You can later sort vocabulary into professional and academic walls.

Do not spend too much time focusing on the comparison. This can get very complicated as the boundaries sometimes bleed together. In the past, for examples, some cultures did believe the magic of folktales was true. And some folktales do come from ancient myths. The point is that you show which kind of tales you will study, and where they fit into the realm of their "profession," folkloritsts who study folktales.

16. Reading the chart with the students, point out that they are oral narratives: they are passed orally by storytellers and from person to person, and they are narratives. (A *narrative* is another word for story.)

Explain that the main difference between myths, legends, and folktales is that myths and legends were believed by a culture at one time to be true. People thought that the gods were real in myths, and people thought that the characters in legends had really lived. (And some did—like Johnny Appleseed.) Folktales are made up or "fictional." Still, these boundaries are tricky, and students should not be too worried about them.

## HOMEWORK: COMPOUND WORDS

17. Distribute Handout 1.3: Homework. This assessment provides independent practice.

## HANDOUT 1.1
# UNIT PREASSESSMENT

**Directions:** Circle the correct answer.

1.  Hercules is the son of the Greek god, Zeus, and a mortal woman. He had super strength and fought dragons and monsters. This type of story is a:
    a. fable                          c. legend
    b. fairy tale                     d. myth

2.  The wicked queen was jealous of Snow White because the magic mirror said she was more beautiful. The story about Snow White is a:
    a. fable                          c. legend
    b. fairy tale                     d. myth

3.  "A dog held a bone as he crossed a bridge. When he looked in the water, he saw the reflection of a dog with a bone that he wanted as well. He snaps at the other dog, and loses his bone." A story like this that ends with a moral is a:
    a. fable                          c. legend
    b. fairy tale                     d. myth

4.  A bucket is a:
    a. pail                           b. pale

5.  _____ swim in the ocean.
    a. Wails                          b. Whales

6.  The postal carrier delivers:
    a. male                           b. mail

7.  The store has clothes on:
    a. sail                           b. sale

## HANDOUT 1.1, CONTINUED

8. Put checkmarks next to the animated Disney movies that you have seen. Summarize the plots.

   ❑ Snow White and the Seven Dwarfs

   ❑ Cinderella

   ❑ Aladdin

   ❑ The Lion King

   ❑ Sleeping Beauty

   ❑ The Little Mermaid

   ❑ Beauty and the Beast

**Fairy Tales**

# FOLKTALE RECORDING CHART

| Folktale | Never heard of it | Title is familiar | Can summarize it |
|---|---|---|---|
|  |  |  |  |
|  |  |  |  |
|  |  |  |  |
|  |  |  |  |
|  |  |  |  |
|  |  |  |  |
|  |  |  |  |

## HANDOUT 1.3
# HOMEWORK

**Directions:** Divide the compound words into two words. If it cannot be divided into two separate words, the word is not a compound. Circle the words that are not compound words.

*Example:*

Dog/house  (crocodile)

1. folktale
2. fairytale
3. deathbed
4. mailbox
5. folklore
6. princess

7. woodsman
8. folksong
9. outside
10. legend
11. myth
12. gentleman

**Bonus:** Can you think of any other compound words?

# LESSON 2
# Folktales: What and Why?

## MATERIALS

- ✓ Teacher's copy of "The Boys and the Frogs" (available at http://www.gutenberg.org/files/19994/19994-h/19994-h.htm#Page_33)
- ✓ Teacher's copy of "The Frog Prince (or Iron Henry)" (available at http://www.pitt.edu/~dash/grimm001.html)
- ✓ Handout 2.1: Lesson 1 Homework Answer Key
- ✓ Appendix B2: Grouping Plan Chart

- Folktales have different purposes—to instruct and/or to entertain.
- Folktales can help us feel empathy for others.

## OBJECTIVES

Students will:

- ✓ apply knowledge of language structure, language conventions, and genre to create, critique, and discuss print and nonprint texts;
- ✓ read a wide range of literature to build an understanding of human experience; and
- ✓ apply a wide range of strategies to comprehend, interpret, evaluate, and appreciate texts.

- Fable
- Fairy tale
- Purpose
- Moral
- Plot
- Astonished
- Plaything
- Vanished
- Weep
- Creeping
- Bewitched

171

# SEQUENCE

## WARM UP

1. Provide students with the answer key to the homework from Lesson 1 (Handout 2.1) and have them score their homework papers. Ask if there are any questions.
2. As you collect the homework, ask students to give examples of other compound words. Ask if *homework* is a compound word.

## READ ALOUD

3. Read "The Boys and the Frogs" aloud.
4. Introduce *plot*. Tell students: *When we talk about what happened in the story, we are discussing the plot.* With students, record the sequence of events in "The Boys and the Frogs" on the board. Tell students: *If we were to summarize this tale, we would choose the most important parts of the plot and try to write them in one or two sentences.* Model a verbal summary for students.
5. Add *plot* to the word wall.
6. Review the plot of "The Boys and the Frogs." Ask: *What are the most important things happened in the story?* Underline the most important events listed on the board.

 Ask students to write a summary based on the events underlined.

## DISCUSSION: FABLES VERSUS FAIRY TALES

7. Read "The Frog King (or Iron Henry)" aloud.
8. Assign students to random groups and assign one of the stories to each group ("The Boys and the Frogs" or "The Frog King"). Ask each group to record the plot sequence and to write a plot summary. Review their responses.

 **2E**
For students struggling with or who have disabilities in written expression, an oral summary or drawing may substitute for a written summary. This will enable teachers to assess these students' comprehension of the fairy tale's plot.

9. Ask the students to draw a Venn diagram that shows the similarities and differences between the stories. (Model one on the board.) Ask children to compare the stories with a partner, recording the things the stories had in common in the area where the two circles intersect. Ask: *What*

> • Before reading the moral at the end of the story, ask students: *What is this story about? What is its message?*
> • Tell students: *A moral is a lesson that you learn from a story. Some stories have them. Some don't.*

*was different? Did the stories have similar characters?* If needed, record student ideas for the whole class on a Venn diagram on the board.

10. Using the concept map (Appendix B1), point out that there are two kinds of folktales—simple and complex. Fables have a simple plot (usually one episode or event). Also, most fables have animals—but not all. Fairy tales have a complex plot ("multiepisodic" or many events).

11. Explain that the purpose of both fairy tales and fables is to entertain the listeners. (Entertainment can be funny, happy, or even sad.) However, the additional purpose of fables is to teach a lesson.

12. Ask students if they have ever heard, "The moral of the story is . . . " The moral is the lesson in the story. Explain that fables and fairy tales are also different because in fables the morals are stated. In fairy tales the moral is not stated. Some fairy tales do not have a moral.

13. Add to the word wall: *purpose, moral, plot, setting.*

14. Have students answer the following question with a partner: *Did you think there was moral in "The Frog King (or Iron Henry)?" If so, what was it?*

## PREPARATION: FORMATIVE ASSESSMENT 1

15. In their journals or as an exit card, have students respond to the following questions:
    ✓ Which has a more complex plot: a fable or a fairy tale?
    ✓ Did you think there was a moral in "The Frog King (or Iron Henry)?" If so complete the sentence: "The moral of the story is . . . "
    ✓ How would you describe what *folklore* means to a friend who doesn't know that word?

16. **Using the assessment data:** Use responses to ensure that students understand key concepts of fables, fairy tales, and folklore. Students who correctly answer all three questions should be placed in Group A. Students who correctly answer two questions should be placed in Group B. Students who correctly answer one or no questions should be placed in Group C. A sorting chart is provided (Appendix B2).

## HANDOUT 2.1
# LESSON 1 HOMEWORK ANSWER KEY

1. folk/tale
2. fairy/tale
3. death/bed
4. mail/box
5. folk/lore
6. (princess)

7. woods/man
8. folk/song
9. out/side
10. (legend)
11. (myth)
12. gentle/man

# LESSON 3

# Magic Tales

## MATERIALS

- ✓ Teacher's copy of "The Little Match Girl" (available at http://www.gutenberg.org/files/1597/1597-h/1597-h.htm#link2H_4_0015)
- ✓ Handout 3.1: Word Work, *Pathos*
- ✓ Handout 3.2: Word Splash (one per group of 3–4 students)
- ✓ Handout 3.3: Fairy Tale Timeline
- ✓ Handout 3.4: Homework

- Folktales can help us feel empathy.
- Folktales have formulaic elements.

## OBJECTIVES

Students will:

- ✓ apply knowledge of language structure, language conventions, and genre to create, critique, and discuss print and nonprint texts;
- ✓ read a wide range of literature to build an understanding of human experience; and
- ✓ apply a wide range of strategies to comprehend, interpret, evaluate, and appreciate texts.

| | |
|---|---|
| • Purpose | • Universal |
| • Setting | • Empathy |
| • Character | • Sympathy |

# SEQUENCE

- Write the names of the tales read so far on the board as reminder to the students as they work on the task of summarizing.
- Consider a filing system (box or file folders) where students can file their exit/assessment cards after they finish a task.

## WARM UP

1. Write the following sentences on the board:
   - ✓ The woodsman can't kill Snow White.
   - ✓ Will you read me stories at bedtime?
   - ✓ The tablecloth covered the table.
   - ✓ She is happy to see her grandmother.
   - ✓ The snowstorm was blinding.

2. Students should write the compound word from each statement on an index card and separate the two smaller words with a slash (e.g., woods/man).

3. On the back of the card, have students summarize the tales they have read thus far. Ask students to include one important lesson learned when studying the tale and to give an example. Collect the cards. (You can use this formative assessment data to determine if students understand big ideas from previous lessons. It can also serve as a preassessment of students' ability to summarize.)

 Have students who finish early work on Handout 3.1: Word Work, *Pathos*. You can differentiate this activity by student readiness. You can draw a web on index cards and write in one of the words (e.g., "sadness").

 For students struggling with or who have disabilities in written expression, an oral summary or drawing may substitute for the written summary. This will enable you to assess these students' retention of narrative from yesterday and preassess students' ability to summarize.

## READ ALOUD

4. Tell students: *"The Little Match Girl" tells the story of a child who is desperately poor, hungry, and cold on New Year's Eve and dies. However, it is not technically a "traditional" folktale—a story originating from a community and passed down—but is a fairy tale—the 19th-century name given to magical stories for children. Hans Christian Andersen, as we will learn, created many now-famous fairy tales (in the time when they were also being collected and printed in anthologies). Read "The Little Match Girl."*

• For this lesson, the distinction between traditional and literary fairy tale is not crucial, merely the content. "The Little Match Girl" is a fairy tale that evokes empathy or strong emotion in students. You are laying the foundation of empathic thinking that fairy tales can evoke.
• The difference between a traditional fairy tale (a folktale with magical elements) and a literary fairy tale (an invented tale, not originating orally from a culture) will be investigated later. There is no need to make the distinction for students at this point.

## WORD WORK

5. Discuss with students that words can mean almost the same thing but have slight differences. Ask how students felt toward the little match girl. (Possible responses: *I felt sad. I felt sorry for her.*) Record answers on the board.

6. Ask children to explain why they felt that way. The "whys" will expose a feeling of sympathy or empathy. For example, if they have felt cold themselves, they are feeling empathy. If they felt sad because she didn't get to eat a nice Thanksgiving dinner like they have with their family, they felt sympathy.

7. From students' answers distinguish between the two terms: Circle the examples that show sympathy. Explain that you feel sympathy when you feel sad for someone. Underline the examples that show empathy. Explain that you feel empathy when you feel sad for someone, because you have experienced something similar.

• *Empathy* (noun): "The ability to identify with or understand the perspective, experiences, or motivations of another individual and to comprehend and share another individual's emotional state."
• *Sympathy* (noun): "A feeling or an expression of pity or sorrow for the distress of another; commiseration."

• This prompt is the first step in developing empathic thinking in the students.
• Give students a short, allotted amount of time to write (3–5 minutes).

8. Give students the opportunity to react to "The Little Match Girl" in their journals. Ask them to respond to the following questions: *How did you feel about the character and what happened to her? Did you ever experience something similar?*

## ACTIVITY: WORD SPLASH

9. Display Handout 3.2: Word Splash and/or distribute it to students. Students must determine how the words and phrases are related to fairy tales.

You may desire to write the fairy tale words (i.e., *wicked*, *woods*, etc.) on index cards and then display them in a cluster in order to create a motif word wall. This cluster will later be renamed "motifs" or rearranged in a "motif" column.

- *Wicked*: Typical description of witches or fairies
- *Woods*: Typical generic setting where fairy tales are set
- *Number 3*: The most common number in fairy tales
- *Wishes*: The most common element in fairy tales
- *Once upon a time*: Formulaic opening
- *Happily ever after*: Expected outcome of fairy tales
- *Beauty*: The way most princesses or good female characters *must* look
- *Magic sleep*: Motif found in stories like "Sleeping Beauty" and "Snow White"

Generate a list of fairy tales to display on the board. This list will be helpful as students consider how words relate to fairy tales they know.

10. In small groups or with a partner, have students create a 2-column grid by folding a piece of paper in half (or using a page in their folklorist journal). In one column, have students record the word or phrase, and in the other their guess about how it relates to fairy tales.

11. Share responses as a class. After gathering student thoughts, guide students toward consensus. Students should leave with an understanding of how these words relate to fairy tales.

## DISCUSSION: FAIRY TALES

12. Tell students: *We will be studying a particular type of folktale, the fairy tale.* Explain that *fairy tale* can be written as one word or two. Ask students to write the word in their journals. Based on your knowledge of compound words, what type of stories should fairy tales be? (Possible answer: Stories about fairies.)

13. Model dividing the word into *fairy/tale*. This name is confusing because not all fairy tales even feature fairies; in fact, few do. But they almost all have some magical elements. A more accurate name would be magic tales. Specialists in the field actually prefer this term. They also refer to such stories as wonder tales.

14. Distribute Handout 3.3: Fairy Tale Timeline showing the genesis of the term *fairy tale*. Have students work in pairs to study the timeline showing how folktales became known as fairy tales. Together they need to write a short explanation of why this happened—they will be reading and interpreting a timeline, summarizing the events, and putting them in their own words.

Refer to the groups from Formative Assessment 1 in Lesson 2.

## WORD WORK

15. Write *sympathy and empathy*. Ask students to suggest a good place to divide the word. Try different suggestions, ultimately dividing the prefix from the word root: *sym/pathy*. Underline the suffix. Ask: *Is this a compound word? Can you think of a good way to remember which words are compound words and which words are made up of prefixes and suffixes?*

## CLOSE

16. Return to words and phrases from the Word Splash activity (Handout 3.2). Explain that there are elements that are universal in many fairy tales. Students will see them occur over and over. Read the following statements.

> If students think it is a universal situation, that it is something that happens everywhere to all people, they should give a thumbs up. If it is not universal, not something that happens everywhere, they should give a thumbs down.
> - Children are sometimes scared of the dark.
> - It snows in winter.
> - People have birthdays.
> - People have birthday parties.
> - Children have drinking fountains in their schools.

- *Universal:* (Latin) universalis; "of or belonging to all"
- Make up your own statements that encourage children to see that children share similar thoughts and feelings all over the world.

## HOMEWORK

17. Handout 3.4: Homework contains summaries of fairy tales with which children may identify. They will empathize, sympathize, or feel neither, and explain why.

**Name:** _____  **Date:** _____

## HANDOUT 3.1

# WORD WORK, *PATHOS*

### DEFINITION
**pa·thos** (pā′thäs′, -thôs′)
*noun*
    The feelings of pity, sorrow, sympathy, or compassion brought about by something experienced or observed

### ETYMOLOGY
    Greek: Suffering, disease, feeling

### EXAMPLE
    Pathos names that quality, in a real situation or in a literary or artistic work, which evokes sympathy and a sense of sorrow or pity.

**Directions:** Write your responses on an index card. Try to answer as many as you can.

1. Put the word in the center of a word web. Draw lines from the circle, and write as many synonyms as you can think of.

2. Have you read a fairy tale where you felt pathos because of what happened to one of the characters in the fairy tale?

3. What does the suffix *-pathy* have to do with *pathos*?

4. Write a kid-friendly definition of *pathos*.

## HANDOUT 3.2
# WORD SPLASH

# HANDOUT 3.3
# FAIRY TALE TIMELINE

## 1697

Marie-Catherine D'Aulnoy, French writer, publishes a book of fantasy stories called, *Tales of Fairies* (in French, *Les contes des fees*)

**Featuring:**
*Cinderella, The Sleeping Beauty, Little Red Riding Hood*

## 1812–1815

Folklorists, the Grimm brothers, collected a book of folktales called *Children and Household Tales* (in German, *Kinder- und Hausmarchen*)

**Featuring:**
*The Frog King, Hansel and Gretel, Rumpelstiltskin, Snow White and the Seven Dwarfs*

## 1868

The Grimm book is translated **badly** from German to English as *Grimms' Fairy Tales*

## 1872

Hans Christian Andersen's collection of stories, *Fairy Tales Told for Children*, is translated into *Hans Andersen's Fairy Tales*

**Featuring:**
*The Little Match Girl, The Princess and the Pea*

## HANDOUT 3.4

# HOMEWORK

**Directions:** You feel sympathy when you feel sad for someone. You feel empathy when you feel sad for someone because you have experienced something similar. Read the passages from the stories below. For each one, decide if you sympathize, empathize, or don't feel either. Explain why.

1. Hansel and Gretel get left alone in the woods:

> Gretel shared her piece of bread with Hansel, who had scattered his by the way. Then they fell asleep and evening came and went, but no one came to the poor children. They did not awake until it was dark night, and Hansel comforted his little sister and said, "Just wait, Gretel, until the moon rises, and then we shall see the crumbs of bread and they will show us our way home again."

I (sympathize/empathize/don't feel either) because . . .

2. The queen puts a pea under the mattress of the princess, and then asks the princess how she slept:

> "Oh simply terribly! I didn't sleep a wink all night! I felt like I was lying on something hard, and I'm black and blue all over!"

I (sympathize/empathize/don't feel either) because . . .

## HANDOUT 3.4, CONTINUED

3. The Little Mermaid wishes she could see the human world above the sea.

> No joy was greater to the youngest princess than hearing about the human world above . . . None of the sisters was filled with as much longing as the youngest, who had the longest to wait, and who was so quiet and thoughtful.

I (sympathize/empathize/don't feel either) because . . .

# LESSON

# 4 Once Upon a Time . . .

## MATERIALS

- ✓ Index cards
- ✓ Handout 3.4: Homework
- ✓ Handout 4.1: "Once Upon a Time" (cut into strips, 1 set per group)
- ✓ Handout 4.2: Character Types

Folktales can be recognized by their formulaic elements. They have:
- stock or set openings and closings,
- generic, unspecified settings, and
- stereotyped characters.

## OBJECTIVES

Students will:

- ✓ apply knowledge of language structure, language conventions, and genre to create, critique, and discuss print and nonprint texts;
- ✓ read a wide range of literature to build an understanding of human experience; and
- ✓ apply a wide range of strategies to comprehend, interpret, evaluate, and appreciate texts.

- Stereotype
- Character
- Setting
- Plot
- Motif

185

# SEQUENCE

## WARM UP

1. Students will work with a partner to review the homework from Lesson 3 (Handout 3.4). Ask students to compare answers and discuss any differences in their responses.

2. Students should share with a partner one character with whom they empathized and explain why. If a student did not empathize with any of the characters, ask them to explain why.

 Empathy is an important life skill. This activity encourages students to consider the context in which the text is situated by making personal connections with the characters.

## ACTIVITY: FAIRY TALE OPENINGS/SETTINGS

- You need to make multiple sets of Handout 4.1 cut into strips.
- The individual responses will provide insight into students' complexity of thought.

3. Review the conclusion from Lesson 3 (Fairy tales have universal elements; for example, how they begin).

4. Cut Handout 4.1 into strips. Distribute strips to groups based on prior assessment of levels of understanding. Students should read one strip, then pass it to the person next to them.

5. Display the full handout. Ask: *Why do you think fairy tales start like this?*

6. Independently, students should write their answer on an index card. Then, with their group, students can share ideas and pick their favorite or best answer to share with the class. The more advanced group should also be asked to generate three more ways a fairy tale could begin that follows the same idea as the ones they read.

7. Display the following quote:

> "Once upon a time," "In a certain country," "A thousand years ago, or longer," "At a time when animals still talked," "Once in an old castle in the midst of a large dense forest"—such beginnings suggest that what follows does not pertain to the here and now that we know. (Bettelheim, 1976, p. 62)

8. *Ask: How is this similar to an answer we came up with?* Explain that these openings signal that we have entered a fairy tale place. Say: *They also tell us we are in a place that could be anywhere—even though it set a long time ago, the woods are so general, they could be our woods.*

The forest is a recurrent image in German fairy tales, in part because over a quarter of the country is comprised of forest land. In the Grimms' tales, the forest is a supernatural world, a place where anything can happen and often does. (Heiner, 1999)

- Ask students if they have a wooded area or a forest near their homes—or perhaps a place they visited. Did the forest have any fairy tale like qualities? If you are in a large city, ask how the tall buildings in their city could be like the forest or woods.

## ACTIVITY: CHARACTER TYPES

9. Distribute Handout 4.2: Character Types. The first two passages in each section have very similar, stereotypical characters (e.g., handsome prince, greedy witch, or beautiful, sweet daughter), and the third passage features a nonstereotypical character.

Students may work with the same groups as earlier in the lesson. Less advanced groups can make Venn diagrams of similarities and differences in the characters. The more advanced groups can be asked to identify the stereotype and find other stereotypes in fairy tales they have read.

- Why do fairy tales have "stock" settings and characters? One reason is so that listeners can personalize the stories more easily. Another is that they are easier for storytellers to remember.
- The "Say Something" strategy can be used in partner reading while rereading for fluency.

10. Have students use a "Say Something" reading strategy in their groups: One student reads his or her passage aloud. The other students must then say something at the end of the passage. The statement can be factual, inferential, even an opinion. The only restriction is that they not repeat what the other child said.

## WORD WORK

11. Ask: *What characters did you encounter (e.g., princess)?* Record the types of characters on the board. These will become word webs, so spread them out on the board.

12. Ask: *What adjectives describe the characters (e.g., pure)?* Record answers on the web, with the character in the center circle. Ask: *In which passage is the character a little different?* "Beautiful Princess" Passage 3 has a nonstereotypical character. At this age, students may not yet be saturated with character types, so they may not choose the "odd" character. They needn't find the right answer.

13. Explain that most characters in fairy tales are stereotypes. They appear over and over in different tales—a universal type. Because these character types are very predictable, they are called *stereotypes*.

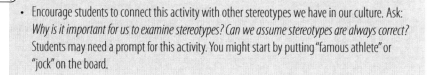

- *Stereotype* (noun): "A conventional, formulaic, and oversimplified conception, opinion, or image;" (verb) "to give a fixed, unvarying form to."

  ‣ **Kid-Friendly Definition:** A *stereotype* is a character that is very simple, usually described with one or two words.

- Encourage students to connect this activity with other stereotypes we have in our culture. Ask: *Why is it important for us to examine stereotypes? Can we assume stereotypes are always correct?* Students may need a prompt for this activity. You might start by putting "famous athlete" or "jock" on the board.

14. Tell students that the word *stereotype* is a noun. Ask for a definition of noun. Write the following sentence on the board: *Fairy tales often reinforce the stereotype of a beautiful princess.*

15. Explain that *stereotype* can also be a verb. (Some words can be both.) You can stereotype someone when you make an overly simplified judgment about someone. Write the following sentence on the board: *People stereotype princes as handsome and brave.*

## CLOSE

16. Ask students to respond to the following question in their journals: *Can you think of a time that you stereotyped a person, then found out there was more to him or her?*

## HANDOUT 4.1
# "ONCE UPON A TIME"

ONCE UPON A TIME, THOUGH IT WAS
NOT IN MY TIME OR IN YOUR TIME,
OR IN ANYBODY ELSE'S TIME . . .

IN OLDEN TIMES WHEN WISHING STILL HELPED . . .

THERE ONCE LIVED UPON THE
EARTH A POOR MAN . . .

ONCE UPON A TIME, THERE WAS A
CASTLE IN A WILD PLACE . . .

ONCE UPON A TIME THERE LIVED IN A CERTAIN
VILLAGE A LITTLE COUNTRY GIRL . . .

IN LONG-PAST TIMES THERE WAS A
CHIEFTAIN OF A COMPANY OF MICE . . .

BEFORE, BEFORE, IN THE BEGINNING OF
THINGS, PEOPLE WORE THEIR BEAUTY
AS THEY WORE THEIR CLOTHES.

## HANDOUT 4.2

# CHARACTER TYPES

## "THE YOUNGEST" GIRL

### PASSAGE 1

Once upon a time there was a poor man who had so many children that he didn't have much food or clothing to give them. Pretty children they all were, but the prettiest was the youngest daughter, who was so lovely that there was no end to all her loveliness.

—"East O' The Sun and West O' the Moon"

### PASSAGE 2

Once upon a time there lived a widow with two daughters. The elder was often mistaken for her mother, so like her was she both in nature and in looks; parent and child being so disagreeable and arrogant that no one could live with them.

The younger girl, who took after her father in the gentleness and sweetness of her disposition, was also one of the prettiest girls imaginable. The mother doted on the elder daughter—naturally enough, since she resembled her so closely—and disliked the younger one as intensely. She made the latter live in the kitchen and work hard from morning till night.

—"The Fairies"

### PASSAGE 3

"It is a beautiful flower," said the woman, and she kissed the red and golden-colored leaves, and while she did so the flower opened, and she could see that it was a real tulip. Within the flower, upon the green velvet stamens, sat a very delicate and graceful little maiden. She was scarcely half as long as a thumb, and they gave her the name of "Thumbelina," or Tiny, because she was so small.

A walnut-shell, elegantly polished, served her for a cradle; her bed was formed of blue violet-leaves, with a rose-leaf for a counterpane. Here she slept at night, but during the day she amused herself on a table, where the woman had placed a plateful of water. Round this plate were wreaths of flowers with their stems in the water, and upon it floated a large tulip-leaf, which served Tiny for a boat. Here the little maiden sat and rowed herself from side to side, with two oars made of white horse-hair. It really was a very pretty sight. Tiny could, also, sing so softly and sweetly that nothing like her singing had ever before been heard.

—"Thumbelina"

## HANDOUT 4.2, CONTINUED

# "BEAUTIFUL PRINCESS"

## PASSAGE 1

By this time, the Queen's little daughter was growing up. She had a kind heart and a beautiful face, and a golden crown on her forehead.

—"The Twelve Brothers"

## PASSAGE 2

As time went on, all the wishes of the fairies came true. The Princess grew up so gracious, merry, beautiful, and kind that everyone who knew her could not help but love her. And because she was mischievous and clever as well, she was called Briar Rose.

—"Sleeping Beauty"

## PASSAGE 3

A very long time ago, when all the countries you've ever heard of were in different places on the map, and the world was still full of the dark, wide forests where fairies tend to live, a princess was born who was not beautiful.

But by the time Rose was thirteen, the maximum possible age for developing beauty in those days, there was still no trace of beauty about her. She had a wonderful character and a quick mind, and everybody liked her. She was buck-toothed and skinny, though, with freckles and hair cut too short for those glamorous styles that beautiful princesses were required to wear. Rose was always running, climbing, and riding bareback, and she knew that if she had to spend as much time on her hair as [her sisters] Asphalt and Concrete did she'd have no time left for anything fun.

—"The Ugly Princess and the Wise Fool"

## HANDOUT 4.2, CONTINUED

# "YOUNGEST BOY"

## PASSAGE 1

There once was a man who had three sons. The youngest was called Simpleton. He was teased and hated by the others and kept in the shadows.

—"The Golden Goose"

## PASSAGE 2

There was once a woodcutter and his wife who had seven children, all boys. The eldest was only twelve years old, and the youngest was five. None of them was large enough have a job and earn money, so their parents had to work very hard to get food and clothes for them. To make matters worse, the youngest child was sickly and weak, and he was so small that his father and mother called him Hop-o'-my-Thumb. Yet the little, weak boy was gifted with a great deal of sense, and though he never had much to say, he noticed all that went on around him.

—"Hop-O'-My-Thumb"

## PASSAGE 3

"They were very poor, and their seven children inconvenienced them greatly, because not one of them was able to earn his own way. They were especially concerned, because the youngest was very sickly. He scarcely ever spoke a word, which they considered to be a sign of stupidity, although it was in truth a mark of good sense. He was very little, and when born no bigger than one's thumb, for which reason they called him Little Thumb.

The poor child bore the blame of everything that went wrong in the house. Guilty or not, he was always held to be at fault. He was, notwithstanding, more cunning and had a far greater share of wisdom than all his brothers put together. And although he spoke little, he listened well."

—"Little Thumb"

## HANDOUT 4.2, CONTINUED

# "WICKED STEPMOTHER"

## PASSAGE 1

Cinderella's house and Cinderella's life were ruled by a cold, hard woman with a face of stone and a heart sick with envy. This woman hated anything beautiful: the small yellow birds in the trees, the soft rabbits in the gardens, even the roses that bloom in the summer fields. And she hated Cinderella most of all.

—Walt Disney's *Cinderella*, retold by Cynthia Rylant

## PASSAGE 2

Once upon a time there was a poor man, who had a wife and two children, a boy and a girl. He was so poor that he possessed nothing in the world but the ashes on his hearth.

His wife died, and after a time he married another woman, who was crabby and bad-natured, and from morning till evening, as long as the day lasted, she gave the poor man no peace, but snarled and shouted at him.

The woman said to him, "Do away with these children. You cannot even keep me. How then can you keep all these mouths?" For was she not a stepmother?

—"The Little Boy and The Wicked Stepmother"

## PASSAGE 3

When their stepmother saw the children, she acted not like a woman, but a perfect fury; crying aloud, wringing her hands, stamping with her feet, snorting like a frightened horse, and exclaiming, "What fine piece of work is this? Is there no way of ridding the house of these creatures? Is it possible, husband, that you are determined to keep them here to plague my very life out? Go—take them out of my sight! I'll not wait for the crowing of cocks and the cackling of hens; or else be assured that tomorrow morning I'll go off to my parents' house, for you do not deserve me. I have not brought you so many fine things, only to be made the slave of children who are not my own.

—"Nennillo and Nennella"

## HANDOUT 4.2, CONTINUED

# "OGRES"

## PASSAGE 1

His mother was ugly and his father was ugly, but Shrek was uglier than the two of them put together. By the time he toddled, Shrek could spit flame a full 99 yards and vent smoke form either ear. With just a look he cowed the reptiles in the swamp. Any snake dumb enough to bite him instantly got convulsions and died.

—"Shrek"

## PASSAGE 2

Then off she ran again until she came to a great castle where a terrible Ogre lived. He was such a fierce and powerful Ogre that he lived all alone, and no one would ever come near him. But Puss-in-Boots pulled the bell boldly, and when the Ogre opened the door and glared out, she bowed politely and walked in with little, silly steps, showing off her yellow boots. And the Ogre was so astonished to see such a visitor that he could only stare with his mouth open.

"Good-afternoon, your Mightiness," said Puss calmly. "I have heard so much about you that I thought I would call and see you. Is it really true that you can turn yourself into a wild beast?"

"Just wait and see!" bragged the Ogre, for he was very proud of the wonderful things he could do.

—"Puss in Boots"

## PASSAGE 3

In those days there lived a huge ogre, eighteen feet high and nine feet round; his fierce and savage looks were the terror of all who beheld him.

He dwelt in a gloomy cavern on the top of the mountain, and used to wade over to the mainland in search of prey; when he would throw half-a-dozen oxen upon his back, and tie three times as many sheep and hogs round his waist, and march back to his own abode.

The giant had done this for many years when Jack resolved to destroy him.

—"Jack and the Beanstalk"

# LESSON 5

# Understanding Culture

## MATERIALS

- ✓ Teacher's copy of "The Ant and the Grasshopper" (available at http://www.gutenberg.org/files/19994/19994-h/19994-h.htm#Page_34)
- ✓ Handout 5.1: Character Cards
- ✓ Handout 5.2: Adjective Cards
- ✓ Handout 5.3: Tale Cards

- Fairy tales, myths, legends, and fables are all categorized as oral folklore.
- Folktales have different purposes—to instruct and/or to entertain.
- Folktales can help us feel empathy for others.

## OBJECTIVES

Students will:

- ✓ read a wide range of literature to build an understanding of human experience and
- ✓ apply a wide range of strategies to comprehend, interpret, evaluate, and appreciate texts.

- Folk
- Myth
- Setting
- Folklore
- Oral

- Character
- Folktale
- Purpose
- Universal
- Fairy tale

- Moral
- Empathy
- Culture
- Legend

# SEQUENCE

## READ ALOUD

1. Read "The Ant and the Grasshopper" aloud. When you have finished reading the story, ask students to summarize in one sentence the moral of the story.

Now ask students to think about the moral of the story; then divide them into two groups for discussion:

- Group 1: Ask students to think about why we would need to warn others about the risks of not storing food for winter.
- Group 2: Have students complete the same task as Group 1, as well as list all the other ways we should prepare for the future (e.g., next season, next year, or many years in the future).

Ask students to think about ways in which people in their community plan for the seasons, such as planting herbs or vegetables, hunting, etc.—even shopping for back to school clothes or supplies can be an example of preparing for the next season.

## ACTIVITY: WHAT IS CULTURE?

2. Tell students that many folktales and fables were told to teach people about a *cultural norm*. Ask students to brainstorm with a partner about what a *cultural norm* might be. Ask groups to share out and write responses on the board.

- Prompt students by asking them what *norm* might be short for (normal).
- *Culture* is a difficult concept to define. Simply, it is the collection of experiences, beliefs, values, arts, knowledge, and so forth in a society. It's important to understand that there are many different types of culture. There's not one, single U.S. culture, for example. There might be a comprehensive piece of culture that others recognize about the U.S. (e.g., form of government); however, within the U.S. there are many different types of cultural beliefs (e.g., different religions have different cultural beliefs).
- For this unit, students should learn that stories passed down from generation to generation not only become part of the culture but they in fact convey beliefs held by a particular culture.

3. Next, draw a simple iceberg on the board (see Figure 4).

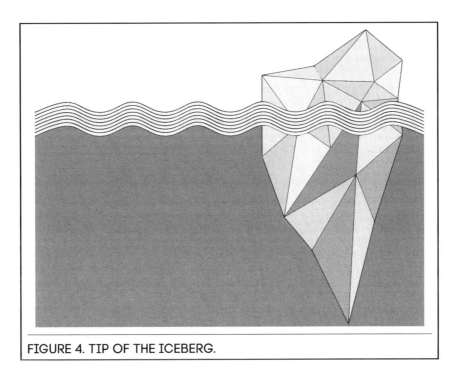

FIGURE 4. TIP OF THE ICEBERG.

4.  You want to illustrate that the "tip of the iceberg" is just that! Students should recognize that the majority of the iceberg is under water.
5.  Next, label the parts of the iceberg (see Figure 5).

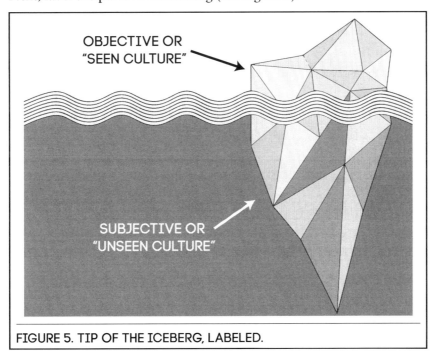

OBJECTIVE OR "SEEN CULTURE"

SUBJECTIVE OR "UNSEEN CULTURE"

FIGURE 5. TIP OF THE ICEBERG, LABELED.

Ask students if they recognize the word *objective*. Does it sound like another word they know? (Object.) *Ob-* is a prefix meaning to, on, or toward; *-ject* is a suffix meaning to throw (as in eject, inject, project, reject). Give students a few minutes to see if they can make meaning out of the word *objective* by telling them it is something seen and/or that people can agree on. Students will likely need support during this activity. You can say: *A ball is an object. It can be seen. Or, in the U.S., the Executive Branch is one of three branches of government.*

6. After students have thought about the word *objective*, ask: *What parts of a culture can we see?*

7. Have students work with a partner to think about what can they "see" in a culture. What is objective? Tell them to pretend they live in another country, and they are taking a trip to visit the U.S. What kinds of things could they learn about the U.S. from searching on the Internet?

8. After students have an opportunity to work together, collect class ideas on the board. The list should include things like: language, religions, holidays, music, government, money, etc.

9. Now, repeat the activity with *subjective* or unseen parts of culture. What are parts of a culture that are unseen or harder to see (e.g., values, beliefs, traditions)? It might help to say: *If we go to Italy, we might know that they speak Italian and have a type of currency called a lira and that the capital is Rome. However, we might not know how two neighbors talk to each other if they pass each other in the street.* Depending on your students, you can share that many people in the world think that everyone in America is rich. You can discuss why others would think that, and if it is true. Sometimes we "see" parts of a culture but that seen culture might not tell the whole story or might not include the "unseen" parts.

Ask students to think about the prefix *sub-*. What other words start with *sub* (e.g., submarine, subtract)? What do these words have in common (e.g., under, lower, beneath)?

10. Ask students to draw an iceberg in their notebooks and to choose a culture they are familiar with. They can choose their families, school, church, neighborhood, etc. The seen culture might be where they live, number of siblings, parents' name; whereas the unseen parts might include the special traditions the family has (pizza or movie night, a family reunion, a special song or prayer they sing, a vacation spot they return to each year). It's important to stress that everyone has a culture or cultures they belong to. Students can complete this assignment for homework. They will later use this work to brainstorm writing ideas for their own folktale or fable.

## INSTRUCTION: CHARACTER

11. Ask: *What are some characters we've encountered in the tales we have read so far?* Distribute Handout 5.1: Character Cards. Ask students to cut out all of the cards or precut them before this lesson. Have students group characters according to similar characteristics and then brainstorm adjectives to describe that type of character. If students have difficulty, display the character types passages (Handout 4.3) and have volunteers underline examples of characters and adjectives on the overhead.

## ACTIVITY: REVIEW

12. Distribute Handout 5.2: Adjective Cards. Ask the students to cut out all of the cards or precut them before the lesson.

13. Students should sort cards using the following instructions, starting with the first. Tell students to see how far they can go:
    - ✓ Match characters from the tales we have read to adjectives (closed sort).
    - ✓ Match words that go together (open sort).
    - ✓ Match in a way you invent (open sort).

14. Have students record sorts on paper.

 You may have students complete this task independently or in reciprocal peer tutoring pairs where a student with a learning or emotional disability is paired with a comparably able student without a disability.

## ACTIVITY: TALES AND ELEMENTS

15. Distribute Handout 5.3: Tale Cards. Ask: *How many different ways might you sort these tales?* For each sort, describe the criteria you used to do the sorting. Tell students to record sorts on the same paper as their adjective sorts.

## PREPARATION: FORMATIVE ASSESSMENT 2

16. At the end of Lesson 5, administer Formative Assessment 2. Students have learned about plot, characters, empathy, and culture. Have students respond to the following in their journals or as an exit card:
    - ✓ How do folk tales help us feel empathy?
    - ✓ What is an example of objective culture?
    - ✓ What is an example of subjective culture?

- These sorting activities will assess students' understanding and retention of tales from previous week.
- If you incorporated tales that are different from the curriculum, put them on cards as well. Use tales covered in the first week.

17. **Using the assessment data:** Use responses to ensure that students understand key concepts of empathy and culture. If necessary, use the beginning of the next class to reinforce these concepts for those students who did not respond correctly to the questions.

## HANDOUT 5.1

# CHARACTER CARDS

| | |
|---|---|
| BROTHER | SISTER |
| STEPMOTHER | WITCH |
| KING | PRINCESS |
| OGRE | PRINCE |
| QUEEN | FAIRY |
| GODMOTHER | |

**HANDOUT 5.2**

# ADJECTIVE CARDS

| | |
|:---:|:---:|
| WICKED | BRAVE |
| BEAUTIFUL | PURE |
| JEALOUS | GREEDY |
| CLEVER | CRUEL |
| | |
| | |

## HANDOUT 5.3

# TALE CARDS

| | |
|---|---|
| "HANSEL AND GRETEL" | "LITTLE RED RIDING HOOD" |
| "SNOW WHITE AND THE SEVEN DWARFS" | "SLEEPING BEAUTY" |
| "PUSS IN BOOTS" | "THE LITTLE MATCH GIRL" |
| "THE FROG KING" | "BOOTS WHO ATE A MATCH WITH THE TROLL" |
| "THE ANT AND THE GRASSHOPPER" | "THE BOYS AND THE FROGS" |
| "CINDERELLA" | "THE PRINCESS AND THE PEA" |

# LESSON 6

# Variants

## MATERIALS

- ✓ Thumbtacks or sticky note tabs
- ✓ World map for classroom wall
- ✓ Titles of "Cinderella" tales on small sticky notes or slips of paper
- ✓ Teacher's copy of "Cinderella" (available at http://www.gutenberg.org/files/11027/11027-h/11027-h.htm#cinderella)
- ✓ Teacher's copy of "Cinderella" in German (available at http://www.grimmstories.com/de/grimm_maerchen/aschenputtel)
- ✓ Teacher's copy of "Cinderella" in French (available at http://www.iletaitunehistoire.com/genres/contes-legendes/lire/cendrillon-biblidcon_029)
- ✓ Handout 6.1: Can You Guess the Tale?

- • Folktales come from many different countries.
- • One tale can "come from" many places.

## OBJECTIVES

Students will:

- ✓ read a wide range of literature to build an understanding of human experience;
- ✓ apply a wide range of strategies to comprehend, interpret, evaluate, and appreciate texts;
- ✓ apply knowledge of language structure, language conventions, and genre to create, critique, and discuss print and nonprint texts; and
- ✓ develop an understanding of and respect for diversity in language use, patterns, and dialects across cultures, ethnic groups, geographic regions, and social roles.

Responses to this prompt give teachers insight into students' complexity/depth of thought. Sometimes challenging or open-ended journal prompts will alert teachers to deep thinkers who, perhaps, don't speak up often in class.

**Cultural Sensitivity:** Please remind students that certain things that could not be explained scientifically were sometimes explained incorrectly in myths and fairy tales (e.g., the issue of blindness in "Cinderella").

• Variant

## SEQUENCE

### READ ALOUD

1. Read "Cinderella" aloud.
2. Display the following quote from Jane Yolen: "Folktales from the oral tradition carry the thumbprints of history" (1998, p. 5).
3. Ask students to think about the discussion of culture in the previous lesson. History is a part of culture. Ask students to respond in their journals to the following question: *What do you think the quote means?*
4. After writing for 5 minutes, students should share their ideas, either with the whole group or with a partner.

### ACTIVITY: FOLKTALES ARE UNIVERSAL

5. Display "Cinderella" in German and French. Ask if any student can recognize the languages and/or read the languages. Looking at the title, ask if they can guess the tale.
6. Explain that folktales originate all over the world. Ask if anyone can locate France on the world map. Provide a thumbtack, tape, or sticky tab to that student, who will mark the location of, for instance, "Cinderella."

If a student can read the language, invite them to read the opening sentences of the tale.

Remind students that finding a country on the map and knowing the language spoken there are examples of objective culture. Ask: *What does "Cinderella" teach us about subjective culture in the variants told from different countries?*

### ACTIVITY: CAN YOU GUESS THE TALE?

7. Distribute Handout 6.1: Can You Guess the Tale? The tales on the page get progressively longer and more difficult. Either assign students the appropriate passage to read based on their readiness level or, better yet, ask them to start at the top of the sheet and see how far they can go. All tales are versions or variants of "Cinderella":
   ✓ **USA:** Walt Disney's *Cinderella*, retold by Cynthia Rylant

✓ **Georgia:** "Conkiajgharuna, the Little Rag Girl"
✓ **Ireland:** "Fair, Brown, and Trembling"
✓ **Germany:** "Aschenputtel"
✓ **France:** "The Little Glass Slipper"
✓ **Italy:** "La Cenerentola"

8. Explain that sometimes the same folktale, like "Cinderella," appears in different countries but with slight differences. They are variations of one story, or as folklorists call them, variants.

 Instruct students who finish early to use the folktale list they have been keeping in their folklorist journal, and map the tales they have read so far. On a small sticky note, have students write the tale, the country, and the language that is spoken there. Students can then place the sticky note in their journal next to the appropriate folktale.

9. Provide each student with the title of a "Cinderella" tale with the country on the back of thin strips of paper. Have them locate it on their own map, then place it on the class map.

## WORD WORK

10. Explain to students that words in English originate from other languages.
11. Remind students that Grimms' first collection of folktales was called *Kinder- und Hausmärchen* (*Children's and Household Tales*). Write the title in German on the board. Ask: *Do you see a familiar word? What is that similar to?* (Possible responses: Kinder = kindergarten, haus = house.)

- If students wonder what *kindergarten* means, ask what *garten* looks like. That's right, *garden*. Ask what *kinder* looks like. That's right, *kid* or *children*.
- *Kindergarten*: Coined in 1840 by a German referring to his method of developing intelligence in young children, brought to the U.S. by a German Catholic priest. Taken into English untranslated.

12. Ask students to write the word *vary* on their word wall, which means "to alter or change something."
13. Explain that many words originate from older languages like Latin. Some words that originate from Latin sound the same in many modern languages. For example:
    ✓ Vary (English)
    ✓ Varier (French)
    ✓ Variar (Spanish)

14. Students should share what they wrote in their journals. Synthesize their responses. The final definition should include the fact that variants differ only slightly from something else.

15. Write the words vary and variant and draw a line before -*ant*. Have children pronounce the words with you.

16. Display words that end in -*ant* or -*ent*. Have students copy words and draw a line before the suffix (-*ent*, -*ant*).

| | | |
|---|---|---|
| ✓ pleasant | ✓ elegant | ✓ different |
| ✓ peasant | ✓ significant | ✓ innocent |
| ✓ merchant | ✓ constant | ✓ intelligent |
| ✓ servant | ✓ accident | ✓ absent |

- -*ant*: a suffix forming adjectives and nouns from verbs, occurring originally in French and Latin loanwords (pleasant; constant; servant).
- -*ant* can be added only to bases of Latin origin, with very few exceptions, such as coolant.
- It is easier to understand the effect prefixes (*un-, re-, in-, dis-*) have on words than suffixes whose meanings are more abstract (i.e., "the state of").

## CLOSE

"The fairy tale has no landlord." —Italian proverb

17. Display the second half of Jane Yolen's quote: "Each place, each culture, each teller leaves a mark" (1998, p. 5).

18. At the end of class or as homework, ask students to review their journal response from the beginning of the class and the first half of the Jane Yolen quote. Then ask students to answer the following question in their journal: *How does the second half of this quote change your original answer to the question, what do you think the quote means?* You might have to state the entirety of the quote for students: "Folktales from the oral tradition carry the thumbprints of history. Each place, each culture, each teller leaves a mark."

## HANDOUT 6.1
# CAN YOU GUESS THE TALE?

**Directions:** Fill in the blank with the name of the fairy tale you believe the passage is from.

1. This is a story about darkness and light, about sorrow and joy, about something lost and something found. This is a story about love. (USA)

   Can you guess the tale? _____

2. There was and there was not, there was a miserable peasant. He had a wife and a little daughter. So poor was this peasant that his daughter was called Conkiajgharuna. Some time passed, and his wife died. He was unhappy before, but now a greater misfortune had befallen him. He grieved and grieved, and at last he said to himself, "I will go and take another wife; she will mind the house, and tend my orphan child." So he arose and took a second wife, but this wife brought with her a daughter of her own. When this woman came into her husband's house and saw his child, she was angry in heart. (Georgia)

   Can you guess the tale? _____

3. King Aedh Cœrucha lived in Tir Conal, and he had three daughters, whose names were Fair, Brown, and Trembling. Fair and Brown had new dresses, and went to church every Sunday. Trembling was kept at home to do the cooking and work. They would not let her go out of the house at all; for she was more beautiful than the other two, and they were in dread she might marry before themselves. (Ireland)

   Can you guess the tale? _____

4. Once upon a time there was a rich man who lived happily for a long time with his wife. Together they had a single daughter. Then the woman became ill, and when she was lying on her deathbed, she called her

## HANDOUT 6.1, CONTINUED

daughter to her side, and said, "Dear child, I must leave you now, but I will look down on you from heaven. Plant a little tree on my grave, and when you want something, just shake the tree, and you shall get what you want. I will help you in time of need. Just remain pious and good." Then she closed her eyes and died. The child cried, and planted a little tree on her mother's grave. She did not need to carry any water to it, because her tears provided all the water that it needed." (Germany)

Can you guess the tale? _____

5. Once there was a gentleman who married, for his second wife, the proudest and most haughty woman that was ever seen. She had, by a former husband, two daughters of her own humor, who were, indeed, exactly like her in all things. He had likewise, by another wife, a young daughter, but of unparalleled goodness and sweetness of temper, which she took from her mother' who was the best creature in the world. (France)

Can you guess the tale? _____

6. There once lived a prince, who was a widower, but who had a daughter, so dear to him that he saw with no other eyes than hers; and he kept a governess for her, who taught her chain-work, and knitting, and to make point-lace, and showed her such affection as no words can tell. But after a time the father married again, and took a wicked jade for his wife, who soon conceived a violent dislike to her stepdaughter; and all day long she made sour looks, wry faces and fierce eyes at her, till the poor child was beside herself with terror, and was for ever bewailing to her governess the bad treatment she received from her stepmother. (Italy)

Can you guess the tale? _____

# LESSON 7
# Collectors of Tales

## MATERIALS
- ✓ Teacher's copy of "Puss in Boots" (available at http://www.pitt.edu/~dash/perrault04.html)
- ✓ Handout 3.3: Fairy Tale Timeline
- ✓ Handout 7.1: Anticipation Guides
- ✓ Handout 7.2A: The Brothers Grimm Biography (easiest)
- ✓ Handout 7.2B: Charles Perrault Biography
- ✓ Handout 7.2C: Andrew Lang Biography (hardest)

- Folktales don't have authors—they are collected by scholars from the people.
- Variants are different versions of one folktale as recorded by different people and/or in different countries.

## OBJECTIVES
Students will:
- ✓ read a wide range of literature to build an understanding of human experience;
- ✓ apply a wide range of strategies to comprehend, interpret, evaluate, and appreciate texts;
- ✓ apply knowledge of language structure, language conventions, and genre to create, critique, and discuss print and nonprint texts; and
- ✓ develop an understanding of and respect for diversity in language use, patterns, and dialects across cultures, ethnic groups, geographic regions, and social roles.

- Folklorist

# SEQUENCE

## READ ALOUD

1. Read "Puss in Boots" aloud.
2. Ask students to respond to the following in their journals: *What do the stories "Puss in Boots" and "Cinderella" have in common?* (Possible answer: Both stories are about a person in a lowly position who, with the help magical or supernatural assistance, makes a "good marriage," according to folklorist D. L. Ashliman [2004].)

- Journal responses could instead be gathered on index cards and placed as data in the student's folder.
- This response measures students' abilities to make higher level connections.

## DISCUSSION: INTRODUCING FOLKLORISTS AS COLLECTORS

3. Ask students: *Do you have a favorite book? Who wrote your favorite book? Do you have a favorite author? What do you know about him or her?*
4. Explain that real, oral folktales do not have authors—they are recorded by someone who collects tales that people tell. Explain to students that there are three very famous collectors of folktales—Charles Perrault, Andrew Lang, and the Brothers Grimm. Tell students: *We will learn about all of them, but small groups of you will become specialists on one of them.*
5. Distribute Handout 7.1: Anticipation Guides. Tell students the guides make statements about what they will learn in the upcoming days. Explain to students that they will read each statement, decide if they agree or disagree, discuss it with the group, and circle an answer in the "Before Reading" column. Have students work through all of the statements. They will not find out the answers immediately!

Anticipation guides give students a reason to plunge into a nonfiction passage. By first making predictions, they are motivated to find the answers in the text to confirm or reject them.

- Distribute Handouts 7.2A–C, grouping students by reading level. The biographies are leveled from easiest to hardest: (1) Grimm, (2) Perrault, (3) Lang.
- Have students read the biographies independently to find out if their guesses were correct. Students should underline or highlight where they find the correct answer or support for the correct answer.

6. After they have finished reading, groups should reconvene to confirm if their predictions on Handout 7.1 were correct. Then, have groups present their anticipation guides to the class. The class will orally agree and disagree with the statements. Have presenting groups guide the discussion by correcting the answers and reading the justification for the correct answers from the biographies.

## CLOSE

7. Tell students: *In 1878, the Folklore Society was born; its quarterly journal is called Folk-Lore. Its interest is primarily the origin of variants: Do folktales they all stem from one place? The prevailing theory was that folktales originated in India. In 1893, in the first book-length attempt to provide solid data to prove or disprove this, Marion Cox published 345 versions of "Cinderella." Modern folktale scholarship began.*

8. Ask students: *Where do these dates fit on the Fairy Tale Timeline?* Have students add these dates to Handout 3.3: Fairy Tale Timeline.

**Fairy Tales**

## HANDOUT 7.1
# ANTICIPATION GUIDES

## CHARLES PERRAULT

| Before Reading | | Statement | After Reading | |
|---|---|---|---|---|
| ❑ I agree | ❑ I disagree | Charles Perrault invented fairy tales. | ❑ I agree | ❑ I disagree |
| ❑ I agree | ❑ I disagree | Mother Goose was a man. | ❑ I agree | ❑ I disagree |
| ❑ I agree | ❑ I disagree | Cinderella did not originally have a fairy godmother. | ❑ I agree | ❑ I disagree |
| ❑ I agree | ❑ I disagree | Little Red Riding Hood was eaten by a wolf and was not saved by a woodsman | ❑ I agree | ❑ I disagree |

## ANDREW LANG

| Before Reading | | Statement | After Reading | |
|---|---|---|---|---|
| ❑ I agree | ❑ I disagree | Andrew Lang invented fairy tales. | ❑ I agree | ❑ I disagree |
| ❑ I agree | ❑ I disagree | A folklorist can be important, but not collect stories from "the common people." | ❑ I agree | ❑ I disagree |
| ❑ I agree | ❑ I disagree | Teachers used to think fairy tales were too scary for children. | ❑ I agree | ❑ I disagree |
| ❑ I agree | ❑ I disagree | Fairy tales should teach a lesson. | ❑ I agree | ❑ I disagree |

## THE BROTHERS GRIMM

| Before Reading | | Statement | After Reading | |
|---|---|---|---|---|
| ❑ I agree | ❑ I disagree | The Brothers Grimm invented fairy tales. | ❑ I agree | ❑ I disagree |
| ❑ I agree | ❑ I disagree | The Brothers Grimm changed the stories when they wrote them down. | ❑ I agree | ❑ I disagree |
| ❑ I agree | ❑ I disagree | *Sleeping Beauty* is also called *Briar Rose.* | ❑ I agree | ❑ I disagree |
| ❑ I agree | ❑ I disagree | The Brothers Grimm were American. | ❑ I agree | ❑ I disagree |

## HANDOUT 7.2A

# THE BROTHERS GRIMM BIOGRAPHY

> Our first aim in collecting these stories has been exactness and truth. We have added nothing of our own, have embellished no incident or feature of the story, but have given its substance just as we ourselves received it.
> —From *Children's and Household Tales*
> by the Brothers Grimm

Some folklorists wrote or collected fairy tales for children but not the Brothers Grimm! They did not collect tales for little children. Instead, these two patriotic brothers gathered German folktales for other scholars to read. But, children read and loved their tales anyway. In fact, once the stories grew popular among children, the brothers started to change details. In their later books, the stories became less violent and more about teaching a moral lesson.

Some folklorists argued that the Grimms should not have changed their stories. The brothers were accused of rewriting tales in their own words instead of reporting exactly what the original storyteller said. The Grimms claim their stories came directly from peasants, when really they changed some of the details. Also, once the stories were translated into other languages, the stories were very different from the originals.

Still, many of today's most popular fairy tales come from the Grimms: "The Frog King," "Rumpelstiltskin," "Snow White and the Seven Dwarfs," "The Bremen Town Musicians," "Hansel and Gretel," and "Rapunzel." They also collected tales similar to those recorded by Charles Perrault, especially "Aschenputtel" ("Cinderella") and "Briar Rose" ("Sleeping Beauty").

### HANDOUT 7.2B
# CHARLES PERRAULT BIOGRAPHY

Mother Goose is not a goose at all—or a mother. Mother Goose is actually a man! If J. K. Rowling reimagined wizardry and gave the world Harry Potter, then Charles Perrault, the writer of *Tales From Times Past*, or *Tales of Mother Goose* (1967), reimagined popular fairy tales. He is sometimes called the creator of the modern fairy tale.

Even though older variants existed, Perrault's most popular tale, "Cinderella," was made new with a magical pumpkin coach and rat coachmen. Cinderella did not pick lentils out of the fireplace. There is no tree or ghost of her mother. Instead of having the stepsisters cut off their toes and heels, Perrault added a fairy godmother and a glass slipper. It's no wonder that Walt Disney based his movie on Perrault's version, where Cinderella forgives her selfish sisters in the end. The Disney movie influenced the way most people now know the tale.

Perrault's conclusion in "Cinderella" is consistent with his belief that folktales should have a moral ending. He wrote his stories to teach children how to behave and to warn them against making poor choices or being thoughtless in their behaviors. For example, in Perrault's "Little Red Riding Hood," the girl gets eaten by the wolf without being rescued by a huntsman. The tale ends with a moral: "Children, especially attractive, well-bred young ladies, should never talk to strangers, for if they should do so, they may well provide dinner for a wolf."

Like the Harry Potter books, Perrault's stories were very popular. They became some of the most translated works of French literature. They have remained popular for centuries. He wrote that his stories would be "modern fables," and thought that one day his stories would be as important as myths and legends. He was right.

## HANDOUT 7.2C
# ANDREW LANG BIOGRAPHY

Ever since I could read, and long before I ever dreamed that fairy-tales might be a matter of curious discussion, those tales have been my delight. I heard them told by other children as a child, I even rescued one or two versions which seem to have died out of oral tradition in Lowland Scots; I confess that I still have a child-like love of a fairy-story for its own sake; and I have done my best to circulate Fairy Books among children.

—Andrew Lang

When the Harry Potter series was first published, fans would line up at bookstores (often at midnight!) to buy the latest book. Andrew Lang's popular "fairy books" had the same effect. English and Scottish children looked forward to a new colored fairy book every few years.

Lang lived in Scotland and was an important folklorist. He did not collect his folktales from "the people" but rather collected fairy tales from *other* collectors. He put the stories together in a series of "fairy books," first published in 1889. At that time, English fairy tale collections were rare, and some believed they were inappropriate. Adult critics argued the stories were too silly for grown-up readers, and teachers thought the traditional tales were too brutal and scary for kids.

Folklorists of his day also had strong opinions about folktales. Even the Folklorist Society, which was formed when Lang was writing his books, argued with him! For example, many folklorists believed fairy tales originated in India a long time ago, but Lang disagreed.

However, Lang did agree with other folklorists that the purpose of fairy tales was to amuse children and to teach them a moral lesson. (He lived during the Victorian era, which was a time when teaching manners was very important.) As a result, he usually chose tales where bad behavior was punished and good behavior was rewarded.

His collection of tales showed his beliefs, which is why the females were usually gentle and well behaved. And because his books were so popular,

## HANDOUT 7.2C, CONTINUED

those female heroes became the most famous. Many girls in older fairy tales were wilder and braver. They just weren't made famous.

### ANDREW LANG'S FAIRY BOOKS

>> *The Blue Fairy Book* (1889)  >> *The Violet Fairy Book* (1901)
>> *The Red Fairy Book* (1890)  >> *The Crimson Fairy Book* (1903)
>> *The Green Fairy Book* (1892)  >> *The Brown Fairy Book* (1904)
>> *The Yellow Fairy Book* (1894)  >> *The Orange Fairy Book* (1906)
>> *The Pink Fairy Book* (1897)  >> *The Olive Fairy Book* (1907)
>> *The Grey Fairy Book* (1900)  >> *The Lilac Fairy Book* (1910)

### ANDREW LANG'S INTRODUCTION TO *THE GREEN FAIRY* BOOK

To the Friendly Reader

This is the third, and probably the last, of the Fairy Books of many colours. First there was the Blue Fairy Book; then, children, you asked for more, and we made up the Red Fairy Book; and, when you wanted more still, the Green Fairy Book was put together. The stories in all the books are borrowed from many countries; some are French, some German, some Russian, some Italian, some Scottish, some English, one Chinese. However much these nations differ about trifles, they all agree in liking fairy tales. The reason, no doubt, is that men were much like children in their minds long ago, long, long ago, and so before they took to writing newspapers, and sermons, and novels, and long poems, they told each other stories, such as you read in the fairy books. They believed that witches could turn people into beasts, that beasts could speak, that magic rings could make their owners invisible, and all the other wonders in the stories.

Then, as the world became grown-up, the fairy tales which were not written down would have been quite forgotten but that the old grannies remembered them, and told them to the little grandchildren: and when they, in their turn, became grannies, they remembered them, and told them also. In this way these tales are older than reading and writing, far older than printing. The oldest fairy tales ever written down were written down in Egypt, about Joseph's time, nearly three thousand five hundred years ago.

## HANDOUT 7.2C, CONTINUED

Other fairy stories Homer knew in Greece nearly three thousand years ago, and he made them all up into a poem, the Odyssey, which I hope you will read some day. Here you will find the witch who turns men into swine, and the man who bores out the big foolish giant's eye, and the cap of darkness, and the shoes of swiftness, that were worn later by Jack the Giant-Killer. These fairy tales are the oldest stories in the world, and as they were first made by men who were childlike for their own amusement, so they amuse children still, and also grown-up people who have not forgotten how they once were children.

Some of the stories were made, no doubt, not only to amuse, but to teach goodness. You see, in the tales, how the boy who is kind to beasts, and polite, and generous, and brave, always comes best through his trials, and no doubt these tales were meant to make their hearers kind, unselfish, courteous, and courageous. This is the moral of them. But, after all, we think more as we read them of the diversion than of the lesson. There are grown-up people now who say that the stories are not good for children, because they are not true, because there are no witches, nor talking beasts, and because people are killed in them, especially wicked giants. But probably you who read the tales know very well how much is true and how much is only make-believe, and I never yet heard of a child who killed a very tall man merely because Jack killed the giants, or who was unkind to his stepmother, if he had one, because, in fairy tales, the stepmother is often disagreeable. If there are frightful monsters in fairy tales, they do not frighten you now, because that kind of monster is no longer going about the world, whatever he may have done long, long ago. He has been turned into stone, and you may see his remains in museums. Therefore, I am not afraid that you will be afraid of the magicians and dragons; besides, you see that a really brave boy or girl was always their master, even in the height of their power.

If we have a book for you next year, it shall not be a fairybook. What it is to be is a secret, but we hope that it will not be dull. So good-bye, and when you have read a fairy book, lend it to other children who have none, or tell them the stories in your own way, which is a very pleasant mode of passing the time.

# LESSON

# 8

# Type Index

## MATERIALS

- ✓ Teacher's copy of "The Silkie Wife" (available at http://www.pitt.edu/~dash/type4080.html#silkiewife)
- ✓ Teacher's copy of "The Feathery Robe" (available at http://www.pitt.edu/~dash/swan.html#brauns)
- ✓ Teacher's copy of "The ATU System" (Types 1–750, available at http://oaks.nvg.org/folktale-types.html)
- ✓ Handout 8.1A: "The Seal's Skin" (easiest)
- ✓ Handout 8.1B: "The Swan Maiden" (on-level)
- ✓ Handout 8.1C: "The Monkey Husband" (hardest)
- ✓ Handout 8.2: Fairy Tale List
- ✓ Handout 8.3: Fairy Tale List With ATU Numbers

- Variants are different versions of one folktale as recorded by different people and/or in different countries.
- Types are numbers assigned by folklorists to tales with a dominant motif.
- Folklorists created (and altered over a span of many years) the ATU system to universally categorize folktales by number.

## OBJECTIVES

Students will:
- ✓ read a wide range of literature to build an understanding of human experience;
- ✓ apply a wide range of strategies to comprehend, interpret, evaluate, and appreciate texts;
- ✓ develop the skills to participate as knowledgeable, reflective, creative, and critical members of a variety of a literary community; and

✓ apply knowledge of language structure, language conventions, and genre to create, critique, and discuss print and nonprint texts.

- Type
- Motif
- ATU system
- Summarize

# SEQUENCE

## WARM UP

1. Tell students: *We will do a 5-minute round of "Say Something!" Based on the things we read and learned about folktale collectors in the previous lesson, we all need to say something. The trick, of course, is that you can't repeat what someone else has said. You can state facts, opinions, ask questions—as long as it pertains to the "say something" subject.*

## READ ALOUD

2. Read "The Silkie Wife" aloud.

> . . . the myth of the Swan-maiden, one of the most widely distributed, and at the same time one of the most beautiful, stories ever evolved from the mind of man.
>
> —Edwin Sidney Hartland, 1904

## ACTIVITY: INTRODUCE TYPES

Students don't need to know what "type" of tale they are reading yet.

3. After listening to "The Silkie Wife" as a class, ask students to list the events from the tale. Record their recollections on the board.
4. Based on class discussion and coming to consensus, circle 3–4 of the most important things that happened in "The Silkie Wife."
5. Distribute Handouts 8.1A–C and instruct students to read their tale individually.

 Handouts 8.1A–C are loosely leveled—distribute them by reading readiness levels as determined by prior assessments.

6. Upon finishing their tale, students should begin to record their story's main events in their Folklorist journals. Once all students have finished reading independently, they should gather in groups with other stu-

dents who read the same tale. Together, they should narrow the plot points to the most important. Finally, the group should choose a leader to distill the ideas into one oral summary to share with the class.

7. Regroup as a class. One member of each group should go to the board (or on chart paper) and record the three most important events in their plot. Another will share the oral summary.

8. Ask: *What do all these tales share in common?* (Possible answer: A human steals the skin/fur/feathers of a creature to keep her for a wife. These are the common motifs in these sealskin/swan maiden stories.)

## WORD WORK

9. Write the word *motif* on the board. Have students record it on their personal wall. Take *magic sleep* from the folktale wall and ask students, again, what this has to do with fairy tales. (Possible answers: Snow White ate an apple and fell into magic sleep. Sleeping Beauty pricked her finger, etc.) Explain to students that a motif is an element that happens in many tales, like someone falling into a magic sleep. Motifs are very important to the plot. Ask: *Was Snow White falling asleep very important? Why?*

 **Kid-Friendly Definition:** A *motif* is an important event or object that occurs over and over in fairy tales.

To be considered a motif, the event can't be normal, such as, "He walked down the hall." If he "walked down the hall in his invisibility cape to escape the witch," then the action is unique enough to be a motif.

> A motif is a basic narrative element used in constructing a story. A simple tale may consist of a single motif. Tales typically include a number of motifs, which can be, and often are, used in more than one story.
>
> —D. L. Ashliman, 2004, p. 198

10. Using a Venn diagram, illustrate what the sealskin/swan maiden stories (Handouts 8.1A–C) have in common. Ask students to point out the differences. Record those on the diagram as well. (For example, in all of the tales, a female creature loses a covering. The covering varies; the setting varies; some are happily married; some are not.)

## INSTRUCTION: TYPE INDEX

11. Tell students: *As soon as folklorists started to realize that certain stories appeared in different places with important similarities, they needed a system to catalogue or keep track of the variants. It was a huge, difficult job. The universal version used today is the ATU Type Index, which catalogues stories by their overall plots and gives them a number.*

12. Display the ATU System, Types 1–750. Explain that students are only looking at some of the types. Tell students: *The tales we read today were of Type 400. How does the ATU system categorize them? Did you think that was the most important part of the plot? Note that one problem with the ATU system is that it only catalogues certain tales—it leaves out Native American and African tales, for example.*

13. Display "The Feathery Robe" from Japan. Ask: *Do you think this should be a Type 400 (i.e., forcing a female into marriage by stealing an item of her clothing and/or transformation by skin)?*

- *Type* is a description of narrative content or a "bundle of motifs" that often appear together to make a story.

- A *type index* refers us to other stories with similar events (though not similar themes). In other words, tales could have dissimilar "messages," but have some similar things happen in them, and, hence, share a type

- Type indexes do not index literary fairy tales, only oral tales, even when literary tales are rewritten variants. Ask students: *How are books grouped in the library? Where do these groupings come from?*
- Because these numbers, until a few years ago, were only ATU types—searching by type on the Internet was a frustrating process. Type 400 in the AT system is the "The Quest for a Lost Bride." Another source calls Type 400 "Transformation by Skin." For this reason, do not hold students accountable to types. They simply must know that systems exist, and the ATU number is the most widely used.
- Many websites organize tales by type, such as:
  > http://www.surlalunefairytales.com (the section on "annotated tales" and "similar tales from other countries")
  > http://www.pitt.edu/~dash/folktexts.html
  > http://www.grimmstories.com/en/grimm_fairy-tales/classification

## ACTIVITY

14. Display and/or distribute Handout 8.2: Fairy Tale List. Students should choose a tale that they know and, on an index card, write a short summary of the plot—only the most important things that happen. Referring to the ATU chart, students should try to determine in what number range it should fall and write it on the card.

15. After all students' cards have been turned in, display and/or distribute Handout 8.3: Fairy Tale List With ATU Numbers.

Because some students with disabilities have difficulties in written expression, you may choose an alternative method for summarizing the fairy tale such as bulleting, drawing, or orally summarizing.

## ACTIVITY: INTEREST/STRENGTH OF ANALYSIS

16.  Tell students: *Pick a number and list as many tales as you can to fit that number range.*

17.  Then, let students select a tale to read and have them pick the ATU they feel describes it best.

## HOMEWORK

18.  Ask students to respond to the following in their journals for homework: *A deficiency of the ATU system is that it leaves out tales from Native Americans and Africans, among others. If you could create your own system, that included all tales we've studied, and others, how would you group them? How would you make it simpler for kids?*

## HANDOUT 8.1A

# "THE SEAL'S SKIN"

### ICELAND

One morning, a man was walking along the cliffs and neared a cave. He could hear playful noises and dancing. As he looked inside, he saw a pile of sealskins. Looking them over, he picked one up, brought it home with him, and locked it away.

Later that day, he returned to the cliffs. A beautiful young girl was sitting there. She was naked and crying. It was her skin that the man had brought home. The man gave the girl some clothes, offered her comfort, and invited her home with him.

She eventually got used to the man, but did not get along well with others. She would often just sit and stare at the sea. After some time the man married her. They had many children.

The man had locked the skin in a trunk, and he carried the key with him at all times.

Many years later, the man rowed out to sea and forgot he left the key at home under his pillow. Some people say that the man went to a church service with his family, but that his wife had been sick and stayed home. They say that he forgot to take the key out of the pocket of his everyday clothes when he changed for church. When he got home the trunk was open, and his wife was gone. She had found the key, looked through the trunk, and found the skin.

The wife could not resist the sea. She said farewell to her children, put on the skin, and threw herself into the water.

Before she jumped into the sea, it is reported that she said:

This I want, and yet I do not,
I have seven children at sea
And seven here on land.

This touched the man's heart. From that day on, when he went fishing, a seal often swam around his boat. Tears seemed to run from its eyes. From that day, he always caught many fish.

*Note.* Adapted from "The Sealskin" translated by D. L. Ashliman, 2000, retrieved from: http://www.pitt.edu/~dash/type4080.html#sealskin.

## HANDOUT 8.1B
# "THE SWAN MAIDEN"

## SWEDEN

A young peasant, who often amused himself with hunting, saw one day three swans flying toward him. The birds settled upon the strand of a sound nearby. Approaching the water, he was surprised to see the three swans remove their feathery covering, which they threw into the grass, and three beautiful maidens step forth and dive into the water. After playing in the waves awhile they returned to the land. They put their feathery coverings back on and flew away in the same direction from which they came.

The hunter could not forget the bright image of one creature—the youngest and fairest. His mother noticed something was wrong with her son, because he had lost interest in hunting, which had been his favorite pleasure. She asked him finally the cause of his sadness, and so he told her what he had seen. He declared that there was no longer any happiness in this life for him if he could not marry the fair swan maiden.

"Nothing is easier," said the mother. "Go at sunset to the place where you last saw her. When the three swans come, remember where your chosen one lays her feathery garb, take it, and run away."

The young man listened to his mother's instructions, and, so hid that evening near the sound. He waited impatiently for the coming of the swans. The sun was just sinking behind the trees when the young man heard a whizzing in the air, and the three swans settled down upon the beach.

As soon as they had slipped off their swan skins, they were again transformed into the most beautiful maidens. From his hiding place the young hunter took careful note of where his enchantress had laid her swan feathers. Stealing softly, he took them and slipped back behind the bushes.

Soon he heard two of the swans fly away, but the third, in search of her clothes, discovered the young man. She fell upon her knees and asked for his help. The hunter, however, would not lose his beautiful prize. He did not tell her he had her feather dress. He threw his cloak around her and carried her home. They were married in a grand wedding and lived lovingly together.

One evening, seven years later, when they were much in love, the hunter told the girl the truth about how she became his wife. He showed her the white swan feathers of her former days. But, no sooner were they feathers in her hands than she transformed once more into a swan, and instantly flew out the open window. In breathless shock, the man stared wildly after his vanishing wife. Before a year and a day had passed, he was laid, with his longings and sorrows, in the village churchyard.

## HANDOUT 8.1C
# "THE MONKEY HUSBAND"

### INDIA

One very hot afternoon, a group of children were playing in a fountain, when a Hanuman monkey snatched up the cloth, which one of the girls had left on the bank, and ran up a tree with it. When the children came out of the water, they found one dress missing. Looking about, they saw the monkey with it up in the tree. They begged and begged, but the monkey only said, "I will not return it, unless its owner consents to marry me."

The children ran and told the parents of the girl whose cloth had been stolen. They called the villagers who went with bows and arrows and threatened to shoot the monkey if he did not give up the cloth. He still refused, unless the girl would marry him. They shot all their arrows at him, but not one hit him.

The villagers said, "This child is fated to belong to the monkey. That is why we cannot hit him."

The girl's father and mother began to cry and sang: "Give the girl her cloth, her silk cloth, Monkey Boy!

The monkey answered: "If she consents to marry me, I will give it. If she consents, I will put it in her hand."

So the girl herself begged for the dress. The monkey dropped one end of the cloth to her, and when she caught hold of it, he yanked her up into the tree. There he wrapped the cloth around her and ran off with her on his back. The girl called out as she was carried away, "Never mind, Father and Mother. I am going away."

The Hanuman took her to a cave in the mountains where they lived on fruit. Normally, the monkey would climb the trees and shake the fruit down. But if the girl saw teeth marks in the fruit, she knew that the monkey had bitten it off, instead of only shaking it down, and she would not eat it.

Finally the girl tired of fruit to eat and demanded rice. So the monkey took her to a bazaar and left her on the outskirts of the village under a tree. He stole all the ingredients from the merchants and brought them to the girl. She collected sticks and lit a fire and cooked a meal. The monkey liked the cooked food, and asked her to cook for him every day. They stayed there several days.

Soon the girl wanted new clothes, and the monkey tried to steal them too, but the shopkeepers drove him away. Next, the girl tired of sleeping under a tree, so they moved back to the cave. The monkey gathered mangos and let her sell them in the market, so she could buy cloth. But she stayed in the village and never returned to the monkey.

The monkey watched for her and searched for her in vain, and returned sorrowfully to his hill. But the girl stayed on in the village and eventually married one of the villagers.

## HANDOUT 8.2
# FAIRY TALE LIST

- ✓ "The Frog Prince (or Iron-Henry)"
- ✓ "Beauty and the Beast"
- ✓ "Cinderella"
- ✓ "Little Red Riding Hood"
- ✓ "Rumpelstiltskin"
- ✓ "Snow White and the Seven Dwarfs"
- ✓ "Hansel and Gretel"
- ✓ "Rapunzel"
- ✓ "Sleeping Beauty"
- ✓ "The Seal's Skin"

## HANDOUT 8.3

# FAIRY TALE LIST WITH ATU NUMBERS

| Tale | ATU Type | Explanation Of Type |
|------|----------|---------------------|
| "The Frog Prince (or Iron-Henry)" | 440 | Slimy suitors |
| "Beauty and the Beast" | 425C | Supernatural or enchanted husband |
| "Cinderella" | 510 A | The persecuted heroine |
| "Little Red Riding Hood" | 333 | Red Riding Hood |
| "Rumpelstiltskin" | 500 | Name of the helper |
| "Snow White and the Seven Dwarfs" | 709 | Little Snow-White |
| "Hansel and Gretel" | 327 | Abandoned children |
| "Rapunzel" | 310 | The maiden in the tower |
| "Sleeping Beauty" | 410 | Sleeping Beauty |
| "The Seal's Skin" | 400 | Quest for a lost bride |

# LESSON

# 9

# Storytellers Carry Culture

## MATERIALS

- ✓ Teacher's copy of "Why Tigers Never Attack Men Unless They Are Provoked" (available at http://www.heritage-history.com/?c=read&author=barker&book=folktales&story=provoked)
- ✓ Handout 9.1: Culture Cards (precut for pairs of students)
- ✓ Handout 9.2A: Storyteller Article (Japan)
- ✓ Handout 9.2B: Storyteller Article (China)
- ✓ Handout 9.2C: Storyteller Article (Africa)
- ✓ Appendix B3: Topic Bag Objects

- • Storytellers are revered in cultures around the world and throughout history.
- • Storytellers "deliver" tales with specific audiences in mind and choose their words accordingly.

## OBJECTIVES

Students will:

- ✓ develop an understanding of and respect for diversity in language use, patterns, and dialects across cultures, ethnic groups, geographic regions, and social roles; and
- ✓ develop the skills to participate as knowledgeable, reflective, creative, and critical members of a variety of a literary community.

- • Culture

# SEQUENCE

## WARM UP

1. Tell students: *It has been said that storytellers hold "culture in their mouths." Talk with a partner, what do you think that might mean? Then, in your journals, write your own definition of culture.*

If necessary, remind students: *A few lessons back we talked about culture.* Share the following dictionary definition with students, if needed. Ask students how their definition or understanding of culture is similar or dissimilar to the dictionary definition.

- *Culture* (noun): The totality of socially transmitted behavior patterns, arts, beliefs, institutions, and all other products of human work and thought.
  > **Kid-Friendly Definition:** *Culture* is the way of life for a society—the sports they watch, the music they listen to, the clothes they wear, the religions they believe in, etc.—passed on through families.

## READ ALOUD

2. Read "Why Tigers Never Attack Men Unless They Are Provoked" aloud.

In this lesson, insert the culture from any community or society students have studied this year—Greeks, Romans, Americans, Native Americans, etc.

## WORD WORK

3. Ask students to volunteer their answers from their journal.
4. Display a semantic map with culture at the center (see Figure 6). Explain to students that the culture of a society can be broken down into different elements like the leaders, art, activities, food, and beliefs of a place. Tell students: *The story you heard is from the famous Mali culture, the wealthy empire that dominated West Africa from around 1200–1600.*

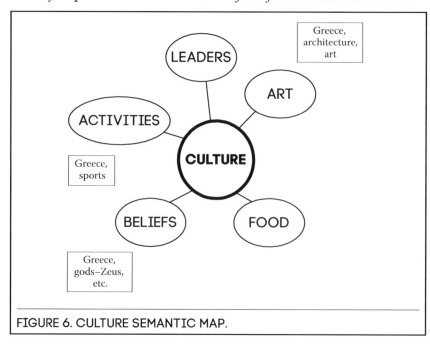

FIGURE 6. CULTURE SEMANTIC MAP.

Connect learning to students' sense of place or community. It may be helpful for students to start with a "home" culture or a culture represented in the school or in the community.

## ACTIVITY: GET THAT CULTURE OFF MY BACK

5. Distribute Handout 9.1: Culture Cards (precut) to pairs of students.

6. With a partner, have one student draw a Culture Card from the deck and tape it to their partner's back. Have students guess what is on their back, by asking their partner only "yes" or "no" questions (e.g., "Can you wear this cultural object?").

## INSTRUCTION: TOPIC BAGS

7. Tell students you are about to learn about a different job you can have if you like folktales. You are not, however, going to tell them what it is . . . yet. You will be pulling objects or pictures of objects (Appendix B3) from a bag that have something to do with the job. Students should write down the object, and as the clues unfold, they can guess what the job is. Once they have guessed (or not) reveal that they will become storytellers for a few days. First, though, they will learn a little about them.

8. Create groups based on prior assessments.

- For the average and struggling learners, distribute one of the Storyteller Articles (Handouts 9.2A–C) to each group. Each article provides informational text pertaining to their storyteller.
- Assign advanced students to find information about storytellers from other cultures on the Internet—the Norse skalds or the Celtic shanachies are good examples. After they have found other examples of storytellers, have them create articles like those being distributed. This would be a good point to introduce the idea of paraphrasing, to caution against plagiarism, and to have students practice writing for a particular audience. They should also complete the task below on the storytellers they identify.
- For students needing additional support, consider giving them the article on China (Handout 9.2B), as it has the least abstract details. Give students time to read the article silently. Then, you may want to read it aloud to the group so they can decide together what items to draw.

9. Once the groups have read their article they should create a topic bag on their culture with 3–4 drawings that represent special things about that culture and the types of storytelling traditions they have. They should place these pictures into a brown paper bag. In the next lesson, the class will have to guess what country the teller is from, based on the objects inside of the bag, so if students give a geographical clue, suggest they make it the last clue, because it would be the strongest hint.

## WORD WORK

10. The following words and their variations will be important words to know for comparing and responding to folklore in upcoming units, especially in journal writing:
    - ✓ different/difference
    - ✓ important/importance
    - ✓ affluent/affluence
    - ✓ ignore/ignorance
    - ✓ ambulance
    - ✓ finance

## CLOSE

11. In their journals, have students respond to one of the following quotes by explaining what the quote means and why they agree or disagree:
    - ✓ "Every human, regardless of race or culture, is a leaf from one giant tree." (Baba Wagué Diakité, storyteller from Mali)
    - ✓ Poet and novelist Pat Schneider once said storytelling is like "writing on the wind."

## HANDOUT 9.1
# CULTURE CARDS

*Music*: **Djembe "talking" drum**
"The drum with a thousand faces"

A grail-shaped hand-drum with goatskin covering its head. An experienced djembe drummer can coax enough sound from the drum to make it seem like an exchange between several drums is taking place.

---

*Music*: **Kora**

A harp-like stringed instrument with 21 strings stretched over a long neck. It is a sacred instrument and the choice of the "jails" or "griots"—the storytellers of the Malis.

---

*Rituals:* **Dama**

A highly religious ceremony ending a period of mourning. The masks used by the Dogon for their religious rituals are only known to the Dogon. Their meanings are secret and are only worn by members of the Awa, a secret masking association.

---

*Jewelry*: **Gold**

Jewelry is important to men and women in Mali. Some women wear such heavy gold earrings they are wrapped in silk to protect the ear.

## HANDOUT 9.1, CONTINUED

*Legends:* **Sundiata**

Founder of the Mali Empire, famous ruler. The famous
tale, "The Lion King," is based on his life.

*Leaders:* **Jalis (or griots)**

Special historians who used to serve a ruler, now
carriers of history in song—storytellers.

*Costume/Clothes:* **Anaga**

A symbol of the Dogon tribe. It is so well known that
is often used as an emblem of the Mali Republic. It
looks like a bird of prey with outspread wings.

*Costume/Clothes:* **Kanaga**

A mask topped with a short pole intersected by two
parallel blades. At the ends of the blades are boards. The
face is encircled by dyed fibers. Used in ceremonies.

*Textiles:* **Bogolan Cloth**

Woven and dyed with crushed leaves, and painted
with mud that has been in a pot for a year.

## HANDOUT 9.2A
# STORYTELLER ARTICLE (JAPAN)

Storytelling is a strong tradition in Japan. The "*Biwa Hōshi*" were blind storytellers who had shaved heads and long robes. They traveled around Japan telling adventure stories of the samurai and playing music on a lute or *biwa*—which looks like a small guitar with a teardrop shape and a skinny neck.

Later, Japanese storytellers told "paper dramas" or *Kamishibai* (*kah-mee-she-bye*). The *kamishibai* rode a bicycle with a small stage attached to it. The storyteller would ride into a village and then clasp together two blocks, indicating to the children that it was story time. The storyteller would use sets of large printed or painted cards to tell a story. He also sold candy, and the children who bought it sat close to the stage.

Very dramatically, the storyteller began the story, holding up the pictures one by one as the story unfolded. And just when the plot got exciting—he stopped! The *kamishibai* never finished a tale. Instead, he stopped the story so that children would come running the next time he rode into town.

When television was invented, this tradition of storytelling started to vanish. They even called TV the "electric *kamishibai*." The artists who made a living making the drawings for the cards became manga (comic book) and anime artists.

The art of *kamishibai* is popular in Japanese schools. The storyteller stacks sheets of thick paper. The front of the paper has an illustration. The back has the words to the story. The pages slide in and out of a special frame.

## HANDOUT 9.2B
# STORYTELLER ARTICLE (CHINA)

Long and long ago, there were different types of storytellers in China. Storytellers who preformed in the street were called "artists of the bazaar." Other storytellers looked down on them. The highest class was those who retold history, and just below the history tellers were storytellers who recounted tales of love, and also ghost stories.

In Chinese storytelling, there are two kinds of stories, or *pingtan*— *pinghua* (stories without music) and *tanci* (stories with music). *Tanci* stories (often love stories) have two performers who sing and also tell the stories. Sometimes teams of storytellers work together, and sometimes the storytelling alternates between chanting and then singing. If a team chooses to sing, it sings part of the story and then ends the story with a question. Then, the other team repeats what the first team sang, telling more of the story, and ending with another question. The storytelling goes on until one team cannot answer a question.

Historical storytellers wanted to control who could perform and charge fees, so they formed "guilds." Today, the Chinese government regulates the storytellers. Students who want to learn *pingtan* go to a storytelling school. There, these students also learn to play a *pipa* (a 40-stringed lute), and they must also learn Chinese history, literature, and politics. They are tested on how well they memorize scripts, too. Even after they finish school, they must study more with a master storyteller.

A Chinese proverb says: "To memorize the master's words a thousand times is not as effective as seeing the master in actual performance, and to see the master's performance a thousand times is not as effective as performing it yourself."

## HANDOUT 9.2C
# STORYTELLER ARTICLE (AFRICA)

Storytellers have great significance in West Africa. At one time, the *griots* or *jalis* (as they are also known) were so important that they even helped kings make decisions, and even taught the king's children. After the fall of Sundiata, the Lion King, *griots* often worked for rich families. Besides telling stories, they gave the families advice, even helping to arrange marriages and settle arguments, because the *griots* knew the histories of the families for generations.

*Griots* know so much because any time a family asked, the *griot* had to sing about the history of a tribe or family, going back seven generations. Some places expected the *griot* to also know songs that would summon spirits and songs that would get approval from the ancestors.

Over time, the *griots* or *jalis* have become the official musicians and historians of the culture. They play an instrument called a *ngoni*, or a *kora*, which is a cross between a lute and a harp. Most *griots* are women, but some are men.

Most *griots* move from family to family because a single family cannot afford their own *griot*. Families ask *griots* or *jalis* to perform at special events like weddings and baptisms. Today, *griots* know a little bit about a lot of people, instead of knowing a lot about one family.

Many of Africa's famous pop stars are actually *griots*. These present day *griots* take traditional songs and make them more modern. African storytellers also tell stories in order to pass on lessons or morals. One famous African writer, Chinua Achebe, said: "The storytellers worked out what is right and what is wrong, what is courageous and what is cowardly, and they translated this into stories."

All over the world, if we listen to storytellers, we learn about people and their cultures.

# LESSON 10
# Delivering Stories

## MATERIALS
✓ Jokes for students to tell (optional)
✓ Teacher's copy of "Little Red-Cap" (available at http://www.gutenberg. org/files/2591/2591-h/2591-h.htm#link2H_4_0023)

 Storytellers must tell their stories with their audiences in mind and choose their words accordingly.

## OBJECTIVES
Students will develop an understanding of and respect for diversity in language use, patterns, and dialects across cultures, ethnic groups, geographic regions, and social roles.

• Culture
• Audience

## SEQUENCE

### WARM UP
1. Have students present the topic bags they created in Lesson 9. Other students should guess what country the storyteller is from. Remind students to show a clue that is least obvious first, so that the other students have to use their best detective skills.

### READ ALOUD
2. Read "Little Red-Cap" aloud.

## WORD WORK

3.  Display the following Jane Yolen quote and read it aloud:

> The blind beggar sings for his supper and so is constrained to change his story to suit the listening audience, the better to be paid for his tales. The nurserymaid changes stories to suit what she assumes are the **appetites** and **moral** needs of her young charges . . . (Yolen, 1988, p.6)

- Students are not reading this quote for mastery. Ultimately, the premise of the sections on storytellers (and retellers) is based on this quote. Teachers can model comprehension strategies using this difficult passage.
- Students may need an explanation for the phrase "sings for his supper."

4.  Tell students: *Let's break down the first sentence. Is there a word we don't know? "The blind beggar sings for his supper and so [is constrained to] change his story to suit the listening audience, the better to be paid for his tales." We can try to understand the meaning by looking at the words before and after for context clues. "So" is a signal word that something will happen "as a result" of something: "The beggar sings for his supper [as a result] . . . change[s] his story to suit the listening audience."*

*Empathy:* Discuss with students that the word *beggar* is an old-fashioned word that they may see in folktales. Ask if they feel it is not a nice word.

5.  Ask if someone can put the following quote in his or her own words, or explain what it means: "The nurserymaid changes stories to suit what she assumes are the appetites and moral needs of her young charges."
6.  Ask: *What is a "nurserymaid?" Can we break the compound word into two smaller words to look for clues?* Have students make educated guesses about the job of a nursery/maid.
7.  Ask students for the meaning of appetite. Ask: *Do you think the nursemaid is changing stories because the children are hungry?* Explain that words can have multiple meanings.

## INSTRUCTION: DELIVERY

8.  Ask students to name some things that can be delivered. (Possible responses: Pizza, flowers, letter, package, birthday card, bad news, a baby, a joke, etc.)

9. Model a joke badly told. Forget words, restart, talk too fast, etc. Tell students: *I need to work on my delivery.* Ask: *What does it mean to deliver a story?*

 **Optional Activity:** Have students learn a joke with a partner and practice telling it. Ask students if jokes might be a form of folktale.

## ACTIVITY: CHOOSING STORYTELLING DETAILS

10. Explain to the students that many original fairy tales contained "raw" elements that were later eliminated, such as the Grimm Brothers' version of "Cinderella," when the stepsisters actually cut off their feet to try and fit them into the glass slipper, and then they later had their eyes pecked out by little birds. This is because fairytales were originally written for adults but were then changed for children to enjoy.

11. Review this part of the Yolen quote: "The nurserymaid changes stories to suit what she assumes are the appetites and moral needs of her young charges . . . " Ask: *Would you tell the Read Aloud story to little kids? How would you change it to tell to preschoolers? What about "The Little Match Girl"? Is it too sad?*

12. Have students respond to the following question in their journals: *What kinds of stories do third graders have an* appetite *for?*

## CLOSE

13. Ask: *How might you change stories for audiences of little children?* Gather students' thoughts on chart paper. Save these suggestions for review in the storytellers' seminar during the end of the unit.

- Students may need to be reminded that a moral is a lesson to be learned from some folktales. "Moral needs" are the lessons the nursemaid thinks they should have.
- Some students may not remember "The Little Match Girl." Ask one of the students who knows the story and is an advanced storyteller (this may be a student who is not necessarily the most advanced traditional learner) to share the story like a storyteller would. Asking the student to come to the front of the room and tell the story will enhance the sense of performance.

# LESSON 11

# Storytellers

## MATERIALS

- ✓ Paper or folklorist journals
- ✓ Markers, crayons, or map pencils
- ✓ Teacher's copy of "The Frog Prince (or Iron Henry)" (available at http://www.pitt.edu/~dash/grimm001.html)
- ✓ Teacher's copy of "The Little Match Girl" (available at http://www.gutenberg.org/files/1597/1597-h/1597-h.htm#link2H_4_0015)
- ✓ Teacher's copy of "The Little Mermaid" Opening Paragraphs (available at http://www.gutenberg.org/files/32572/32572-h/32572-h.htm#Page_124)
- ✓ Handout 11.1A: Formative Assessment 3 (easiest)
- ✓ Handout 11.1B: Formative Assessment 3 (on-level)
- ✓ Handout 11.1C: Formative Assessment 3 (hardest)

- Characters are usually stereotypes with "set" descriptions.
- Characters are usually described using a single adjective.
- Storytellers use adjectives that are evocative, not limiting. (We want the story to take place in the reader's mind.)
- Folktales have stock or set openings and closings (to help storytellers remember).

## OBJECTIVES

Students will:
- ✓ read a wide range of literature to build an understanding of human experience;
- ✓ apply a wide range of strategies to comprehend, interpret, evaluate, and appreciate texts;
- ✓ develop the skills to participate as knowledgeable, reflective, creative, and critical members of a variety of a literary community; and
- ✓ apply knowledge of language structure, language conventions, and genre to create, critique, and discuss print and nonprint texts.

# SEQUENCE

## WARM UP

1. Return to openings:
   - ✓ "Once upon a time . . ."
   - ✓ "In olden times when wishing still helped . . ."

2. Ask: *Why do you think stories begin this way? Storytellers had to remember so many tales; it helped to have repeated descriptions and characters.*

## READ ALOUD

3. Read the first three opening paragraphs to "The Little Mermaid" aloud. Instruct the students to close their eyes and to pay close attention to how the writer presents the tale and the words he uses. Ask the students to try to visualize what is being read.

## ACTIVITY: LIMITING VERSUS EVOCATIVE ADJECTIVES

Students are not required to know or use the word *evocative*, only to understand that characters can be described in two ways. Another way to explain the difference: adjectives can either be "author's choice" or "reader's choice." With a *limiting adjective*, the author chooses what the character is like. With an *evocative adjective*, the reader gets to use his or her imagination.

4. Now, read the first paragraph of "The Little Match Girl." Have students quickly illustrate the character as accurately as possible. Then, read the first paragraph of "The Frog Prince (or Iron Henry)." Have students quickly illustrate characters as accurately as possible.
5. Have students compare their drawings with their neighbors'.
6. Display the two fairy tales on the overhead. Circle the adjectives from the first paragraph in "The Little Match Girl" (i.e., *poor, little, bareheaded*). Then repeat this with the second fairy tale (i.e., *youngest, beautiful*). Ask: *Which words or descriptions let you use your imagination to draw your own picture? Which word creates a specific image?*
7. Tell students: *In writing descriptions, we sometimes learn to use very specific adjectives and descriptions. In storytelling, however, we want to choose adjectives that are not too specific, but are evocative—words that that let the reader draw their own picture. This is especially important with oral folktales that will be listened to, not read. Literary fairy tales or modern tales, which we will examine next, are sometimes more detailed and descriptive.*

**Kid-Friendly Definition:** A limiting adjective **tells** what something looks like; an evocative adjective **suggests** what something looks like. Tell students: *For example, if I tell how to do something, you do it that way. If I suggest how to do something, you can do it that way or do it another way.*

8. On the displayed fairy tales, circle the *evocative adjectives.* Underline the *limiting adjectives.* Examples include:
   ✓ Blue eyes
   ✓ ⟨Dancing, sparkling eyes⟩
   ✓ Five feet tall
   ✓ Petite, slight stature

## PREPARATION: FORMATIVE ASSESSMENT 3

9. For homework, challenge students to select a character type and write an evocative description (a reader's choice) and limited description (a writer's choice) using Handouts 11.1A–C. Give lower level readers A, on-level readers B, and above level readers C.

## ACTIVITY: TELLING A GROUP STORY

10. In Lesson 12, students will try their hand at storytelling in the safety of a group. Toward the end of Lesson 11, students should select a folktale from the list of tales they have studied so far, or a one from an anthology or picture book. They do not, however, have a lot of time to decide, so it is best they choose a tale that they are familiar with. Students who select the same or similar folktales should be put in a group so they are grouped by interest.

11. Once they decide what tale to tell, groups must divide the story and decide who will perform which parts. Students may divide the story by paragraph or by event. They may have some students only read dialogue. They may read their individual sections, or they may retell them in their own words.

 In storytelling you must begin and end strong. If students cannot organize themselves within their groups, step in and assign students parts that better address their readiness levels or interests.

## CLOSE

12. Ask: *Do you think Hans Christian Anderson's opening to "The Little Mermaid" is good for storytelling? Can you imagine it in your head, or is it too specific?*

## HANDOUT 11.1A
# FORMATIVE ASSESSMENT 3

**Directions:** The following tale needs to be edited for a storyteller, not a reader. Fill in the blanks with the *evocative* description, not the *limiting* description. Remember: Select the words that let the *readers* choose the picture in their head, not the *writer*.

One cold morning the _____ Water-rat
                          (Dark grey, old)

poked his head out of his hole. He had _____
                                       (beady, round)

eyes and _____ whiskers, and his tail was
         (3-inch-long, proud)

like _____. The little ducks
     (a whip, a long piece of black-india rubber)

were swimming about in the pond, looking just like

_____, and their mother, who was
(five or six bright yellow canaries,
        a whirl of yellow)

_____ with _____ legs, was trying
(white, pure)      (quick, red-striped)

to teach them how to stand on their heads in the

water.

*Note.* This excerpt is adapted from Oscar Wilde's tale, "The Devoted Friend."

## HANDOUT 11.1B
# FORMATIVE ASSESSMENT 3

**Directions:** The following tale needs to be edited for a storyteller, not a reader. Fill in the blanks with the *evocative* description, not the *limiting* description. Remember: Select the words that let the *readers* choose the picture in their head, not the *writer.*

One cold morning the _____ Water-rat

poked his head out of his hole. He had _____

eyes and _____ whiskers, and his tail was

like _____. The little ducks

were swimming about in the pond, looking just like

_____, and their mother, who was

_____ with _____ legs, was trying

to teach them how to stand on their heads in the

water.

*Note.* This excerpt is adapted from Oscar Wilde's tale, "The Devoted Friend."

## HANDOUT 11.1C
# FORMATIVE ASSESSMENT 3

**Directions:** Select a character and write two descriptions—one *evocative* description (words that let the *readers* choose) and one *limiting* description (words that let the *writer* choose.) Consider these examples of characters: ogre, witch, princess, prince, frog, coyote, fox, woodsman.

## EVOCATIVE DESCRIPTION

## LIMITING DESCRIPTION

# LESSON 12

# Storytellers Mini-Product

## MATERIALS
- ✓ Handout 12.1: How to Tell a Story
- ✓ Handout 12.2: Homework

- Characters in folktales are usually stereotypes with "set" descriptions.
- Characters in folktales are usually described using a single adjective.
- Folktales have stock or set openings and closings (to help storytellers remember).

## OBJECTIVES
Students will:
- ✓ use spoken language to accomplish their own purposes (e.g., for learning, enjoyment, persuasion, and the exchange of information), and
- ✓ develop the skills to participate as knowledgeable, reflective, creative, and critical members of a variety of a literary community.

- Storyteller
- Audience

## SEQUENCE

### WARM UP
1. Distribute Handout 12.1: How to Tell a Story. Have students read and underline the pieces of advice they think are the most important and would help them be a good storyteller.

• Students' first venture into storytelling is a group effort to provide some safety for more introverted students. Students are all required to give each profession a brief try so they develop an understanding of what their preferences are.

• This is a discovery activity in that students will discover the best way to divide the story, to retell or read, how long stories take, etc.

2. Have students choral read the handout. Afterward, ask students to underline the pieces of advice they think are the most important for storytellers to remember in order to be a good storyteller.

## ACTIVITY: GROUP STORYTELLING— PRACTICE AND PERFORM

3. In the previous lesson, students worked in groups to select a familiar story and assign parts for storytelling practice. In this lesson, students will have the opportunity to experience the storytelling aspect of folkloristics. Remind students that they will be performing the story they chose in the last lesson. Allow students to break into their groups in order to practice. Remind students that they are not being graded. It's okay to stumble or get stuck. Peers should be supportive of one another. This may not be for everybody, but you don't know until you try!

## DISCUSSION: ANALYZE PERFORMANCES

This post-performance evaluation will give students ownership on what their performance goals should be.

4. Discuss successes and challenges of today's performances. Ask:
   ✓ What did performers do well today?
   ✓ What was difficult for you about this task?
   ✓ What should performers always do?
   ✓ How did the audience affect your performance?

5. Collect students' thoughts on chart paper. This can be turned into a checklist for the storytellers' seminar in Lesson 17. Students can add suggestions to the list of advice previously distributed.

## HOMEWORK

6. Ask: *How much did you like being a storyteller? What did you like about it? Dislike? For example, did you like to perform? Were you good at memorizing?* Distribute Handout 12.2 for students to complete as homework.

**HANDOUT 12.1**

# HOW TO TELL A STORY

1. **Time yourself beforehand.** Keep stories to less than 10 minutes. (Three written pages might take 15 minutes when you tell the story aloud.) Long stories can bore your audience!

2. **Tell it in your own words.** Don't try to memorize every word. Remember some of the plot, and let it come out. Use your imagination. But do remember to practice telling your story.

3. **If you forget something, just keep going.** Don't stop, apologize, or say, "oops!"
   - ✓ One trick is to describe details of sounds, colors, smells, clothes, etc., to give yourself time.
   - ✓ Or stay silent and look into people's eyes—they will believe you are pausing on purpose to build suspense.
   - ✓ Don't look around the room trying to remember. If you act naturally, the audience will never notice your pauses. Be confident.
   - ✓ Remember: There are no mistakes. If you make up something new this time, it may be something great to keep for the next storytelling.

4. **Accept the applause!** Look at your audience. Smile and bow. Clapping means they enjoyed it.

_Note._ Some strategies are adapted from _Tim Sheppard's Storytelling Resources for Storytellers_ by Tim Sheppard, 2014, retrieved from http://www.timsheppard.co.uk/story/faq.html.

**HANDOUT 12.2**

# HOMEWORK

1. What did you like about today's activity?

2. What did you dislike about today's activity?

3. Rate the following statements, circle your response:

   1. I like to perform—to sing, dance, tell jokes, act, etc.

      (1) a lot!          (2) sometimes          (3) not at all!

   2. I like to memorize things.

      (1) a lot!          (2) sometimes          (3) not at all!

   3. I like to tell stories.

      (1) a lot!          (2) sometimes          (3) not at all!

   4. I like to talk in front of the class.

      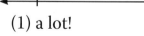

      (1) a lot!          (2) sometimes          (3) not at all!

   5. I like to talk to little kids.

      (1) a lot!          (2) sometimes          (3) not at all!

# 13

# Re-Tellers

## MATERIALS

- ✓ Disney's *Snow White* (film)
- ✓ Teacher's copy of the Grimms' beginning of "Little Snow-White" (available at http://www.pitt.edu/~dash/grimm053.html)
- ✓ Teacher's copy of the Grimms' ending of "Little Briar Rose" ("Sleeping Beauty") (available at http://www.pitt.edu/~dash/type0410.html#grimm)
- ✓ Student copies of the Grimms' "Little Snow-White" (1812; available at http://www.pitt.edu/~dash/type0709.html#snowwhite)
- ✓ Student copies of the Grimms' "Little Snow-White" (1857; available at http://www.pitt.edu/~dash/grimm053.html)
- ✓ Student copies of Joseph Jacobs's "Snowwhite" (1916; available at http://www.gutenberg.org/files/26019/26019-h/26019-h.htm#SNOW WHITE)

 Folktales change when they are written down.

## OBJECTIVES

Students will:

- ✓ read a wide range of literature to build an understanding of human experience;
- ✓ apply a wide range of strategies to comprehend, interpret, evaluate, and appreciate texts; and
- ✓ apply knowledge of language structure, language conventions, and genre to create, critique, and discuss print and nonprint texts.

 • Influential

# SEQUENCE

## WARM UP

1. Tell students: *With a partner, retell the story of Snow White as well as you know it—what happened first, second, etc.*

## READ ALOUD

2. Read the Grimms' beginning of "Snow White" aloud.

## ACTIVITY: COMPARING TALES

3. Tell students they are starting to compare fairy tales that are deliberately changed from the traditional tale. Show the beginning of Disney's *Snow White* film.
4. Draw a Venn diagram to compare/contrast the movie opening with the original tale.
5. Display picture books that have been "retold" (or other retellings of "Snow White"). Allow students to do a gallery walk in which they peruse the books, flip through them, and look at the covers and pictures. Ask your librarian for help finding retellings!
6. Distribute the three versions of "Snow White" according to readiness, and have students read their version independently.

If *Snow White* cannot be rented, nearly any Disney fairy tale can be compared to a Grimm version.

**2E** If the text seems too difficult for some students, struggling readers can be grouped with the teacher to do a choral read where the teacher models fluent reading. Use Joseph Jacobs's version with the least advanced readers. Grimms' 1812 version is the most raw and should be assigned to the most mature students.

For readers who might struggle with the length of these passages, students can read these as homework prior to class.

7. After students have completed their reading, ask: *What is similar compared to the original? What is different?* Students should record their ideas in their journals.

## ACTIVITY: REREAD WITH PURPOSE

8. Redistribute the collectors' articles (Handouts 7.1A–C). Students should skim or reread the same article to answer the following in their journals: *Why did the collectors change the original folktales?* (Grimm and Lang changed tales for their child audience. Perrault and Lang thought tales should have a moral.)

 Have students who finish early read one of the other articles on a collector of interest to the student.

If reading the "Snow White" endings takes too long, this rereading can be done for homework. Or the point can simply be made as direct instruction.

## INSTRUCTION: RETELLINGS

9. Review the original list of Walt Disney fairy tales from the Unit Preassessment (Handout 1.1). Explain that Walt Disney is probably the most modern influential re-teller because his versions are the ones most people know.

10. Ask students the following questions about the tales they read. Different groups will have different answers:
    - ✓ How does the wicked queen trick Snow White?
      - ▪ In Disney's *Snow White*, she transforms through potion. In the Grimm version, she disguises herself.
    - ✓ What happens to the queen at the end of the story?
      - ▪ In the Grimms' tales, she must dance in burning metal shoes until she dies. In Jacobs's, she throws herself out the window. In the Disney version, the dwarves chase her off the cliff.

> If you are interested in purchasing a book for this unit, consider Walt Disney's *Cinderella*, retold by Cynthia Rylant (2015). This story is a great example of a retelling of a classic fairy tale, and the original artwork is from Perrault's version of the tale.

11. Have students refer back to their journal entry from earlier in the lesson. Ask: *How else did your tale differ from the story you know?*

12. Share the following quote from Jane Yolen: "Occasionally, of course, a particular transcriber is so able, so, effective, so inventive, that the story itself is changed forever." Then, tell students: *The first re-teller to make his versions popular was Charles Perrault, the Disney of the 1800s. His version of Cinderella is the considered the "normal" type now. A translation error changed the glass slipper; Perrault added the fairy godmother and the plump mice. Perrault also added the famous red hood to Little Red.*

## CLOSE

13. Read the Grimms' ending of "Sleeping Beauty" aloud. Encourage students to listen closely to this version of "Sleeping Beauty" and to think about how the story begins, the characters, the order of events, the conflict, and the resolution. Tell the students that in the next lesson, they will be comparing this version to a different retelling of "Sleeping Beauty." After reading, discuss the story elements.

# LESSON 14 Literary Tellers

## MATERIALS

- ✓ Folktale motif cards (from the Word Splash activity, Lesson 3)
- ✓ Teacher's copy of Lang's ending of "The Sleeping Beauty in the Wood" (available at http://www.sacred-texts.com/neu/lfb/bl/blfb07.htm)
- ✓ Student copies of excerpts from Hans Christian Andersen's "The Little Mermaid" (optional; available at http://www.gutenberg.org/files/27200/27200-h/27200-h.htm#li_merma)
- ✓ Handout 4.3: Character Types
- ✓ Handout 5.2: Character Cards
- ✓ Handout 14.1: Word Continuum Cards
- ✓ Handout 14.2: Fairy Tale Patterns

For students' copies of excerpts from "The Little Mermaid," you will want to include the first paragraph ("Far out in the ocean . . ."to" . . . for the diadem of a queen.") and the climax through the ending ("I know what you want . . ."to" . . . added to our time of trial!").

- When a folktale is altered and embellished, it becomes a "literary folktale," usually more stylishly written than traditional folktales.
- Some folktale writers are not re-tellers at all, but creators of brand new tales, "literary tellers."

## OBJECTIVES

Students will:

- ✓ read a wide range of literature to build an understanding of human experience;
- ✓ apply a wide range of strategies to comprehend, interpret, evaluate, and appreciate texts;
- ✓ employ a wide range of strategies as they write to communicate with different audiences for a variety of purposes;
- ✓ apply knowledge of language structure, language conventions, and genre to create, critique, and discuss print and nonprint texts; and
- ✓ adjust their use of spoken, written, and visual language (e.g., conventions, style, vocabulary) to communicate effectively with a variety of audiences and for different purposes.

- Adjective
- Purpose

The group work may be more successful if it is modeled first, with the whole class, although it will extend the time.

- When students explain why one word is more intense than another, they will often say it just "feels" bigger or hotter. Students are recognizing word connotation, that different words have a certain "feeling." This should be validated.

- Remind students that intense or "big" words may not always be best. For example, *enormous* may be better than *astronomical* given context. Ask students why this is the case and how they will make their decisions.

- Record the adjectives on the word wall to use in the storytelling activity at the end of the lesson.

# SEQUENCE

## WARM UP

1. Revisit the discussion from the end of the last lesson. Ask: *How did the Grimms' version of "Sleeping Beauty" end?* Explain that now you will read a different ending to the tale. Encourage students to listen closely to the story and to think about the differences and similarities they hear in this version compared to the Grimms' version.

## READ ALOUD

2. Read aloud Lang's ending to "The Sleeping Beauty in the Wood," beginning after the prince awakens Sleeping Beauty ("They had but very little sleep . . . ") to the end.

3. Ask: *What differences did you hear in the two versions of "Sleeping Beauty"?*

## WORD WORK

4. Distribute to groups of mixed ability one of the word cards (Handout 14.1)—size (big or small), behavior (good or bad), appearance (ugly or pretty). Students need to brainstorm adjectives that describe the noun on the front of the card. The adjectives need to be synonyms for one or both of the words in parenthesis (e.g., appearance: beautiful, gorgeous, hideous, ugly).

5. After brainstorming for about 3–5 minutes—students can use a thesaurus—have students select their five strongest words and write them in large letters on separate pieces of paper. One by one, groups should stand at the front of the room and have the class arrange the words on a continuum from "the least" to "the most." Guide the class discussion as they explain the "whys" behind their placements (e.g., size: big, huge, enormous, astronomical, etc.).

6. Ask students to consider that literary folktales are often considered to be more descriptive than oral tales. Their purpose is to create a picture in the reader's mind, but writers can provide more evocative detail. Ask students to consider the advantage writers might have over oral storytellers.

## INSTRUCTION: LITERARY FAIRY TALES

7. Tell students: *In the mid-1600s, telling fairy tales became very trendy at parties in Paris. These special parties, called* salons, *were especially popular with women who weren't allowed to go to college and had to keep their opinions to themselves. Before this time, fairy tales were not valued by educated people, but were limited to the nurses and maids to tell to the children of the wealthy. These French women retold and created new tales. Charles Perrault was influenced by the new tales and his famous book of tales was even called* Tales of My Mother Goose. *The famous version of "Beauty and the Beast" came from these salons in 1756 by Madame Leprince de Beaumont. One-hundred years later Hans Christian Andersen became the most famous of the literary tellers. He carefully mixed the power of oral tales with a "literary" voice. He read versions of his stories out loud to friends to get them perfect.*

 Write these quotes on the board or read them aloud to the class. Discuss each. Ask: *How does each speaker feel about literary tellers?*
- "These are contrived literary creations, based only marginally on folklore" (Ashliman, 2004).
- "Nobody can write a new fairy tale; you can only mix up and fess up the old, old stories" (Lang, 1922).
- "Since the mid-eighteenth century European creative writers have been mixing up and dressing up the old, old stories" (Ashliman, 2004).

## INSTRUCTION: FAIRY TALE STRUCTURE

8. According to famous folklorist D. L. Ashliman, "After 'Once Upon a Time' the main character, usually a human, follows a typical pattern (like a hero quest) that is fixed by magic" (2004). Share another plot pattern found in fairy tales such as (1) childhood, (2) conflict, or (3) marriage.
9. With a partner, students should use Handout 14.2: Fairy Tale Patterns to analyze the pattern of a tale they have studied.

## OPTIONAL ACTIVITY: CLASS STORY

10. Help students list the narrative elements that are the building blocks of folktales—character, setting, motifs. Ask students to brainstorm examples of each found in fairy tales.
11. Distribute folktale motif cards (from the Word Splash activity, Lesson 3) to small groups of students. The must deal each player two cards. (Every third person should get a character card.) The student with the "Once upon a time card" begins the story with one sentence. Students will then go around the circle adding a sentence to the story using their word. The person with the "Happily ever after" card must end the story.

Students may need additional support for this activity. Consider posting all tales read thus far and having students identify patterns. Ask: *How is childhood or marriage a plot pattern?*

Teachers may want to model this activity with the whole class first.

## ACTIVITY: PREWRITING

12. Tomorrow students will be writing a folktale. They can (a) turn a basic folktale into a literary one, (b) write a new tale given a set of elements, or (c) write an original tale.

13. Tell students: *Decide which type of tale you would like to write. Write ideas in your folklorist journal, and choose one to write about. You can think about this tonight or talk with your family at home. You may choose to write about something else, but write down one idea now to think about.*

## OPTIONAL ACTIVITY (OR HOMEWORK ACTIVITY)

This story is a perfect example of Andersen's mixing of fairy tale styles.

14. Most students will probably have heard of the "The Little Mermaid." If so, have them write the basic plot with bullet points or numbers (e.g., (1) mermaid wants to be human, (2) meets the sea witch, (3) sea witch tricks mermaid). Then, have students read excerpts from the fairy tale. Ask the students to consider and reflect: *Did Andersen's plot match to the one they know from Disney? Were there any differences?*

**HANDOUT 14.1**
## WORD CONTINUUM CARDS

# SIZE
### (BIG OR SMALL)

# BEHAVIOR
### (GOOD OR BAD)

# APPEARANCE
### (UGLY OR PRETTY)

## HANDOUT 14.2
# FAIRY TALE PATTERNS

**Directions:** Select a tale and find out if it fits the following fairy tale patterns as suggested by folklorist D. L. Ashliman. Fill in the details for evidence.

1. "Once upon a time" style opening:

2. A typical plot pattern (like a hero quest—character goes out into the world):

3. A problem is fixed by magic:

4. Childhood:

5. Conflict:

6. Marriage:

# LESSON

# 15 Literary Tellers 2

## MATERIALS

- ✓ Handout 15.1: Letter to Parents
- ✓ Handout 15.2: Folklore Festival Product Options
- ✓ Handout 15.3: How to Plan a Storytelling Program

 Projects require planning and having clear goals and strategies can help you work efficiently.

## OBJECTIVES

Students will:

- ✓ employ a wide range of strategies as they write to communicate with different audiences for a variety of purposes, and
- ✓ apply knowledge of language structure, language conventions, and genre to create, critique, and discuss print and nonprint texts.

- Salon
- Society
- Workshop

## SEQUENCE

## READ ALOUD

1. Explain that for the last part of the unit students will be literary tellers, like Hans Christian Andersen or a French salon writer.
2. Ask for a volunteer to select a tale to read aloud.

## ACTIVITY: WRITE A TALE

3. Using their prewriting notes from yesterday, have students use class time to write a folktale.

Encourage students to use the allotted time. If they finish early, they should revise and edit their draft.

## PREPARATION: FOR NEXT LESSONS

4. Distribute Handout 15.1: Letter to Parents and Handout 15.2: Folklore Festival Product Options.
5. Using Handout 15.2, review students' professional options for the final lessons (Lessons 16–18) leading up to the Folklore Festival (Lesson 19). Each profession will meet with others of the same profession:
   ✓ **Folklorist Society:** Folklorists will form a society, like the original one formed in the mid-1800s. In the society, scholars will discuss different fairy tales and how to catalogue them.
   ✓ **Storytellers' Workshop:** Storytellers will meet at workshops where they practice their craft and learn new techniques.
   ✓ **Literary Tellers' Salon:** Writers will meet in a "salon" like the French fairy tale writers of the 1700s. When writers gather, they will discuss each of the pieces they are working on.

6. Explain to students that they will take Handouts 15.1 and 15.2 home and should discuss the product options with their parents/guardians to help decide which final product they will choose for the class Folklore Festival.
7. Begin preplanning with students. Display and discuss Handout 15.3: How to Plan a Storytelling Program. Discuss each aspect of the Folklore Festival and invite one student to serve as a scribe to write down the ideas that are decided upon for each section.

Depending on the time of year and your school, you may invite a pre-K or kindergarten class, another class from your grade level, parents, principals, or a class from a neighboring school. The teacher should plan these logistics earlier than the week before to have availability of a location (an auditorium, the library) and to coordinate with other teachers' schedules.

## CLOSE

8. Reread the Jane Yolen quote from Lesson 10, but add the ending:

"The blind beggar sings for his supper and so is constrained to change his story to suit the listening audience, the better to be paid for his tales. The nurserymaid changes stories to suit what she assumes are the appetites and moral needs of her young charges . . . And the clerk is the literary teller, writing down stories that suit the needs of an audience of one, the self."

9. Reinforce the idea that today students have been tellers, writing for themselves.

## HANDOUT 15.1
# LETTER TO PARENTS

Dear Parent/Guardian,

We have been working as scholars in the field of folkloristics. We are now planning a Folklore Festival in which students will showcase what they have learned as folklorists, storytellers, and literary tellers. After the festival, students will complete a formal assessment to capture what they have learned during this unit of study. All work for the assessment will be completed in class; however, students will bring home progress cards to remind them of what they need to accomplish during the next lesson. Feel free to use these cards as talking points to provide support and guidance on the project.

Each product will require the student to show what he or she understands about folktales: types of characters, settings, and motifs. Students will be given options on how to demonstrate this knowledge based on their interests and learning styles. Each product has equal rigor, but different products will appeal to different students. Consider discussing these options with your child.

On the night before the festival, students can bring home final drafts in case they would like to add extra artwork or props to their final project. Although added flourishes will not be part of the grade, they are encouraged to take pride in their work! Product options are attached.

Thank you for your support!

Sincerely,

## HANDOUT 15.2
# FOLKLORE FESTIVAL PRODUCT OPTIONS

## FOLKLORIST: FOLKLORIST SOCIETY— SPONSORS OF THE FOLKLORIST FESTIVAL

1. **Introduction to the anthology:** Write an introduction to the Literary Tellers anthology. This project requires that you:
   - ✓ write a general overview of folklore and fairy tales,
   - ✓ talk to all the literary tellers to find out what tales they are writing, and
   - ✓ write briefly about each of the literary tellers and a little bit about their tale.

2. **ATU for kids:** Create your own cataloguing system like the ATU system, based on how you think fairy tales should be grouped for kids to best find a tale they like. This project requires that you:
   - ✓ choose 5–10 folktales to categorize,
   - ✓ sort the tales into a system (groups) based on common characteristics,
   - ✓ write short summaries of each tale, and
   - ✓ collect summaries into one system on a document for other scholars to use.

3. **Festival program:** Create a program for guests at the Folklorist Festival. This project will require you to:
   - ✓ look at other programs for festivals for ideas on what makes a good program;
   - ✓ write a description of the festival—who will be performing, what tales they will perform, where people can get copies of the anthology, etc.;
   - ✓ talk to each of the storytellers to find out what tale they are going to tell;
   - ✓ write a brief summary of the tale to put in the program; and
   - ✓ illustrate the program

## HANDOUT 15.2, CONTINUED

## STORYTELLERS: PERFORMERS OF FOLKTALES

**Perform:** Deliver a folktale at the festival in front of an audience. This project will require you to:
- ✓ select an appropriate fairy tale,
- ✓ choose what details to include in your telling,
- ✓ make sure to create characters,
- ✓ practice with peers,
- ✓ perform, and
- ✓ write a summary of the tale and why you chose it (for the program).

## LITERARY TELLERS: CONTRIBUTE TO STUDENT ANTHOLOGY

**Write a new tale:** Based on what you've learned, write a new fairy tale to go in a class anthology. This project will include:
- ✓ prewriting and writing a draft,
- ✓ editing and revising,
- ✓ meeting with colleagues to help revise their tales, and
- ✓ (optional) reading a passage from your tale (decide which passage to read, practice reading it aloud).

## HANDOUT 15.3
# HOW TO PLAN A STORYTELLING PROGRAM

- ✓ Consider the size of the audience.
  - ▪ Will we need a sound system or microphone?
  - ▪ Will we need an adult to run lights or the sound system?

- ✓ Consider the way the stage is set up.
  - ▪ Will the audience sit on the floor?
  - ▪ Will they sit at tables or desks or in rows of chairs?

- ✓ Consider the types of stories.
  - ▪ Will we feature a mixture of fables and folktales?
  - ▪ Will we do stories based around a motif?
  - ▪ Will we do variations on a type?

- ✓ Grab the audience with the first story, and close with a strong story.
  - ▪ Which storyteller will open the show?
  - ▪ Which storyteller will close the show?

# LESSON 16 Festival Prework

## MATERIALS

- ✓ Class rotation chart
- ✓ Index cards (class set to be used as planning cards)
- ✓ File folders (class set to be used as project folders)
- ✓ Handout 1.2: Fairy Tale Recording Chart
- ✓ Handout 16.1: How to Choose, Learn, and Tell a Story (for students who have selected Storyteller profession)

 Professionals meet with colleagues.

## OBJECTIVES

Students will assume the roles of professionals in the field by:
- ✓ sorting tales,
- ✓ prewriting a folk tale, or
- ✓ selecting a tale to perform.

 • Fakelore

## SEQUENCE

### WARM UP

1. Tell students: *In 1950, an American folklorists coined a new term called "fakelore" to describe stories that weren't really recorded traditionally from a culture, but made up. To be fakelore, though, they have to be presented as "real"—the writers have to be tricking the public. Some folklor-*

*ists, for example, regard the story of Paul Bunyan as fakelore, although the character was a real folk hero from stories told by loggers.*

2. Ask students to respond to the following in their journals: *Were the Grimm Brothers "fakelorists?" Why or why not? What evidence do you have to support your answer?*

## ACTIVITY: ROTATIONS

3. Students will begin professional folklore work today and will move through the following rotations:
   - ✓ Teacher meeting
   - ✓ Work with colleagues
   - ✓ Independent work

If a student did not decide since the last lesson or is unsure, assign him or her to a group once all of the other students have made their selections. This will just be a temporary group for now——the undecided students should be the first to have a teacher meeting.

4. Students should select their group—folklorist, storyteller, literary teller—and follow that group's rotation. When students are not with the teacher, students can choose whether they will work in a small group or independently based on the work they have to do (perhaps with some input from the teacher), and should place their name card appropriately on the class rotation chart (see Figure 7 for an example chart).

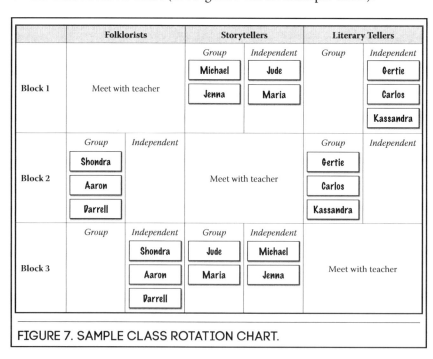

| | Folklorists | | Storytellers | | Literary Tellers | |
|---|---|---|---|---|---|---|
| | | | *Group* | *Independent* | *Group* | *Independent* |
| **Block 1** | Meet with teacher | | Michael  Jenna | Jude  Maria | | Gertie  Carlos  Kassandra |
| | *Group* | *Independent* | | | *Group* | *Independent* |
| **Block 2** | Shondra  Aaron  Darrell | | Meet with teacher | | Gertie  Carlos  Kassandra | |
| | *Group* | *Independent* | *Group* | *Independent* | | |
| **Block 3** | | Shondra  Aaron  Darrell | Jude  Maria | Michael  Jenna | Meet with teacher | |

FIGURE 7. SAMPLE CLASS ROTATION CHART.

5. Before students begin rotations, briefly re-explain the expectations for each product. Then, have students write what their goals should be for the day:

✓ **Folklorists:** Collect tales to sort and look through Folklorist Notebook for notes on tales, lists of tales.

✓ **Storytellers:** Review tales studied or find a new tale to perform.

✓ **Literary Tellers:** Begin prewriting by brainstorming about the characters, setting, and motifs.

For storytellers, distribute Handout 16.1: How to Choose, Learn, and Tell a Story.

6. During today's teacher meetings, spend 5 minutes explaining the product options again to students. Determine who is confident in his or her choice and who still needs guidance. It is important to meet with your unsure or struggling students first. Check in with the students who started off on-track if there is time, or meet with them first during the next lesson.

✓ **Folklorists:** Folklorists have the following options: Introduction to the Anthology, ATU for Kids, Festival Program.

✓ **Storytellers:** Storytellers are the main attraction at the festival. They will perform a fairy tale.

✓ **Literary Tellers:** Literary tellers will create a new folktale based on typical folktale elements. The tales will be collected in an anthology like Andrew Lang's *The Blue Fairy Book*—a mass-marketed book distributed by peddlers for consumption by the lower classes and peasants.

The folklorists have more product options. The Introduction to the Anthology and the Festival Program are similar (different in that the anthology includes information about literary tellers and the festival program includes information about storytellers.) If there are not enough tales to make an anthology or enough storytellers to make a program, one product can be dropped. Teachers should be flexible on the group program.

## PREPARATION: PLANNING CARD

7. Have students respond to the following on a planning card: *What do I need to do tomorrow?* Students must turn in drafts or notes for teacher review.

# HOW TO CHOOSE, LEARN, AND TELL A STORY

## CHOOSING A STORY

✓ Consider "logistics," such as performance time, possible size of the audience, what the audience expects, where the show will take place.

✓ Consider *the average age of the audience.*

- Little children may wander away if there is no audience participation or if it is too long.
- Adults like more complex stories that are longer or with more characters.

✓ What kind of stories does your audience expect?

- Be sure your invitation or flyer gives a hint (e.g., funny stories from West Africa, classic Disney fairy tales, a mixture, etc.).

✓ Choose stories that you like or write stories you would like to hear.

- Remember stories you loved as a little kid and tell those.

✓ Figure out how long it takes to tell the story.

- Practice telling your story aloud with a timer. It will take longer when you perform. A good time is 5 to 15 minutes.
- Decide what details to leave out, what to leave in (e.g., in "Snow White," will you tell about all three times the witch came and visited the house or just one?)

## LEARNING A STORY

✓ Learn a story like you'd learn a joke:

- Remember the setting, the characters, and what happens (the plot), and certain important phrases.
- When you retell it, though, use your own words.

✓ Don't memorize it!

- Even though the author's words may seem perfect, your own words will have more authority and seem more natural.

## HANDOUT 16.1, CONTINUED

✓ "Tell it to the dog."
  ▪ Practice telling the story out loud.
  ▪ Don't use the mirror—it is hard to watch and listen at the same time, and it could make you self-conscious.

✓ Cut down on the details except as they paint a picture for the audience's imagination.
  ▪ This isn't an oral report or descriptive essay.

✓ Deliver it, don't "perform."
  ▪ The listeners want to focus on the story, not you, so don't be nervous.
  ▪ If you love the story, it will shine through.
  ▪ "Trust the story, then just tell it."

✓ Have fun!

## TELLING A STORY
✓ Incorporate a special talent if you have one.
  ▪ Artists might use markers and chart paper to draw things as they tell their stories.
  ▪ Dancers might want to act out the movements of an animal.
  ▪ Singers may want to hum or sing a tune in the story.

✓ Tell the story in a way that is natural to you.
  ▪ Deliver the story the way you talk. If you are loud and funny, be loud and funny! If you are calm and steady, be calm and steady.

✓ Try to keep the audience involved, especially little kids (older students may like less interaction).
  ▪ Ask simple yes and no questions they can respond to.
  ▪ Ask the audience to make predictions.
  ▪ Add rhymes or chants.

## HANDOUT 16.1, CONTINUED

✓ With your voice you can:
- create characters' accents;
- show emotions—anger, fear, confidence;
- take pauses to create suspense; or
- use sound effects.

✓ With your body you can:
- vary your facial expressions to show emotions or
- make gestures to show what characters are doing.

✓ Imagine all the smells, sights, and sounds of the setting in your story—it will make the tale seem more real to your audience!

*Note.* Some strategies were adapted from "Top Ten Secrets to Finding, Learning and Delivering Folktales" by Mary Grace Ketner, 2008, retrieved from http://www.storyteller.net/articles/232.

# LESSON 17

# Festival Prework, Seminars

## MATERIALS

- ✓ Folklorist journals
- ✓ Project folders
- ✓ Index cards (class set to be used as planning cards)
- ✓ Class rotation chart
- ✓ Handout 17.1A: Folklorist Rubric
- ✓ Handout 17.1B: Storyteller Rubric
- ✓ Handout 17.1C: Literary Teller Rubric

 Professionals work as colleagues.

## OBJECTIVES

Students will develop the skills to participate as knowledgeable, reflective, creative, and critical members of a variety of a literary community.

## SEQUENCE

### WARM UP (OPTIONAL)

1. Folklorists versus storytellers: Share with students the following quote from *Scottish Fairy and Folk Tales* edited by George Douglas (2000):

> . . . is there not [with folkloristics] a loss to the stories themselves? Classified, tabulated, scientifically named, they are no longer the wild free product of Nature that we knew and loved—they have become . . . a collection of butterflies in a case, an album of pressed wild flowers. No doubt they are still very interest-

ing, and highly instructive; but their poetry, their brightness, the fragrance which clung about them in their native air, their native soil, is in large measure gone!

2. Ask: *What is the author trying to say? Do you agree with the quote?*

## ACTIVITY: ROTATIONS

3. Students will continue professional folklore work today and will move through the following rotations:
   ✓ Teacher meeting
   ✓ Work with colleagues
   ✓ Independent work

4. Before students begin rotations, distribute product rubrics (Handout 17.1A–C). Remind students that when they are not with the teacher, they can choose whether they will work in a small group or independently based on what they have to do (perhaps with some input from the teacher), and should place their name card appropriately on the class rotation chart.

5. In teacher meetings:
   ✓ **Folklorists (Organization):** Remind folklorists that they should be starting to write summaries. Review how a summary should be organized.
   ✓ **Storytellers (Word Choice):** Remind storytellers that they should choose words appropriate for their audience. Choose language to create pictures in the listeners' minds.
   ✓ **Literary Tellers (Detail/Voice):** Explore with students how to use their voice in their tales. Are they using metaphors, descriptions, considering word connotation?

6. In small groups, students can review their rubric (Handouts 17.1A–C) with a partner to make sure their product is on the right track.

7. Independently, students should work based on their profession, drafting a summary or tale, or practicing storytelling.

## PREPARATION: PLANNING CARD

8. Have students respond to the following on a planning card: *What do I need to do tomorrow?* Students must turn in drafts or notes for teacher review.

- If you did the poetry unit prior to this unit, a review of figures of speech would be in order here.
- Ask: *What does he mean by "they have become a collection of butterflies in a case"?*
- A good exercise for advanced students would be to look for figures of speech in the folktales they have read.

**HANDOUT 17.1A**

# FOLKLORIST RUBRIC

| Folklorist Product: | 1 Folklorist Needing Retraining | 2 Folklorist-In-Training | 3 Amateur Folklorist | 4 Professional Folklorist |
|---|---|---|---|---|
| Names and describes the important **characters**. | Leaves out important main characters. | Leaves out important main characters or includes too many supporting characters. | Includes mostly main characters and describes without too much detail. | Includes important characters with supporting detail. |
| Tells about the setting. | Does not mention setting. | Leaves out some elements of setting, but it is mentioned. | Tells both time and place but with too much or too little detail. | Includes time and place when describing the setting with supporting detail. |
| Summarizes the **plot**. | Includes too many events and/or relates incorrect events; far too many details. | Includes some key events/conflicts, some unimportant events; and/or too many unnecessary details. | Includes most conflicts/key events with only a couple of unnecessary details. | Includes main conflicts/key events without too much detail. |
| Accurately portrays the **motifs**. | Motifs are not included. | Motifs are included, but unclear or inaccurate. | Some motifs are included. | Motifs are clear and accurate to tales. |

Name: _____ Date: _____

## HANDOUT 17.1B
# STORYTELLER RUBRIC

| Storyteller Product: | 1 Unrehearsed | 2 More Rehearsal | 3 Dress Rehearsal | 4 Professional |
|---|---|---|---|---|
| Names and describes the main and supporting **characters**. | Makes mistakes in describing characters—too descriptive or incorrect detail. | Includes some characters and describes them with evocative, but sometimes limiting, adjectives. | Includes the main characters and most of the important supporting characters; describes them with evocative, not limiting, adjectives. | Includes all of the main characters and important supporting characters with descriptive adjectives. |
| Tells about the setting. | Does not include setting. | Leaves out some elements of setting, but it is mentioned. | Tells both time and place but with too much or too little detail. | Tells both time and place without too much detail. |
| Retells the **plot**. | Tells with few details and noticeable errors. | Retells the plot somewhat out of order, and with noticeable mistakes or few details. | Retells the plot in order and in detail; with few *noticeable* mistakes. | Retells the plot in order and in detail; mistakes are not *noticeable*. |
| Accurately portrays the **motifs**. | Shows no understanding that story has motif—leaves out that part of the story. | Shows some understanding that story has motif, occasionally stresses that part of story. | Motif(s) is evident in the retelling. | Motif(s) is clearly evident and reinforced throughout telling. |

# HANDOUT 17.1C
# LITERARY TELLER RUBRIC

| Literary Product: | 1 Needs Revision With Teacher | 2 Needs Rewrites | 3 Needs One More Draft | 4 Publishable |
|---|---|---|---|---|
| Creates folktale-like **characters**. | Creates characters who are unrelated to folktale-types; and/or descriptions are too limiting. | Creates some characters who are related to folktale types; describes them with evocative, but sometimes limiting, adjectives. | Creates the main characters and most of the important supporting characters as types related to folktales; mostly describes them with evocative, not limiting, adjectives. | Creates main characters and supporting characters who are related to folktale types and describes them with descriptive adjectives. |
| Creates a "folktale" **setting**. | Does not include setting. | Leaves out some elements of setting, but it is mentioned. | Tells both time and place, but with too much or too little detail. | Includes time and place when describing the setting with supporting detail. |
| Writes an strong **plot**. | Plot is confusing and/or seems unrelated to a folktale. | One or two events are confusing in sequence, and is only somewhat related to a folktale-type plot. | One event is confusing in sequence, but is related to a folktale-type plot. | Sequence of events make sense and is related to a folktale-type plot. |
| Includes a folktale **motif(s)**. | Shows no understanding that story has motif—leaves out that part of the story. | Shows some understanding that story has motif, occasionally stresses that part of story. | Motif(s) is evident in the story. | Motif(s) is clearly evident and reinforced throughout story. |

# LESSON

# 18

# Festival Prework, Final Prep

## MATERIALS
- ✓ Folklorist journals
- ✓ Project folders
- ✓ Index cards (class set to be used as planning cards)
- ✓ Class rotation chart
- ✓ Handout 17.1A: Folklorist Rubric
- ✓ Handout 17.1B: Storyteller Rubric
- ✓ Handout 17.1C: Literary Teller Rubric

## OBJECTIVES
Students will:
- ✓ employ a wide range of strategies as they write to communicate with different audiences for a variety of purposes;
- ✓ develop the skills to participate as knowledgeable, reflective, creative, and critical members of a variety of a literary community; and
- ✓ apply knowledge of language structure, language conventions, and genre to create, critique, and discuss print and nonprint texts.

## SEQUENCE

### WARM UP
1. Ask students to list the things they plan to accomplish during today's lesson in their journals.

### INSTRUCTION: REVIEW RUBRICS
2. As a class, review the rubrics (Handouts 17.1A–C). Make sure students understand what is expected of them with their final products.

## ACTIVITY: FESTIVAL PREWORK

3.  Have students continue their professional folklore work in preparation for the Folklore Festival. Remind students that they must turn in their drafts today to go in the class anthology or program.

- Folklorists who finish early can:
  - ‣ read new tales, summarize, and add to new system;
  - ‣ write a keynote address for the festival; or
  - ‣ reread folklorist bios to act as a panelist at the festival.

- Storytellers who finish early can:
  - ‣ find a fable to also perform,
  - ‣ volunteer to read part of a literary teller's new tale at festival, or
  - ‣ listen to a classmate who is practicing aloud and provide feedback.

- Literary tellers who finish early can:
  - ‣ trade stories with another writer for final edits, or
  - ‣ volunteer to edit another writer's tale.

## PREPARATION: PLANNING CARD

4.  Have students respond to the following on a planning card: *What do I need to do for the festival?*

# LESSON 19

# Folklore Festival and Assessment

## MATERIALS

- ✓ Student Anthology to distribute
- ✓ Festival Programs to distribute
- ✓ Equipment for festival (e.g., microphone, chairs, refreshments, etc.)
- ✓ Handout 17.1A: Folklorist Rubric (teacher copies)
- ✓ Handout 17.1B: Storyteller Rubric (teacher copies)
- ✓ Handout 17.1C: Literary Teller Rubric (teacher copies)
- ✓ Handout 19.1: Performance Assessment

## OBJECTIVES

Students will:

- ✓ use spoken language to accomplish their own purposes (e.g., for learning, enjoyment, persuasion, and the exchange of information); and
- ✓ develop the skills to participate as knowledgeable, reflective, creative, and critical members of a variety of a literary community.

## SEQUENCE

1. In this 2-day lesson, students will present their Folklore Festival and complete the unit's summative assessment. The festival will take place on the first day of this lesson, and the wrap-up will take place on the last day. During the wrap-up, the teacher will be able to informally debrief with the students and administer the summative assessment.

2. **Summative Assessment:** During and after the festival, use the appropriate rubrics (Handouts 17.1A–C) to evaluate the storytellers' performances, the literary tellers' tales, and the folklorists' summaries found in their project.

## PREPARATION: PERFORMANCE ASSESSMENT

3. Administer the Unit 2 Performance Assessment (Handout 19.1) during the next lesson or soon after the Folklore Festival. Use the information from the performance assessment to assess students' growth through the unit (i.e., compare this task to responses on the unit preassessment).

## HANDOUT 19.1

# PERFORMANCE ASSESSMENT

## FAIRY TALES TO CONSIDER

| "Little Red Riding Hood" | Type 333 |
|---|---|
| "Hansel and Gretel" | Type 327 (About abandoned children) Includes an episode of type 1121, Burning the Witch in Her Own Oven |
| "Little Snow-White" | Type 709 |
| "Beauty and the Beast" | Type 425C |
| "Frog Kings" | Type 440 (About slimy suitors) |
| "Rapunzel" | Type 310 (The Maiden in the Tower) |
| "Cinderella" | Type 510A |
| "Sleeping Beauty" | Type 410 |

## FAIRY TALE ATU CHART

| Tales of Magic | |
|---|---|
| Supernatural Adversaries | 300–399 |
| Supernatural or Enchanted Wife/Husband or Other Relative | **400–459** |
| Wife | 400–424 |
| Husband | 425–449 |
| Brother or Sister | 450–459 |
| Supernatural Tasks | 460–499 |
| Supernatural Helpers | 500–559 |
| Magic Objects | 560–649 |
| Supernatural Power or Knowledge | 650–699 |
| Other Tales of the Supernatural | 700–749 |

1. Using the Fairy Tales to Consider chart, select three tales and explain why they fall into their ATU range, using the Fairy Tale ATU Chart.

## HANDOUT 19.1, CONTINUED

2. Cinderella has several different endings. Examples include:

She was taken to the young prince, dressed as she was. He thought she was more charming than before, and, a few days after, married her. Cinderella, who was no less good than beautiful, gave her two sisters lodgings in the palace, and that very same day matched them with two great lords of the court.

—Charles Perrault

Then the herald knew that she was the true bride of his master; and he took her upstairs to where the prince was; when he saw her face, he knew that she was the lady of his love. So he took her behind him upon his horse; and as they rode to the palace the little bird from the hazel tree cried out:

> Some cut their heel, and some cut their toe,
> But she sat by the fire who could wear the shoe.

And so they were married and lived happy ever afterwards.

—Joseph Jacobs

As she straightened herself up, she looked into the prince's face, and he recognized her as the beautiful princess. He cried out, "This is the right bride." The stepmother and the two proud sisters turned pale with horror. The prince escorted Cinderella away. He helped her into his carriage, and as they rode through the gate, the pigeons called out:

> Rook di goo, rook di goo!
> No blood's in the shoe.
> The shoe's not too tight,
> This bride is right!

—The Brothers Grimm

## HANDOUT 19.1, CONTINUED

If you were retelling the story to little children, which would you choose? Why?

3. Choose one of the jobs we studied in this unit: folklorist, storyteller, literary teller. How does that job help people feel *empathy*?

4. How does folklore tell us something about what a culture values?

# References

Ashliman, D. L. (2000). The sealskin. *The mermaid and other migratory legends of Christiansen type 4080.* Retrieved from http://www.pitt.edu/~dash/type 4080.html#sealskin

Ashliman, D. L. (2004). *Folk and fairy tales: A handbook.* Westport, CT: Greenwood Publishing Group.

Bettelheim, B. (1976). *The Uses of Enchantment: The Meaning and Importance of Fairy Tales.* New York, NY: Vintage Books.

Burns, D. E. (1987). *The effects of group training activities on students' creative productivity* (Unpublished doctoral dissertation). The University of Connecticut, Storrs.

Callahan, C. M., Moon, T. R., Oh, S., Azano, A., & Hailey, E. (2015). Documenting the effects of an integrated curricular/instructional model for gifted students. *American Educational Research Journal, 52,* 137–167.

Csikszentmihalyi, M. (1990). *Flow: The psychology of optimal experience.* New York, NY: Harper & Row.

Csikszentmihalyi, M., Rathunde, K. R., & Whalen, S. (1993). *Talented teenagers: The roots of success and failure.* New York, NY: Cambridge University Press.

Donovan, M., Bransford, J., & Pellegrino, J. (1999). *How people learn: Bridging research and practice.* Washington, DC: National Academy Press.

Douglas, G. (2000). *Scottish fairy and folk tales.* Courier Corporation.

Heiner, H. A. (1999). Annotations for Hansel & Gretel. *SurLaLune fairytales.com.* Retreived from http://www.surlalunefairytales.com/hanselgretel/notes.html

Howard, P. (1994). *An owner's manual for the brain.* Austin, TX: Leorian Press.

Jensen, E. (1998). *Teaching with the brain in mind.* Alexandria, VA: Association for Supervision & Curriculum Development.

Kaplan, S. (2005). Layering differential curricula for gifted and talented. In F. A. Karnes & S. M. Bean (Eds.), *Methods and materials for teaching gifted students* (pp. 107–132). Waco, TX: Prufrock Press.

Kaplan, S. (2013). Depth and complexity. In C. M. Callahan & H. L. Hertberg-Davis (Eds.), *Fundamentals of gifted education* (pp. 277–287). New York, NY: Routledge.

Ketner, M. G. (2008). Top ten secrets to finding, learning and delivering folktales. *Storyteller.net.* Retrieved from http://www.storyteller.net/articles/232

Lang, A. (Ed.). (1922). *The lilac fairy book.* New York, NY: Longmans, Green, and Company.

National Association for Gifted Children. (2010). *Pre-K to grade 12 gifted programming standards.* Retrieved from http://www.nagc.org/index.aspx?id=546

National Council of Teachers of English, & International Reading Association. (2012). *Standards for the English language arts.* Urbana, IL: NCTE.

Olenchak, F. R. (1991). Assessing program effects for gifted/learning disabled students. In R. Swassing & A. Robinson (Eds.), *NAGC 1991 research briefs* (pp. 86–89). Washington, DC: National Association for Gifted Children.

Reis, S. M. (1981). *An analysis of the productivity of gifted students participating in programs using the Revolving Door Identification Model* (Unpublished doctoral dissertation). University of Connecticut, Storrs.

Renzulli, J. S., & Reis, S. M. (1985). *The schoolwide enrichment model: A comprehensive plan for educational excellence.* Mansfield Center, CT: Creative Learning Press.

Renzulli, J. S., & Reis, S. M. (2001). The schoolwide enrichment model. In K. Heller, F. Mönks, R. Sternberg, & R. Subotnik (Eds.), *International handbook of giftedness and talent* (2nd ed., pp. 367–382). Oxford, England: Elsevier Science.

Rylant, C. (2015). *Walt Disney's Cinderella.* Glendale, CA: Disney Press.

Schack, G. D., Starko, A. J., & Burns, D. E. (1991). Self-efficacy and creative productivity: Three studies of above average ability children. *Journal of Research in Education, 1,* 44–52.

Sheppard, T. (2014). *Tim Sheppard's Storytelling Resources for storytellers.* Retrieved from http://www.timsheppard.co.uk/story/faq.html

Sousa, D., & Tomlinson, C. (2010). *Differentiation and the brain: How neuroscience supports the learner-friendly classroom.* Bloomington, IN: Solution Tree.

Tomlinson, C. A. (1995). *How to differentiate instruction in mixed-ability classrooms.* Alexandria, VA: Association for Supervision and Curriculum Development.

Tomlinson, C. A. (1999). *The differentiated classroom: Responding to the needs of all learners.* Alexandria, VA: Association for Supervision and Curriculum Development.

Wenglinsky, H. (2002). How schools matter: The link between teacher classroom practices and student academic performance. *Education Policy Analysis Archives, 10*(12). Retrieved from http://epaa.asu.edu/ojs/article/view/291

Yolen, J. (1988). *Favorite folktales from around the world.* New York, NY: Pantheon.

# Appendices
# Unit Resources

## APPENDIX A1
# GROUPING PLAN CHART

| GROUP A | GROUP B | GROUP C |
|---|---|---|
| | | |
| | | |
| | | |
| | | |
| | | |
| | | |
| | | |
| | | |
| | | |
| | | |
| | | |
| | | |
| | | |
| | | |

# APPENDIX A2

# CONCRETE VERSUS ABSTRACT ACTIVITY ANSWER KEYS

## GROUP A ANSWER KEY

Underlined = concrete noun.        Double underline = abstract noun.

Line 1: line, end
Line 2: lines,
Line 3: thread
Line 4: none
Line 5: none
Line 6: medals, ribbons
Line 7: none
Line 8: beard, wisdom
Line 9: jaw.
Line 10: none
Line11: victory
Line 12: boat
Line 13: pool, bilge
Line 14: oil, rainbow
Line 15: engine
Line 16: bailer
Line 17: thwarts
Line 18: oarlocks, strings,
Line 19: gunnels, everything
Line 20: rainbow, rainbow, rainbow
Line 21: fish

## GROUPS B AND C ANSWER KEY

Underlined = concrete noun.        Double underline = abstract noun.

| | | |
|---|---|---|
| library | wisdom | school |
| ladder | bone | water |
| trust | memory | peace |
| mouth | children | honesty |
| boat | fish | pool |
| power | engine | rainbow |
| victory | oil | jaw |
| gunnels | thread | ribbon |
| freedom | wish | faith |

# APPENDIX A3
# FOCUS ON THE RUBRIC, PART 1

| | Master | Journeyman | Apprentice |
|---|---|---|---|
| **Choice of language** | ≫ Language is clear and descriptive. <br> ≫ Most language is concrete rather than abstract. <br> ≫ Choice of words is interesting and surprising to the reader. | ≫ Language is clear and descriptive in most sections of the poem. <br> ≫ Most language is concrete rather than abstract. | ≫ Language is unclear and does not help paint a picture of the specific scene in the reader's mind. <br> ≫ Most language is abstract. |

# APPENDIX A4
# FOCUS ON THE RUBRIC, PART 2

| | Master | Journeyman | Apprentice |
|---|---|---|---|
| **Imagery** | ≫ Imagery is used to create a picture in the reader's mind that is unique and surprising; imagery helps the reader see something in a new way. <br> ≫ Imagery is used effectively to connect with more than one of the reader's senses. <br> ≫ Tools such as metaphor, personification, and point of view are used effectively to connect with the reader through imagery. | ≫ Imagery is used to create a clear picture in the reader's mind. <br> ≫ Imagery is used effectively to connect with at least one of the reader's senses. <br> ≫ Tools such as metaphor, personification, and point of view are attempted, but are used inconsistently or are confusing to the reader. | ≫ Imagery does not create a clear picture in the reader's mind. <br> ≫ Imagery does not connect with the reader's senses. <br> ≫ Tools such as metaphor, personification, and point of view are not attempted, or are confusing to the reader. |

# APPENDIX A5
# STATION ROTATION MANAGER SHEET

**Instructions:**

1. Write the names of your students in the first column.
2. Cut along the horizontal lines to make a strip to give to each student with the order of his or her rotation through the four stations.

| Name | Order of Rotation | | | |
|------|---|---|---|---|
| | 1 | 2 | 3 | 4 |
| | 4 | 1 | 2 | 3 |
| | 3 | 4 | 1 | 2 |
| | 2 | 3 | 4 | 1 |
| | 1 | 2 | 3 | 4 |
| | 4 | 1 | 2 | 3 |
| | 3 | 4 | 1 | 2 |
| | 2 | 3 | 4 | 1 |
| | 1 | 2 | 3 | 4 |
| | 4 | 1 | 2 | 3 |
| | 3 | 4 | 1 | 2 |
| | 2 | 3 | 4 | 1 |
| | 1 | 2 | 3 | 4 |
| | 4 | 1 | 2 | 3 |
| | 3 | 4 | 1 | 2 |
| | 2 | 3 | 4 | 1 |
| | 1 | 2 | 3 | 4 |
| | 4 | 1 | 2 | 3 |
| | 3 | 4 | 1 | 2 |
| | 2 | 3 | 4 | 1 |

# APPENDIX A6
# POET'S WORKSHOP CONFERENCE NOTES

Name: _____

Poem title: _____

Teacher conference date and initials: _____

| Area for Feedback | Specific Feedback |
| --- | --- |
| **Concrete descriptions** | |
| **Multiple senses** | |
| **Imagery** | |
| **Spelling/Writing** | |
| **Other** | |

Additional notes: _____

_____

_____

_____

_____

## APPENDIX A7

# FOCUS ON THE RUBRIC, PART 3

|  | Master | Journeyman | Apprentice |
|---|---|---|---|
| **Mechanics** | ≫ Few or no mistakes are evident in the spelling and mechanics of the poem. | ≫ Minor mistakes are evident in the spelling and mechanics of the poem, but these do not detract from the work. | ≫ Mistakes are evident in the spelling and mechanics of the poem to an extent that they detract from the work. |

## APPENDIX A8

# FOCUS ON THE RUBRIC, PART 4

|  | Master | Journeyman | Apprentice |
|---|---|---|---|
| **Poetic Devices** | ≫ The use of tools such as metaphor, personification, point of view, rhythm, and rhyme are used. | ≫ Tools such as metaphor, personification, point of view, rhythm, and rhyme are used some. | ≫ Poetic devices, such as metaphor, personification, point of view, rhythm, and rhyme are not used. |

# APPENDIX A9
# FORMATIVE ASSESSMENT 4 ANSWER KEY

| | | | | |
|---|---|---|---|---|
| 1. | bright | bite | (high) | height |
| 2. | (pale) | gray | stay | bay |
| 3. | shoe | through | (though) | two |
| 4. | (secret) | meat | meet | secrete |
| 5. | high | (under) | cry | untie |
| 6. | eight | undulate | commiserate | (community) |
| 7. | steak | stake | (create) | shake |
| 8. | (towel) | show | stow | toe |
| 9. | (dream) | unclean | serene | machine |
| 10. | soap | hope | heliotrope | (throat) |
| 11. | goad | (odor) | unload | ode |
| 12. | mud | blood | (food) | stud |
| 13. | scare | (scar) | prepare | unfair |
| 14. | (instant) | bled | bread | instead |

# FOLKLORISTICS CONCEPT MAP

*Folkloristics:* The comparative study of folk knowledge and culture.

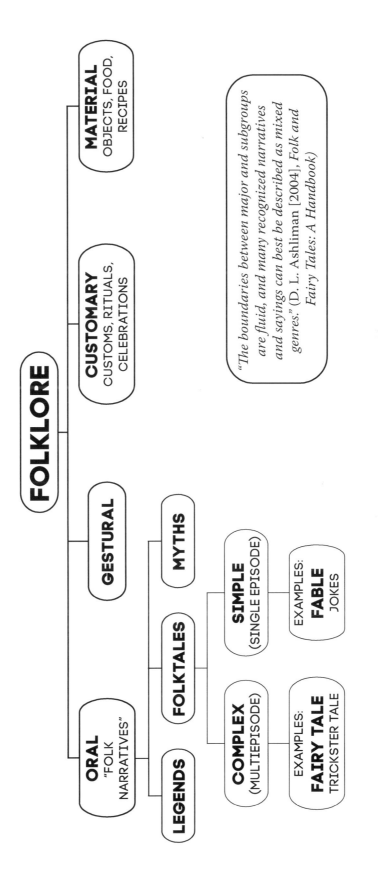

**FOLKLORE**

**MATERIAL** OBJECTS, FOOD, RECIPES

**CUSTOMARY** CUSTOMS, RITUALS, CELEBRATIONS

**GESTURAL**

**ORAL** "FOLK NARRATIVES"

MYTHS

FOLKTALES

LEGENDS

**SIMPLE** (SINGLE EPISODE)

**COMPLEX** (MULTIEPISODE)

EXAMPLES: **FABLE** JOKES

EXAMPLES: **FAIRY TALE** TRICKSTER TALE

*"The boundaries between major and subgroups are fluid, and many recognized narratives and sayings can best be described as mixed genres." (D. L. Ashliman [2004], Folk and Fairy Tales: A Handbook)*

## APPENDIX B2
# GROUPING PLAN CHART

| GROUP A | GROUP B | GROUP C |
|---|---|---|
|  |  |  |
|  |  |  |
|  |  |  |
|  |  |  |
|  |  |  |
|  |  |  |
|  |  |  |
|  |  |  |
|  |  |  |
|  |  |  |
|  |  |  |
|  |  |  |
|  |  |  |
|  |  |  |

## APPENDIX B3
# TOPIC BAG OBJECTS

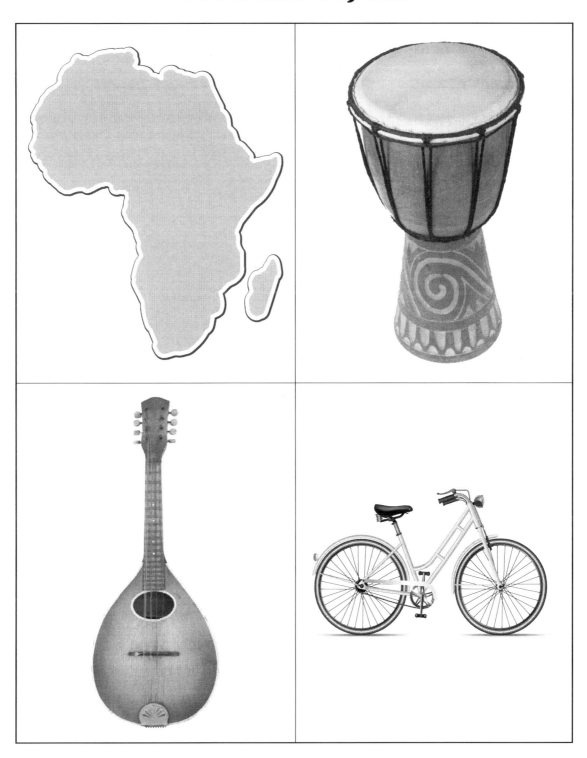

# About the Authors

**Amy Price Azano, Ph.D.,** is an assistant professor of adolescent literacy at Virginia Tech where her research focuses on rural gifted education, place-based pedagogy, and the literacy needs of rural youth. Dr. Azano teaches graduate-level literacy courses to preservice teachers and doctoral students and serves as coprincipal investigator on a 5-year, Jacob K. Javits Department of Education grant seeking to improve gifted education for rural learners. She is also an affiliate faculty member, leading the education research core, with the Virginia Tech Center for Autism Research, and does extensive community outreach in the field of autism. Prior to her current position, Dr. Azano was a researcher and project manager on the "What Works in Gifted Education" study at the National Research Center on the Gifted and Talented (NRC/GT) at the University of Virginia (UVA). Before earning her Ph.D. in English Education from UVA, Dr. Azano taught high school English and served as codirector of UVA's National Writing Project site. Her recent publications can be found in *American Educational Research Journal, English Education, Journal of Advanced Academics, Journal of Research in Rural Education, Journal of Teaching Writing,* and *Teaching Exceptional Children.*

**Tracy C. Missett, Ph.D.,** is an assistant professor at the University of Montana Phyllis J. Washington College of Education and Human Sciences, where she holds the Suzanne and Dave Peterson Endowed Professorship in

Gifted Education. Dr. Missett received her Ph.D. and B.A. from the University of Virginia, her J.D. from the University of California, Hastings College of the Law, and her M.A. from Teachers College, Columbia University. While a doctoral student at the University of Virginia, Dr. Missett was a Graduate Research Assistant on a project of the National Research Center on the Gifted and Talented (NRC/GT) and engaged in research on the effectiveness of the CLEAR Curriculum Model. Dr. Missett has published multiple articles and book chapters on topics in gifted education, and she has received awards in both curriculum and research from the National Association for Gifted Children.

**Carolyn M. Callahan, Ph.D.,** Commonwealth Professor of Education at the University of Virginia, developed and leads the master's and doctoral programs in gifted education, teaches classes in gifted education, and developed the summer and Saturday enrichment programs at UVA. For 20 years she has been the principal investigator on projects of the National Research Center on the Gifted and Talented (NRC/GT), and she has been principal investigator on five Javits grants. Her work with the NRC/GT and with the Javits projects has focused on curriculum development and implementation. As part of her work with the NRC/GT she was coevaluator for the U.S. Department of Education of the Javits program and conducted a national survey of gifted and talented programs. She has conducted evaluations of grant projects including several Javits grants, state-level programs (e.g., the Advanced Placement initiative in Maine), and local-level gifted programs large and small. She has been recognized as Outstanding Professor of the Commonwealth of Virginia and Distinguished Scholar of the National Association for Gifted Children (NAGC). She has served as president of NAGC and the Association for the Gifted, and as editor of *Gifted Child Quarterly*. Dr. Callahan has published more than 200 articles and 50 book chapters on topics in gifted education with one of those publications considered the definitive books on evaluation. She is the coeditor of the recently published book, *Fundamentals of Gifted Education: Considering Multiple Perspectives* and *Critical Issues in Gifted Education*.

# Common Core State Standards Alignment

| Domain | Grade 3 ELA-Literacy Common Core State Standards |
|---|---|
| Reading: Literature | RL.3.1 Ask and answer questions to demonstrate understanding of a text, referring explicitly to the text as the basis for the answers. |
| | RL.3.2 Recount stories, including fables, folktales, and myths from diverse cultures; determine the central message, lesson, or moral and explain how it is conveyed through key details in the text. |
| | RL.3.3 Describe characters in a story (e.g., their traits, motivations, or feelings) and explain how their actions contribute to the sequence of events. |
| | RL.3.4 Determine the meaning of words and phrases as they are used in a text, distinguishing literal from nonliteral language. |
| | RL.3.5 Refer to parts of stories, dramas, and poems when writing or speaking about a text, using terms such as chapter, scene, and stanza; describe how each successive part builds on earlier sections. |
| | RL.3.6 Distinguish their own point of view from that of the narrator or those of the characters. |
| | RL.3.7 Explain how specific aspects of a text's illustrations contribute to what is conveyed by the words in a story (e.g., create mood, emphasize aspects of a character or setting) |
| | RL.3.9 Compare and contrast the themes, settings, and plots of stories written by the same author about the same or similar characters (e.g., in books from a series) |

| Domain | Grade 3 ELA-Literacy Common Core State Standards |
|---|---|
| Reading: Literature, *continued* | RL.3.10 By the end of the year, read and comprehend literature, including stories, dramas, and poetry, at the high end of the grades 2–3 text complexity band independently and proficiently |
| Writing | W.3.3 Write narratives to develop real or imagined experiences or events using effective technique, descriptive details, and clear event sequences. |
| | W.3.4 With guidance and support from adults, produce writing in which the development and organization are appropriate to task and purpose. |
| | W.3.5 With guidance and support from peers and adults, develop and strengthen writing as needed by planning, revising, and editing. |
| | W.3.6 With guidance and support from adults, use technology to produce and publish writing (using keyboarding skills) as well as to interact and collaborate with others. |
| | W.3.10 Write routinely over extended time frames (time for research, reflection, and revision) and shorter time frames (a single sitting or a day or two) for a range of discipline-specific tasks, purposes, and audiences. |